FIRE FOR EFFECT

FIRE FOR EFFECT

USS *Stoddard* and the U.S. Navy's First Shots of the Vietnam War

JOHN F. CALDER

CASEMATE
Pennsylvania & Yorkshire

Published in the United States of America and Great Britain in 2026 by
CASEMATE PUBLISHERS
1950 Lawrence Road, Havertown, PA 19083, USA
and
47 Church Street, Barnsley, S70 2AS, UK

Hardback Edition: ISBN 978-1-63624-598-0
Digital Edition: ISBN 978-1-63624-599-7

A CIP record for this book is available from the British Library

Printed and bound in the United Kingdom by CPI Group (UK) Ltd, Croydon, CR0 4YY
Typeset in India by DiTech Publishing Services

For a complete list of Casemate titles, please contact:

CASEMATE PUBLISHERS (US)
Telephone (610) 853-9131
Fax (610) 853-9146
Email: casemate@casematepublishers.com
www.casematepublishers.com

CASEMATE PUBLISHERS (UK)
Telephone (0)1226 734350
Email: casemate@casemateuk.com
www.casemateuk.com

Front cover image: Foreground, the USS *Stoddard* (U.S. Navy, Wikimedia Commons); background, Da Nang harbor and the surrounding area, taken January 6, 1966. (Picryl: NH 74482, public domain)
Back cover image: The U.S. Navy destroyer USS *Samuel N. Moore* (DD-747) underway circa the late 1940s or early 1950s. (U.S. Navy, Wikimedia Commons)
Title page image: The USS *Stoddard.* (U.S. Navy, Wikimedia Commons)

Contents

Preface

This book is dedicated to honor and thank every serviceman and woman who served our country during the Vietnam War. It was an especially trying time for these courageous warriors: when in-country they were fighting a determined and violent enemy; returning home, they were confronted with a hostile and confrontational citizenry. In Vietnam, the enemy fired shells at us. Returning home, the "enemy" fired derogatory comments, profanity, and in many cases felt a need to spit in our direction. This politically charged environment reminded me of a phrase written by Elmer Davis, and it still applies today: "This nation will remain the land of the free only so long as it is the home of the brave. This republic was not established by cowards; and cowards will not preserve it."

Numerous books and articles have been published about the Vietnam War. The majority of these focused on the brave American Marines and soldiers. By contrast, relatively few have been written about the fearless sailors who served our nation. I'm talking about the men who served on the warships off the coast, in the harbors, and along the rivers of Vietnam. There were a variety of types and sizes of naval vessels, from swift boats to aircraft carriers, with each playing a vital and important role. Attempting to cover the missions and operations of each of these vessels is unrealistic. Therefore, the focus of this book is on the type of vessel I served on: a ship referred to as the Navy's workhorse, the "greyhound of the sea," the destroyer.

Before going any further, while writing this book I came across articles stating less than 30 percent of the military personnel who served in-country in Vietnam saw actual combat. These military personnel were classified as "noncombatants." The absolute coldness of this statistic disturbed me. Let's stop for a moment and realize our combatants, regardless of their branch of military service, were able to execute their duties because of the extraordinary support received from every level of the military. Let me be very clear, regardless of if they were stationed in a combat zone or not, every serviceman or servicewoman who served in-country, was in harm's way and the target of an exceptionally cruel enemy. As an example, most Americans are unaware that more than 7,000 courageous women served in Vietnam; eight of these brave women made the ultimate sacrifice and never returned. Although they may have been classified as "noncombatants," we must remember to honor their memory and thank them for their service. And that applies to the entire heroic staff that supported our fighting force.

One of the destroyer's most important wartime roles is providing NGFS, aka shore bombardment, to the Marines stationed along the coast. Whether it was World War II, Korea, or the Vietnam War, this "weapon" always proved to be a true game changer; it was unique, powerful, and highly flexible. With that said, it was the extraordinarily brave Marine squads/spotters, an equally brave Underwater Demolition Team (UDT), and a crew of exceptional shipmates that inspired me to write this book.

During two consecutive tours in Vietnam, between June 1965 and May 1966, on board two different destroyers, the USS *Stoddard* (DD-566), and later the USS *Samuel N. Moore* (DD-747), I had the honor and privilege of communicating with over 50 Marine spotters (officially known as supporting arms observers), ranging from north of Da Nang, to south of the Mekong Delta.

After being separated from active duty and following numerous conversations with veterans from every branch of service, and several historians, I began to realize the uniqueness of my term of service. This book addresses my entire naval experience, beginning just before boot camp, through radar school, the Gulf of Tonkin incident, and culminating during the earliest stages of the Vietnam War. As you will read, the successes and effectiveness of the ship and its crew were the product of the excellent, professional, and never-ending training provided by the U.S. Navy. At 82, I can say with all sincerity and confidence, the 4½ years I served in the U.S. Navy resulted in some of my most memorable and life-altering experiences. It also set the tone and direction for the rest of my life. I often wonder what I would have become had it not been for the discipline, team building, and excellent training provided by the U.S. Navy!

Before going any further, I'd like to mention that the book addresses a very sensitive topic. While difficult to discuss, it is a vital part or element of the book; I'm talking about "life." While absolutely unfortunate, yet unavoidable, the book contains and discusses a significant loss of life. The loss of life should never be accepted nor taken for granted. I'm confident the majority of wartime veterans would agree; participating in missions or events involving the loss of life makes the most hardened combatant appreciate and respect life so much more.

As you delve deeper into the book, many of you may feel remorse or compassion for the enemy forces and that's perfectly understandable. Please be assured I truly respect those feelings; but as a reader you must also realize, "it's war"! Without question, the fighting between combatants is hell, but you must also understand it is unarguably a true life or death encounter. War is not police action, riot control, or a protest. It's a violent confrontation that involves significant loss of life. It is also financially straining and frequently ends with the warring countries asking, "Could it have been prevented, why did it occur, and what was accomplished?" Probably one of the best descriptions of why war occurs is stated in *Romans 3:10–18*, "Some wars are more 'just' than others, but war is always the result of sin. In a world filled with sin, hatred, and evil, war is inevitable."

It may be important to point out, there never was a time we disrespected or took our enemy for granted. But it's equally important to realize, from the first day we entered the waters off South Vietnam, the duty of every sailor on board was to defend, protect, and support our Marines and the UDT assigned to our ship. As the first Da Nang harbor defense ship, and the first U.S. naval ship to fire a round in the Vietnam War, it was our duty, honor, and privilege to serve with these brave and courageous men. The combined team of Marines, UDTs, and sailors not only disrupted the plans of the Viet Cong (officially known as the National Liberation Front of South Vietnam) but prevented them from capturing and controlling Da Nang harbor and region. In these earliest stages of the war, well before the first round was fired, the Pentagon recognized Da Nang's location as being of critical importance to any future operations. Da Nang was identified as the most strategic asset for mobilizing troops and delivering supplies, weapons, ammunition, etc. It is located 40 miles south of the border with the North, had the second-largest airfield in the country, and contained a deep-water harbor along the shore of the South China Sea.

Shortly after the 3rd Marine Division landed in May 1965, they recognized a rapid buildup of enemy forces in and around Da Nang. Command recognized the immediate need for a "weapon" to manage this evolving situation and, most importantly, prevent the Viet Cong from attacking the base. This weapon had to be quickly mobilized, available to operate around-the-clock, be highly effective, and exceptionally flexible. Finally, while preventing an attack on the base, this "weapon" had to be available to confront situations developing in regions to the north, south, and west of the base. As with every previous war, the weapon of choice was a naval gunship: a gunship to provide NGFS.

While this may have been our assignment and mission, its purpose or effectiveness was best summed up by a young Marine. During an interview he was asked to "describe the impact naval gunfire support was having on their overall effort." Rather than describing a recent mission or battle, he simply replied, "Naval gunfire allowed us to continue breathing air." But with that said, I and every other Vietnam veteran will continue grieving the valiant warriors who paid the ultimate price and never returned.

I'd like to mention, the book is based upon actual events and missions. These events occurred over the first month following the *Stoddard*'s arrival as Da Nang harbor defense ship. When we arrived in Da Nang, there was minimal intelligence available about the enemy, their movements, or their intent. Likewise, the enemy was unaware of the capabilities and destructive power of a U.S. destroyer. Let me emphatically state, I spent the better part of an entire year off the coast of Vietnam, and I can honestly state that first month, serving as Da Nang harbor defense ship, was far and away the most intense, demanding, dangerous, active, and challenging; all others were dwarfed by comparison.

Even before typing the first keystroke, I was committed to providing the reader with an accurate account of our missions. Wanting to avoid using my memory as the sole resource for the book, I began to research documents and data applicable to this period in Vietnam. I also turned to the experiences of many Marine and Navy Vietnam veterans. These discussions spanned from shortly after I was separated from active duty in May 1966 and through to the present day. For their input, I would like to extend my sincere thanks to these veterans for their service, as well as their invaluable counseling and guidance. With that said, please understand some of the information may be less than accurate chronologically and exclude the "documented details" following each battle. However, from a naval perspective, I've provided a general overview and summary of the major campaigns fought in the earliest stages of the Vietnam War. Lacking documented historical data, these summaries describe how the missions developed, were addressed, and executed. The actual date on which they occurred may be less than accurate, as well as the post-battle data describing the equipment or objects destroyed, along with a documented body count.

Finally, in an effort to avoid any questions or concerns on the part of any individuals, families, and crew members, I changed the names of my friends, shipmates, and many of the ships referenced in the book. However, the USS *McDermut* (DD-677, call sign "Gatekeeper"), the USS *Stoddard* (DD-566, call sign "Buckboard"); and the USS *Samuel N. Moore* (DD-747, call sign "Macaroon") are the actual names, hull numbers, and call signs of ships on which I served. In addition, the USS *Craig* (DD-885, call sign "Assassin") is the actual name of a destroyer we operated with during a "mass firing mission." I used the ship's actual name, as it is mentioned in a published press release printed in newspapers nationwide. While never mentioned in official records and occurring a week after Washington authorized the use of NGFS, this mass firing mission was likely our country's first major battle victory in Vietnam. For political reasons, the victory was intentionally ignored by Washington. However, as I look back, I have a better understanding of the reasoning behind this decision.

I would like to thank you for your interest in my book and hope you'll find it educational, eye-opening, and intriguing. But most importantly, I hope you find it a fitting tribute to the many sailors and other Vietnam veterans, as well as all who have served and continue to serve our country; I am most grateful and thank them for their service!

The USS *Stoddard* patch with the Latin motto "Per Mare Ad Astra," meaning "By sea, to the stars." (Author's collection)

CHAPTER I

A Salute to Friendship

It's June 1961, and I've just graduated from Rahway High School in Rahway, NJ. Although I took a college prep course, it would have been a financial strain on my family for me to attend college. In 1961, 41 percent of students graduated high school and that was up from 34 percent in the 1950s. In the 1960s, only 8 percent of students graduated from college.

Like many families in the 1950s and 1960s, we lived "hand to mouth" in this small blue-collar town. It was rare for a family to sit down and discuss their children's future. Most families lacked the financial resources to fund the cost of college tuition, and we were no exception. Instead, following graduation you were more or less on your own. This usually meant finding a job; it was just that way.

Throughout high school, I worked a number of part-time jobs. During most weekday evenings I was employed as an usher at the Rahway Theater. On weekends, I was unloading and reloading cases of beer and soda in the trunks of cars, at a warehouse called Beverage Unlimited. In the evening, I returned to my ushering duties. During my senior year I reduced my hours at the theater; suddenly, $0.50 an hour wasn't cutting it. Instead, I was hired as a short-order cook at Allen Industries; $0.90 an hour was so much better. But none of these jobs offered full-time positions. Within a week following graduation I was hired, along with my friend Angelo Rodrigo, by Quinn & Boden. Q&B was a bookbinding company located in the industrial section of our hometown.

Throughout high school a group of five of us became close friends. We spent many off-hours fishing, playing baseball, chasing girls, and just being teenagers. Let me provide a little background so you have a better understanding of my social circle.

I'll start with Chuck Mauger, whose parents hailed from a coal mining town in northeastern Pennsylvania. With six children, the Maugers were the largest family on the block. It goes without saying, living in a two-bedroom Cape Cod slab foundation house, with a finished attic, posed a challenge, but they did just fine. I never heard any member of the family complain about the living accommodation. Prior to moving to Rahway in 1955, their father worked in a number of Pennsylvania coal mines. He frequently described how he hated every minute being a miner. To escape this unrewarding, unhealthy, if not dangerous job, he found work at a GM Assembly plant in Linden, NJ, and the entire family relocated to Rahway. He worked there until he retired in the early 1970s. Their mom was employed as a waitress at a local diner. As I think back, the Maugers were one of the very few families who had two working parents. It may have been the only way to make ends meet.

Another one in our group was Willard Ludawitz. His family came to Rahway in 1953, from Newark, NJ. His dad was a machinist for a small shop in Irvington, NJ, and his mother was a stay-at-home mom. Willard had a younger sister named Loraine.

Then there's Angelo Rodrigo, who lived on an adjacent street. His siblings consisted of an older sister, Eva, and a younger sister, Marie. His parents were naturalized citizens; his mother was born and raised in Italy, and his father came from Cuba. Angelo had a stay-at-home mom, while his father worked at a factory connected to the textile industry. Like many men at the time, he worked for and retired from the same employer after more than 40 years of employment. Angelo and I were very close; in fact, we enlisted in the Navy under the "buddy system" and remain close friends to this day.

Next was Joseph Rutigliano, who also lived on a neighboring street. He was born in Rahway and sadly lost his father before he was 12. Joey lived with his mom and three sisters. His family was an absolutely fun-loving bunch; everyone loved the Rutiglianos. Somewhere along the line, one of his friends struggled with correctly pronouncing Joey's last name. So, he was given the nickname "Joey Bag of Donuts." Before long, he became known to all as Joey Bagofdonuts. I recall the gym teacher once saying, "Hey Bagofdonuts, grab a bat, you're on deck." In all honesty, he not only liked the nickname but actually relished it; especially after realizing it increased his popularity in a positive way.

Finally, there's my family. I was born at the West Hudson Hospital in Kearny, NJ. At the time, Kearny was a town primarily made up of Scottish and Irish immigrants. Shortly following the death of my grandfather on my mother's side and realizing my grandma would be unable to maintain her Kearny home, my parents moved in with her. This move provided her with some much-needed financial help.

In the early 1950s, immigrants from other European countries began moving to Kearny and the Scottish and Irish began moving out. So, in September 1955, with the proceeds from the sale of Grandma Mary's home, along with a small additional down payment, we moved to a Cape Cod home in Rahway, NJ. Our extended family consisted of my mother (Agnes), father (Harold), a sister (Carol), and my grandmother (Mary). My grandma remained a loved and treasured member of our family until her passing in the late 1960s.

I knew very little of my parents' life as they grew up. My mother, a stay-at-home mom, was born on August 13, 1908, in Passaic, NJ, and passed on June 9, 1989, in Rahway, NJ. My mother's parents were Mary and John Canavan. In the late 1800s, my grandmother, Mary Kendall, immigrated to the United States from Manchester, England, and married my grandfather, an Irish immigrant. They had six children, two of which were stillborn. My grandfather, John Canavan, was killed in an industrial accident in the late 1920s.

My dad was born in Wilmington, Delaware, in 1909. His family included two sisters, Margaret and Grace. They moved to Montgomery, AL, when he was a bit more than a toddler. As fate would have it, my grandfather was tragically killed in a car accident just as my father was finishing the 8th grade. For financial reasons, it forced him to drop out of school and find a job to help support the family. His family struggled for several years and finally decided to relocate to New Jersey, which at the time was ripe with job openings. After working in a number of factories, he finally landed a job as a security guard at Worthington Pump, in Harrison, NJ. He remained there for approximately 30 years, before retiring in the 1970s.

Here's a little insight into our little social group. The late 1950s and early 1960s were a time when people still respected each other and were willing to help those in need. Unfortunately, Joey Bagofdonuts' family struggled financially, as they attempted to recover from the loss of their dad. To supplement their income, one of Joey's sisters, Aida, took a job delivering Sunday newspapers. Much like the current day, the Sunday papers weighed in at several pounds each. The newspaper industry was much less automated than today's factories, so the Sunday paper was printed early Saturday evening and delivered to the carriers sometime between 9 and 10 pm. The newspaper management was amazed by the number of papers Aida was able to deliver and frequently gave her additional routes. Unbeknown to management, the papers were being delivered with assistance from our group of guys. The publishing company only knew, or cared, that they were on their customers' porches when they opened their doors Sunday morning. But that was the end result; let me explain how our small group contributed. Truth be told, during the onset, frequent arguments ensued within the group. They always centered on who would be "honored" to be part of the delivering crew, a position we all desired.

Just after Aida was hired, she bought a used Chevrolet Nomad, circa 1950s. Each Saturday evening, we congregated at Joey's house to unbundle, assemble the commercial ads, flyers, and miscellaneous sections into the Sunday papers. After loading the papers in the car, a crew was chosen to go along for the ride. The riding crew consisted of four—Aida the driver, a "handler" in the back seat, and two "runners" on the tailgate. To avoid fatigue, the tailgate runners and the handler rotated frequently; it was a well-thought-out system.

But delivering the papers isn't what we lived for. Each Saturday night a show aired on the radio called *Make It or Break It*. The show consisted of a DJ playing 45 rpm records of new songs and artists. At the conclusion of airing a new record, people were asked to call in and voice their opinion. They did so by voting on whether the record was good or a flop. If it was deemed "good," the DJ would play it for a second time. If it was judged to be a "flop," he would physically break it on air. The "breaking" would be accomplished with a great deal of fanfare. So, as we were delivering the papers, Aida turned the radio's volume to maximum, so it was heard by the entire crew. To be clear, the broadcast could only be heard by the team; unlike today's radios, it wasn't loud enough to disturb the neighborhoods.

At the end of the song each crew member voiced his or her opinion. Of course, our "reviews" always led to lively debates, especially after the DJ announced the poll results. To keep everyone in the game, when the station was about to reveal the results, Aida would pull over to the side and wait as we commented on the decision … "The song was a Hoover, it really sucked!" … "No, the song is going to be a smash hit; if anything sucks, it's your hearing, open up your friggin' ears" … "You don't have a clue what you're talking about, all of your taste is in your mouth." It always ended with a "mother" reference, the pinnacle of any and all debates. Please understand, the "mother" remarks were taken with a grain of salt. The bantering was never intended to be insulting or demeaning. Instead, the "mother" references represented the ultimate putdown; the apex or zenith of any debate. Aida frequently ended the squabbles by laughing and telling us to "knock it off and let's get these papers delivered." On came another record and the cycle began once again.

We knew the family was struggling to make ends meet, so we pitched in whenever we could. There were even times we included our "dates" in the activity, and they loved it! While we were never financially rewarded, Aida always made sure we had plenty to drink and would occasionally buy a dozen donuts. Her boyfriend worked at the local donut shop, so I'm sure she was given the "proper discount." It was something we frequently mentioned and laughed about.

I hope this gives you a brief glimpse into my life before enlisting in the U.S. Navy. Let me add, you couldn't have found a happier adolescent; a better family, neighborhood, or group of guys to share your teenage years. I still treasure those memories.

Frequently, during the fall of 1961, the five of us would meet at a restaurant. The local hot spot was Walt's 42nd St. Bar & Grill, located on St. Georges Ave, in Linden, NJ. Its draw was the massive parking area to the rear of the restaurant. Every evening, 25 or more teenagers and young adults from Rahway and Linden would "hang out" and pass the time. It was a good group and most of the teens got along very well. If trouble started, it usually involved an "outsider" from a different town starting an argument over some trivial matter.

At Walt's, one could meet up with friends, possibly set up a date, and expend a minimum amount of money. Typically, a hot dog or hamburger, with an order of fries and a soft drink, was under $1.00. To manage the increasing number of teenagers "hanging out," Walt's management hired a cop to "control the gang": Officer Bright. His job was to "move things along" while ensuring those entering the premises were "paying customers." Being teenagers with limited funds, it sometimes took many of us all of two or three hours to finish off a soft drink. Some patrons went as far as refilling their drinks from the trunk of their cars. Officer Bright was considered a "ballbuster" by all, but we also realized he was just doing his job. He generally left us alone unless the crowd got a bit rowdy, and then he'd somewhat forcefully clear the entire parking lot.

Following graduation from high school, our group's favorite pastime was meeting up at Walt's, whining, and complaining about our jobs. That was coupled with the prospect of being drafted into the military. Prior to 1973, every male in the United States, upon reaching the age of 18, was required to sign up for the draft (aka Selective Service System), more formally known as conscription. Following registration, each male was issued a card that assigned the individual a Selective Service Number. Every month a lottery was held and if your Selective Service Number was among the series of numbers drawn, you would receive a letter advising where and when to report for military duty. Being drafted usually meant you would be serving a three-year stint in the Army. Males still in high school or attending college received a deferment. The deferment remained in effect until they graduated or dropped out of either institution. Females were not required nor eligible to register for the draft. Some males preferred to control their own fate by volunteering to have their draft number moved up. Once this request was formally made, the volunteer's number would become part of the next draft lottery.

One evening, while venting our spleen over work and the draft, Chuck mentioned he was thinking about volunteering to have his draft number moved up. Of course, this created some very lively and heated debates; debates that carried over to each evening for well over a week. Finally, we reached a decision; the entire group would volunteer for the draft. Next came explaining our decision to our families. I'm confident you feel this may have been a hard sell. Just the thought of your son or brother joining the military, and being converted into a combatant, could be spine-chilling.

Well, it wasn't! It wasn't because all of our families remembered World War II, as well as the Korean War, and how proud they were to have their men serve our country. The world being at peace also lessened the impact. That's not to say they weren't concerned, because they were. They were as concerned as any other generation. In the 1960s, approximately 18 percent of the male population served in the military, compared to less than 1 percent (combined male and female enlistees) serving in it today. Also, up to the 1960s, all servicemen were respected and strongly supported by their country; unfortunately, that would change for the Vietnam War veteran.

Collectively, we notified the Selective Service Board of our decision to up our draft number. Now it was just a matter of time until we received our orders. Within hours, after filling out the paperwork, I began having second thoughts. Had I thoroughly thought this through? Did I really want to serve in the Army? For the next week or so I found myself losing sleep, as I wrestled with my decision. With each passing day, I became less confident I had made the correct decision: a decision that was "best for me." Bear in mind, I was also dealing with the understanding there wasn't any way of reversing my decision; one way or another, I was going into the military in the near future.

Finally, one night during our evening visit to Walt's, I shared my uneasiness and concern with the others. Instead of getting blasted with all four barrels, each of my friends expressed the same concern. Again, we were all aware our futures involved serving in the military. That was a given. Realizing and accepting the inevitable, the conversation turned in a different direction. By the end of the evening, Chuck and Bagofdonuts decided to keep things as they were, Willard decided he wanted to enlist in the Air Force, while Angelo and I decided the Navy was our choice. For the record, I leaned toward the Navy from the beginning. It was because my Uncle John, my namesake, served in the U.S. Navy during World War II. In fact, his ship participated in the battle of Leyte Gulf. From numerous conversations with him, I felt a connection with his stories, especially what it was like to be at sea. But enlisting in the Navy came along with a four-year commitment, rather than three years as a draftee in the Army. Though Angelo was three months older than me, he was eligible to enlist as a "kiddie cruiser," allowing him to serve a three-year stint. The Navy had a program whereby, if a sailor enlisted at 17 with his parents' written consent, he would only have to serve three years. This also applied to enlistees who were 18 years old. I was serving four years because, after some extensive testing prior to enlisting, I'd been offered a place at a class "A" school. Though the school only lasted nine months (on average), it did mean I had to serve four years.

Let me jump ahead for a moment. After being discharged, my uncle and I spent many evenings sharing our naval experiences. These were conversations that could only be understood and appreciated by wartime sailors. In the fall of 1973, he became ill and was diagnosed with terminal lung cancer. Throughout his hospital and hospice care, I visited him every chance I got. We continued sharing our sea stories right up to the time of his passing. It was extremely difficult to watch as the disease consumed my dearest naval friend. On numerous occasions, following one of our sea tales, one of us would say, "It would have been incredible if only we could have sailed together." With the ringing of eight bells, signaling the end of his final watch, I remember looking back and relishing the many evenings and conversations we enjoyed together. Now as I navigate through my autumn years, I often think or hope, maybe just maybe, someday soon we'll finally get our chance to "sail together."

USS LSM 119
FLEET POST OFFICE

FILE NO.

SERIAL NO.

September 3, 1945

Leyte Gulf, Philippine Islands.

Hello:

Yesterday was official V J day and we had a little celebration out here in the Gulf that was made famous not so long ago when the Jap Fleet was kayoed. There was many a time when I saw a fireworks display back in the States on the Fourth of July, but nothing that took place here last night ever compared to any of those occasions. There must have been a thousand ships here and each one had a couple of thousands thousand dollars worth of pyrotechnics, and we shot the whole bunch of them off at once. Absolutely beautiful! They were all signal flares of one kind and another, and all colors of the rainbow. Some went hundreds of feet in the air, and then burst into clusters of different hues, and others exploded with a color burst and a little parachute that kept the lights burning for many minutes. Watching them all together created a spectacle that was beyond description, and I doubt that I will ever see anything like it again. And then after a few speeches the beer was passed out and the boys became somewhat mellow.

Three fellows on this ship packed up and started for home yesterday to be discharged under the point system, and there must be 5,000 or more on the island waiting for transports back to the States, but... Alas, even though I have enough points, I have to wait for awhile. However, I am not too disappointed, because we are getting underway in a few days to start on what probably will be our last operation... and the most interesting one. I can't tell you where we are going, but you can use your own imagination.

USS LSM 119
FLEET POST OFFICE

FILE NO.

SERIAL NO.

As I told you some time back, Pharmacist Mates, Doctors and anyone connected with the Medicalk Dept. are not as yet eligible under the point system and this will continue under further notice. But I have good reasons for hoping that I will be back home for the holidays if not before. When it does happen that we start home, I sincerely hope that we are transferred to another ship. If we have to go back on an LSM it will be the longest t rip we ever took. Can you imagine going 12,000 miles at about 8 miles an hour ? I'll be a nervous wreck by the time we hit Frisco and the Golden Gate.

Naturally, I am so excited about it all that I just don't know what to say. I am still very thankful that I came out of it safely and also that I was spared some of the things that other poor guys went through, especiall the Marines and soldiers that had to do the real fighting. Once when we w ere on our way to Okinawa we could see the actual fighting and gunfire that was going on near the northern part of Luzon, and that was right near the end of the war. I don't remember whether I told you or not but Doctor Dustin and I had our pictures taken together on the Island of Ie Shima alongside of Ernie Pyle's monument. We just have the negative but no pictures, but as soon as I get a chance I will send you one.

I guess that's all for awhile. Harry should be home by this time or on his way, and I am just looking forward to the day when I climb into a cab at Pennsylvania Station and say, " 25 Grove Street, Kearny."

Bye now, John

JOHN W. CANAVAN CPHM

A copy of a letter my uncle, John Canavan, sent to the family in 1945 at the end of World War II. (Author's collection)

CHAPTER 2

To Sea or Not to Sea, That Is the Question

> The sea is dangerous and its storms are terrible, but these obstacles have never been sufficient reason to remain ashore.
>
> FERDINAND MAGELLAN

Swearing In—and I Never Swore like This Before!

The morning following our decision to enlist in the Navy, Angelo and I headed down to the Naval Recruitment Office in Elizabeth, NJ. Following a series of tests and physicals, we both received orders to report to the Naval Office at Penn Station in Newark, NJ, on January 25, 1962, to be sworn in. Once the swearing-in ceremony was completed, we would board transportation headed for the Great Lakes Naval Training Center, located in Great Lakes, IL. The base is about 40 miles north of Chicago along Lake Michigan. The closest city is Waukegan, IL.

As ordered, on January 25, we arrived early at Penn Station with our family and friends. Angelo and I each had six or seven people who came to see us off. We quickly learned we were about to enter a completely different world. As we reported to the Naval counter, they recorded our presence, told us to say a brief goodbye to those in attendance, and we'd see them in about 8 to 10 weeks. Following the "brief" goodbye, we were "directed" to enter another room through a large, paneled door. In other words, this was it. The "big send-off" was spending a minute or two with our loved ones. I think we were all expecting some type of ceremony to take place, including a speech addressing the new recruits and their guests. And to be honest, after some thought, I realized it was for the best. There weren't any tears or other signs of emotion by the enlistee or his guests but more of a simple farewell and we'll see you in the spring.

Once we entered the room, we immediately were introduced to the Navy. They did so by informing us not to ask any questions, "to keep your traps shut and to listen up for your next orders." Well, this certainly wasn't anything like I was expecting. How about thanking us or expressing some kind of gratitude or appreciation for volunteering. Almost immediately, we were told to remove our shirts, as they began administering a few inoculations; hmmm, I wasn't expecting that either. A few minutes later the door was locked, as a naval officer stood behind a podium and called for our attention. We were about to take the "Oath of Enlistment for Military Service."

We were asked to raise our right hand and repeat:

> I, ___________, do solemnly swear (or affirm) that I will support and defend the Constitution of the United States against all enemies, foreign and domestic; that I will bear true faith and allegiance to the same; and that I will obey the orders of the President of the United States and the orders of the officers appointed over me, according to regulations and the Uniform Code of Military Justice. So help me God.

This may sound like I've already been hitting the rum and coke, but following the swearing-in ceremony, and as the officer announced, "Welcome into the United States Navy," I actually felt different. Let's get on with boot camp; I'm "officially" a United States sailor, Ruler of the Seven Seas.

Angelo and I patiently waited for the train to arrive, along with over 100 other recruits. We began wondering what the next few days, weeks, and months had in store for us. Consistent with the Navy standard of "hurry up and wait," the train arrived several hours later.

As it pulled into the station, we were told to line up and begin marching toward the assigned track. We were also sarcastically reminded we didn't have the foggiest idea how to march. As we were "sashaying" along, I looked around and realized we looked like a pack of prisoners heading back to our cells; all disheveled and disorganized. I couldn't help but think, "What an absolute disgrace. Why did our mothers allow us to go out in the public dressed this way?"

During the 1960s, many rail companies employed Pullman or sleeper cars. Well, if this was true, you sure couldn't prove it by us. We were crammed into a railroad car that had certainly seen better days. The seats were worn, uncomfortable, and the smell reminded me of something from a cheap 5 & 10 store. And we were about to spend in excess of a day confined to our individual seats. The train made a number of stops along the way, picking up additional recruits en route to the Great Lakes Training Center. We were fed sandwiches and slept in the seats. The only time we could get up was to use the restroom (the word "head" was yet to be introduced into our vocabulary). By the end of the trip, nerves were a bit frayed and we were in dire need of some personal hygiene.

What Have I Done?

When we finally arrived in Chicago, a fleet of buses (after all, it is the Navy) were waiting to transport us to the Great Lakes Naval Training Center (aka, Hell, Gehenna, Hades, eternal damnation, etc.) to begin boot training; our worst nightmare begins.

Upon arrival at the base, our drill instructor (DI) was waiting patiently to greet us. Actually, in naval terms DIs are formally referred to as "recruit division instructors." However, by the recruits they are called, both formally and informally, "Satan's Prick" (aka Lucifer, the prince of evil spirits). I think the entire company of recruits immediately recognized "a problem." See, the vast majority of our company was made up of recruits from New York and New Jersey, whereas Lucifer hailed from Macon, GA. Thus, I began my naval training by learning I was a "fucking Yankee," while all the time thinking I was a Dodger fan. There were a few more bits of information he educated us on as well. It was his job to "wean us off our mother's tit; we were a complete and utter disgrace to the entire human race; our ranking fell just below maggots; and our best friend back home was banging our girlfriend like a screen door in a hurricane." Well, screw him, my best friend was standing right alongside me (aka Angelo, though Lucifer referred to him as "Greaseball"—it was a nickname he gave to every dark-haired, olive-skinned person). Also, my other closest friends were either in the Army or Air Force, so the joke was on him. Should I tell him? So, if my girlfriend was cheating on me, it was probably with a stranger. It was rewarding knowing just how wrong he was.

As he "walked" us over to our barracks, Lucifer began preaching about the greatness of the South, and how it was going to "rise again in all its grace and glory." This was followed by one of the "fucking Yankees" saying, "The only reason the South will rise again, is because shit floats." I think we all really enjoyed "marching" the next two hours in our civvies (meaning our civilian clothes).

Following our impromptu exercise, we were lined up outside of our barracks like cattle waiting to be slaughtered. We all wondered what form of torture was about to unfold. After several minutes, Lucifer "marched" us to a large building that seemed miles away. I believe he was beginning to realize a Northerner's marching technique can better be described as a swagger.

When we arrived, we were told to strip completely, place our clothes and personal belongings in a box, and address it to our home. Most of us were left with a wallet and maybe a religious medal. A quick look around revealed a bunch of ne'er-do-wells, all with a confused expression on their faces, standing at attention, while exposing their "third leg." So, modesty isn't exactly a naval attribute; get used to it!

Satan's Son noticed the majority of guys wore a religious medal around their neck. So he offered up some words of wisdom: "Listen up, I notice many of you ladies like wearing jewelry. But remember this, while God may own your soul, the Navy owns your ass!" And he wasn't kidding, which we quickly learned as we began our unofficial transition from civilian life into becoming sailors. This meant transforming from being an individual into being a member of a very well-oiled machine. An organization where one person isn't any more important than any other. If one person excels, it's because of a team effort; but if one individual is a screw-up (yes, it's an official naval term) the entire company suffers the consequences.

Once naked and free from our civvies (and our civilian life), we moved into the next room. Here we were greeted by a stern-faced sailor, who eyeballed each boot (a reference to a recruit who was in boot camp). After surveying us for a few seconds, he wrote a few numbers on a slip of paper and stuck it in our mouths. This slip contained our approximate size and measurements.

As we moved down the line, we held our arms out as we passed from station to station. During this "parade" we were issued our uniforms (dress blues, whites, hats, etc.) and accessories including underwear, peacoat, shoes, and boondockers. (A boondocker is a laced-up, rather striking combat-style boot. This boot would be worn more than 90 percent of the time throughout my enlistment.)

Once the pile of uniforms and accessories extended above our heads, our final stop was where we were issued our sea bag (aka a duffel bag): a sailor's canvas luggage. I'm sure you're wondering why they acted so casual about "sizing" our uniforms, I certainly did. Well, their reasons were very simple, yet spot on. By the time the new recruit graduated to the rank of "seaman apprentice," he realized both a mental and physical transformation. The change was remarkable and rewarding. This was especially true in team building; we learned how to work as a team. Success could only come from the company working together; if one failed, the impact was felt by every member of the company. The country would be a different place if this phase of boot camp could be shared and experienced by every American youth. Besides feeling differently about ourselves, we also felt differently about working with and interacting with others. Sorry, I'm so old I remember when the Dead Sea was alive and occasionally get sidetracked. Let's return to boot camp.

After receiving our uniforms, we "marched" over to the barracks. Barracks on a naval base are quite simple structures. They contain few windows, are completely bare of furniture, and they have walls usually painted an off-white, with a light-colored tiled floor. Within the barracks are row after row of two-tier high bunks. Each bunk has two footlockers at one end. The building also contained two other rooms, one the bathroom (aka the "head" in naval terminology). The head consisted of a row of toilets, urinals, and showers. Noticeably, the heads were open spaces completely void of any partitions, walls, or doors. And this was the case for a very good reason; privacy isn't a consideration or even thought about in the Navy. It was exactly the same on board every destroyer I served upon. The other room was Lucifer's perdition. To the best of my knowledge, no one from the company ever got more than a peek into his abyss. However, from all the beer cans in the trash, we were confident it contained a refrigerator.

After spending a few minutes in the barracks, we marched to another building. Here we received instructions on how to properly fold our clothes and make our beds (aka bunks or racks). We were reminded that deviations from these standards were considered violations and would result in some form of disciplinary action. As we were returning to our barracks, I couldn't help but wonder how the entire duffle bag of government goodies could ever fit into the footlockers. As it turned out, the footlockers were substantially larger than any locker on board a ship.

I'm confident the footlockers were designed to allow easy access for the DI to inspect each locker. It allowed him to verify a recruit's ability to follow Navy protocol when it came to cleanliness, folding articles of clothing, and efficiently using the space allotted. The lockers were simply empty aluminum boxes, lacking any dividers or partitions.

This simplicity also applied to the bunks. They were stacked two high and separated by several feet on either side. On board a ship the bunks were three high, with only inches separating the adjoining bunks on one side. We were completely unaware of the luxury we were experiencing with the sleeping quarters in boot camp.

In today's world, which is so dependent on electronics, it's important to describe how plain and simple barracks life was in the 1960s. I'll do so by addressing everyday items that were *excluded*: there were no radios, televisions, telephones, newspapers, or magazines of any sort. Intentionally, there wasn't any connection or contact with the outside world (bear in mind, the invention of the personal computer was decades away). To take it a step further, we were not allowed to even make a telephone call, write a letter (no pens, paper, or envelopes), nor could we receive mail for at least the first several weeks. By doing so, the Navy was successful in preventing most recruits from experiencing homesickness. Their approach was actually quite simple; they kept the boots busy and prevented any outside influences. If an emergency at home occurred, the recruit was sent to the chaplain's office. Let me conclude by saying, the Navy went as far as discouraging the recruits from even talking with one another. The only time we were free to talk among ourselves was when the "smoking lamp"

The true definition of air mail: a photograph of a helicopter delivering mail for the crew. When in a combat zone, mail from home and outgoing mail was held until the combat zone was exited to prevent a sailor's performance being impacted by bad news from home. When at sea, the only time mail was received was when operating with an aircraft carrier. (Author's collection)

was lit. The phrase "the smoking lamp is lit or out" has become more of a figure of speech in boot camp. In boot camp, "lighting the smoking lamp" allowed the recruits to relax and interact with each other. While at sea, the phrase "the smoking lamp is lit" was generally announced following some drills, refueling, or loading ammunition. During boot camp the "smoking lamp" was lit for less than two hours a day, usually following lunch and an hour or so before lights out.

After receiving and donning the naval uniform (work clothes), the attitude and demeanor of the boots began changing. I think it reached its peak following the GI haircut. Following these two events everyone looked similar and was treated accordingly. This clean-cut look converted us from looking like hoodlums or derelicts into seamen recruits. And it felt great!

***

Here's daily life at boot camp in a nutshell: reveille (consisting of a beer bottle being run around the inside circumference of a metal trash can) was at 5 am; then you wash up, dress, and march over to the mess hall (aka as the "mess deck" on board ship) to stand in a never-ending line for breakfast (remember the Navy phrase "hurry up and wait"). This "waiting" was in temperatures well below freezing and at times nearing zero.

Following breakfast, we lined up and marched back to thoroughly clean the barrack. It was during this activity that we were allowed to use the head. This may be difficult for many to understand, but our days were crammed from sunrise to sunset. Forget the luxury of raising one's hand and saying, "I'd like to use the head." It just didn't fit into the Navy's schedule. As strange as it may sound, all of the recruits were able to move their bowels sometime during the cleaning of the barracks. Once the barrack was clean, Lucifer would conduct his daily inspection. This included checking the bunks to ensure the sheets had "hospital corners" and were tight enough to bounce a quarter off the surface. As he was conducting his inspection, each recruit stood at attention at the end of his bunk, with his thumb reversing the top of his T-shirt under his chin to expose it to view. Lucifer would examine a boot's T-shirt to confirm he had taken a shower and the T-shirt was only worn for one day. Because of the close quarters on board any warship, ensuring personal hygiene was absolutely crucial and had to become a habit-forming event. This daily inspection also included properly shined boots, clean bed linen, and a spotless barrack. He concluded his inspection by examining every footlocker. This was to verify the uniforms were clean, folded, and stored according to naval standards.

Discrepancies during the first several weeks were frequent, immediately corrected, and not expected to be repeated. After several weeks, if a recruit failed inspection more than once, the entire company was disciplined. The discipline could range from shortening the time the "smoking lamp" was lit, to marching an hour or more after dark in near zero-degree temperatures, while holding our rifles over our heads.

Another was being awakened early, marching over for breakfast, and then allowing other companies to go in front of us. While we were disciplined as a company, correcting a repetitive discrepancy was left up to the company. Let me offer up an example. This one involved a recruit who failed inspection, a "violation" involving a personal hygiene issue, for a second time.

On the evening the recruit failed inspection, Lucifer informed us he was giving the company time to "discuss and handle" the matter. He wanted us to find and implement a course of action to promote good hygiene. This course of action should have lasting results for the individual, as well as "the company moving forward." He continued, "Sometimes, only a good 'scrubbing' stimulates an understanding that words just can't convey." He left, saying, "I'm going out for a few beers. I hope a permanent resolution has been reached and implemented by the time I return." Remember the adage "slap me upside my head once, it's your fault; do it a second time and it's mine"; I never heard an adage involving a third time.

Moments following Lucifer's departure, the company agreed to throw a "shower party": a party "in honor" of the boot who struggled with showering. Keep in mind, he had already caused the entire company to be disciplined the first time he failed inspection. So, on with the "party"; he was stripped naked, hauled into the shower, soaked with cold water (no need to waste hot water), and "scrubbed" stem to stern (another nautical phrase), with coarse scrub brushes. As a point of reference, these brushes were normally used for scrubbing our clothes. Every man participated and, in the end, the "pig" looked as if his body was one large birthmark.

During the remaining time I was a member of the company, this recruit was first in line for a shower. Also, prior to the daily inspection, he would ask other recruits to check his T-shirt, shoes, bunk, and footlocker. This "party" also became a reminder to the entire company of what to expect if anyone failed inspection. Even though the warning was clear to all, a week or so later a different recruit failed his second hygiene inspection. Before we were able to "teach" him hygiene must be a high priority, he went AWOL. In military terms, AWOL means "Absent Without Leave." The term AWOL represented any military person leaving their post without permission; bottom line, we never saw him again.

It's necessary to better explain what AWOL was all about. When sworn into the military, you verbally entered into an irrevocable contract with the U.S. government. Unlike a job, where you are interviewed, hired, and free to quit at any time, in the military, you were sworn in and committed to serve for a specific period of time. In most cases, the person going AWOL normally headed back to their hometown and was picked up less than a month after going missing. While I'm not sure if they are granted a second chance, I do know they are subjected to harsh punishment, including a court-martial, brig time (aka, a jail on a warship), and a dishonorable discharge.

***

It's very cold in the Great Lakes area from January through March. Late one night, Lucifer returned smashed and felt we had a bad day. As a form of discipline, he decided we should run the obstacle course in our underwear and boondockers. With many of the boots already suffering from colds, a week or so later about 25 percent of the company came down with pneumonia and were transferred to the base hospital. I was among the sick and one of eight diagnosed with double pneumonia. Due to the high number of sick recruits, the Navy initiated an investigation. While I may not know the full extent of the findings or disciplinary panel actions, I understand following graduation the DI was removed from recruit training. It was at this time when my best friend and shipmate, Angelo, and I were separated. I recovered a little more than a month later and returned to a "new" company. The new company had about the same amount of basic training remaining as I'd had before being hospitalized.

A few years later, I recognized the DI from my first company as I was crossing ships. He was coming up through a hatch covered in oil. I immediately noticed he had been busted (aka reduced in rank) and we were the same grade level. Our eyes met, and I didn't even acknowledge his existence (as a DI, Lucifer was a 1st class machinist mate, and when I saw him his rank had been reduced to 3rd class).

Life in boot camp was very repetitive; we were being converted from thinking and acting as civilians to like military serviceman. Many different topics were addressed during classroom training and testing sessions, but the one constant was the physical training. This physical training included the frequent running of the obstacle course, as well as hour after hour of marching each day. If it snowed, we shoveled it to the side and then marched.

About mid-way through boot camp, we were issued rifles and conducted different routines with these unloaded weapons. My personal favorite was the Queen Anne Salute. And it was frowned upon to refer to your rifle as a gun. See if you can understand Lucifer's simple example showing the difference: "This is my rifle, this is my gun; this is for fighting, and this is for fun!" I'll let your imagination decide the objects he grabbed on during his demonstration.

Along with what seemed to be endless hours of marching came hours devoted to testing, Navy protocol, and standards, as well as other classroom activities. Below is a summary of some of the major classroom topics covered during boot camp:

- Basics of naval life, including wide-ranging physical conditioning and testing (i.e. push-ups, sit-ups, running the obstacle course, swimming, etc.).
- Introduction to the various naval ranks and ratings. This included extensive testing to identify or determine what classification a sailor would be best suited to.
- A detailed overview of the Uniform Code of Military Justice (UCMJ), which is the legal system that governs all members of the U.S. military. The UCMJ covers legal issues from the apprehension and confinement of military personnel to regulations involving the courts for military appeals.

- We were introduced to the Navy chain of command, as well as naval customs and manners.
- We learned the importance of standing a watch. A watch is defined as a period of time when a sailor is assigned specific and detailed responsibilities. He must execute them to the best of his ability, while meeting the expectations of the commanding officer and Navy practices.
- When on board ship, watches are stood both in port and at sea. With the exception of general quarters, standing watch may be the most important and frequent activity on board a warship. When standing watch, a sailor must devote his full attention to his assigned duties. Inattention or negligence can result in serious consequences for the ship and its crew.
- Each recruit is introduced to basic seamanship, including naval jargon or lingo. But this is better taught and understood on board ship.
- Armed conflict lectures, including a detailed explanation of expectations and limitations covered under the Geneva Convention. These lectures included your duties and responsibilities if you were taken prisoner by a foreign government.
- The identification and recognition of naval ships and aircraft.
- The introduction to naval weapons and training in small arms. This included classroom lectures on the safe operation of a number of weapons. If I recall correctly, the rifles we marched with were Springfield bolt action, but the ones we fired were M-14 rifles.
- All recruits received training in shipboard damage control and firefighting. This included techniques for escaping from smoke-filled rooms, fighting a fire, dealing with the opening and closing of watertight hatches. Fire is the primary concern when at sea. All sailors had to be able to swim and practiced how to abandon ship. This was accomplished by having the recruits follow a specific procedure as they jumped off a high platform into a swimming pool. But the worst was being enclosed in a large room and having tear gas introduced, with the recruits testing their skill in properly putting on a gasmask.

When the training was completed, the graduation exercises began. This culminated with a number of companies "passing in review." This was performed in front of the base senior officers and any visitors. At the conclusion of this exercise, the sailors are officially promoted from "seamen recruits" to "seaman apprentices," thus symbolizing the end of boot camp.

***

Weeks prior to completing boot camp, a selected number of future sailors are presented with the opportunity of attending a class "A" school. They are selected based upon the results of extensive testing. The balance received orders to report directly to the fleet, and they would be taught a classification by means of hands-on or on-the job training.

When the Navy offers a class "A" school, the recruit is usually allowed to choose from three possible classifications. In my case, I was offered sonar, electronic technician (ET), and radar school. After some consideration, I chose radar. Close to the conclusion of boot camp, I received orders to report to radar class "A" school. At the time I was completely unaware that only one base, in the entire network of naval bases, taught the duties, requirements, courses, and activities to be classified or certified as a radarman. Just as I was, you're probably wondering: what exotic or beautiful location was I about to spend the next nine months in? Maybe Pearl Harbor, possibly San Diego, or how about Pensacola or Key West? Well, as it turns out, radar class "A" school was located at the Great Lakes Naval Training Center. Yup, only about 300 yards from where I was standing.

One of the benefits of training to be a radarman was advancement. Each time a sailor was eligible for advancement, regardless of his classification, he was required to pass a comprehensive test. Radarmen (as well as sonarmen and electronic technicians) were labeled as "critical" classifications, so they were promoted simply by passing the test. Whereas in less critical classifications (meaning their physical numbers within the Navy were much higher), in order to be promoted a sailor not only had to pass the test but often, they'd have to score within the top 5 or 10 percent of those tested.

Following boot camp, we were given a 10-day leave. As with most sailors, I returned to my hometown to spend time with my family and friends, before reporting for my first assignment. Just prior to departing boot camp, the graduating class is reminded they represent the U.S. Navy and to act appropriately. The final "lecture," before departing boot camp, was given by the base chaplain. It's one I shall always remember.

At the conclusion of his sermon the chaplain provided some excellent advice. He said:

> Remember when you return home, you will be the center of attention. This attention may require getting together with people who are unfamiliar with Navy jargon. This interaction is likely to include parties or dinners with family, neighbors, close friends, or others. It's during these events you must be careful of the words you select when speaking or communicating with civilians. For instance, as dinner is served and after thanking the Lord for such a wonderful meal, it may be inappropriate to say something along the line of "Excuse me Grandma, could you please pass the fucking butter?"

In early June, graduation day had finally arrived. In our "dress" blues, each graduating company marched in perfect step in front of senior officers, the DIs, as well as any family or friends who attended. Let me add, the majority of the "newly promoted" sailors did not have any family or friends in attendance, including me. Traveling during this period was extremely expensive and reserved only for local or the wealthiest of families. Here's an example of what I am talking about. The roundtrip fare from San Diego to Newark Airport in 1962 was approximately $290. In 2022, by searching for inexpensive flights, you could easily beat that fare. Most families couldn't afford such a cost. At the time, my salary was $99 a month. Fortunately, the Navy paid for all fares incurred by traveling between assignments. This included my travel expenses to fly home from boot camp, before returning to the base just on the other side of the fence.

The Good Old Days Just Weren't That Good!

After boarding a plane for the first time in my life, I flew from Chicago to Newark. I was fortunate enough to have been assigned a window seat. As you can imagine, it was an exciting experience, although it was a prop plane. I was absolutely amazed at the thrust of the engines during takeoff and equally impressed as we landed. But I was really taken aback by the number of people who went out of their way to talk to me.

While I may have looked the part of a seasoned sailor, I've always wondered how disappointed they must have been learning I had never been on board a ship. On a more positive side, I actually impressed myself with just how courteous and respectful I had become. I was stunned as the words "Yes sir" and "Yes ma'am" just rolled off my tongue. And it wasn't an act. It was then I began to realize the respect I had for all people, regardless of their race, color, or status. Respect was not a sign of weakness but rather a reflection of good manners. It created an immediate bond with others. Without respect was avoidance and confrontation. And I must say, it was absolutely real and by God, it felt good. Was this the same raggedy-ass kid who boarded the train only last January?

It was a weekday when I arrived at Newark Airport, and the airport was extremely busy. As I deplaned and entered the terminal, I saw my dad waving to get my attention. He had completed his shift and come directly to the airport. I was so excited to see him; I couldn't wait to get into the car and head home. During the entire ride he grilled me with a constant barrage of questions, but I didn't mind one iota. He asked how it felt to be a sailor, what it was like flying in a plane, why I chose radar. His excitement was on the same level as my own; it was so cool.

About an hour later we arrived home, and within a few days my transformation became perfectly clear to all. I must admit, I was beyond proud of what I had become. While the entire family commented and made fun of the "new" me, it impacted my mom the most. And it didn't take long before she began showing signs of being more than casually annoyed with her "new" son. I can vividly recall the expression on her face, as she witnessed me making my bed and picking up after myself; it was absolutely priceless. And she was even less thrilled when I "suggested" bedsheets should include hospital corners. But the straw that broke the camel's back was when she caught me unfolding and refolding my clean laundry, the Navy way. You may be wondering why I didn't go with the flow and let my mom make the bed or fold the clothes while I was on "vacation." Well, I had just graduated boot camp and had little knowledge of what was coming next. Before heading home, I decided I wanted to avoid breaking the good habits I had formed, especially by having things done for me. As it turned out, it was the right decision. Throughout my entire enlistment I made my bed and folded my clothes the Navy way. And, let it be known, this continued for a substantial amount of time after I was discharged.

The word quickly spread around town that I was home on leave. In fact, there was even an announcement in the *Rahway Daily Record.* The paper had a column dedicated to Rahway residents serving in the military. It had become the norm to publish information about local servicemen. While my "closest friends" may not have been there, I received calls from many former high school classmates and was thrilled by their invitation of getting together. Several nights later we met at Walt's, and it turned out to be an absolutely incredible eye-opening experience. And it would be just the first of many similar experiences repeated throughout my leave. I was excited to see my friends and learn about what I missed over the winter. This excitement quickly turned to shock as I learned, with the exception of the temperature, everything basically remained the same. A few of my friends changed jobs, others ended and began new relationships, and a few bought different cars, but that was the extent of it. Not even one person mentioned their future goals or plans. Their life consisted of living at home, going to work, and meeting up at Walt's almost every night. This daily get together could be better described as borderline depressing.

Suddenly, things became unbelievably clear; it was as if time had stood still, then reversed into the night before Angelo and I were sworn in. I began to realize how complete my transformation had become. I was a completely different person. I was a person given a new start, a new life; a life filled with excitement, promise, purpose, with a positive look toward the future. And, by God, I planned to take full advantage of the opportunity. There were even a few times our conversation became a bit touchy, bordering on being somewhat caustic. At its peak, someone would say something along the line of, "So, Sailor Boy, what you're saying is we're no longer good enough for you?" While I may have offered up a less than honest answer, I began wondering if or when they intended to grow up. There was so much more in everyone's future than working and hanging out at Walt's. But as we were talking and, much to my dismay, I began to realize maybe, just maybe, Lucifer was right.

But the highlight of my night occurred when Officer Bright came up, congratulated me on finishing boot camp, and for "doing something with my life." He mentioned he served a stint in the Marine Corps, and suddenly we had something in common. It was a component that changed our relationship entirely. As I looked around, I recall saying to him, "I never want to return to my previous life."

Once again it hits me, boot camp should be a requirement for every teenager following graduation from high school. This should be a prerequisite regardless of if the student is college-bound or entering the workforce. While high school focused on educational material, it lacked even the most basic development involving career potential, human interaction, team building, respect, purpose, and the confidence or focus to move forward. A "future" just doesn't happen; it must be molded, developed, and nurtured. So many young adults sit around and watch the world revolve around them. It's usually too late when they realize life has passed them by, and they end up with nothing more than a rude awakening.

I found the military had a special way of opening one's eyes to understanding "things don't just happen." They happen because we make them happen. It starts with a vision, followed by setting a series of attainable milestones; milestones which lead us to our ultimate goal or goals. Unsurprisingly, these milestones are likely to be tweaked as time passes and our lives change. And our goals should include milestones for both our career and personal life. Unquestionably, the military prepares a young person with an excellent roadmap and vision toward the future.

While it was enjoyable, after interacting with family, neighbors, and friends for 10 days, I was more than ready to return to my Navy life. I was definitely looking forward to radar school, followed by my first shipboard assignment.

CHAPTER 3

Blips, Bogeys, Bandits, and Skunks

Upon returning to the Great Lakes Naval Training Center, I peered through the barbed-wire fence; a fence separating basic training from the rest of the base. There within my view was a group of newly arrived recruits strolling along in their civvies. The first thought that crossed my mind was, "You poor bastards haven't a clue what's ahead."

The difference between boot camp and the regular Navy is like comparing shoelaces and mooring lines; they are just that different. I'm not sure I was prepared for such a dramatic change.

In boot camp you saluted everything that moved; now we only saluted commissioned officers.

While in school, I was temporarily free of watches. In boot camp there was a watch for everything. Some examples involved the waste dumpster (to prevent thieves from stealing our garbage), a "head watch" (to ensure there was an adequate amount of toilet paper available at all times), or a barrack watch (to protect those sleeping from a sudden attack by enemy forces). And these were not disciplinary type watches, but rather run-of-the-mill, everyday watches experienced by every "Boot."

At the end of the day, we were free to leave the base as long as we returned prior to the morning muster (at 0800). Plus, we had weekends totally to ourselves.

During weekdays, reveille was at 0600. We were awakened by a bugle recording that could be heard throughout the base. The time between reveille and when classes started (0800) was controlled by the individual sailor. In other words, we could wash up, eat, and clean the barracks at our own pace. Taps was sounded at 2200, but it only meant lights out. It was up to the individual when he wanted to turn in. Occasionally, the barracks were inspected to ensure they weren't being turned into pigsties. If discrepancies were found, they were immediately corrected. Furthermore, following boot camp, I never witnessed a sailor slacking off when it came to cleanliness or personal hygiene.

A huge change was eating in the mess hall. Rather than marching over for a meal and waiting in endless lines to be fed, the mess hall was open for several hours for each meal. It was left up to the sailor to decide when he wanted to eat. The variety of food was almost unimaginable. During every meal you could select hot or cold food and eat as much as you desired, with great desserts. And for the record, this was an order of magnitude better than the food on any ship. In short order, four radar strikers paired up and ate all our meals together.

When we were out of class, we were free to talk or interact among ourselves. While the barracks remained free from distractions (i.e., TVs, radios, etc.), a sailor could always find relaxation at the base's Enlisted Man's Club (EMC). At the club you could listen to the radio, watch TV, see a movie, play pool, or a variety of other activities. All EMCs, throughout the world, were equipped with bars. However, when it came to consuming alcohol, they followed state and local laws.

Radar school followed a very intense and condensed curriculum. In one of the first classes the instructor asked us to "take a look to your left and right." He continued, "At graduation one of these sailors will have failed or dropped out." Hmm, if that wasn't an incentive or attention getter, I don't know what was.

Most classroom lectures lasted eight hours a day, including breaks and lunch. In addition, there were a few hours of laboratory work and a moderate amount of homework. With classes and labs so concentrated, plus the homework, I can say with a great deal of confidence, I'm unable to recall leaving the base on a weekday.

The barracks were more or less our sleeping quarters. Most of the students in the barracks were in their late teens, so the barracks were more for personal use, sleeping, and "grab ass" activities (i.e., fooling around, playing cards, cribbage, and personal matters). As you can imagine, the barracks were anything but conducive to studying. The classrooms were always open for use by the students; however, the labs were closed. For security reasons, all classified information was securely locked within the labs.

The majority of classes, each involving selected topics, were divided into week-long segments; more complex topics ran for two weeks. Most segments began on a Monday and ended on a Friday. At the conclusion of each segment, the students were given a comprehensive test covering the week's classroom lectures and labs. Passing meant you advanced to the next week. If a student failed, he was allowed to repeat the segment. If a student failed more than one segment, he was released from the school and shipped off to the fleet. At the conclusion of radar school, we were informed that over 60 percent of our original class graduated. From the original class, I was aware of those who failed a segment but unaware of who may have failed a second time. Whenever a student failed and had to retake a course, he was physically relocated to a different barracks. His new barracks was made up of students taking the same segment. It made so much sense; students weren't competing, so it allowed the sailors to share notes and help one another.

During the introduction to radar school, the instructor mentioned there was an incentive for finishing in the top 5 percent of your class. Following the first few classes, we were asked to fill out a profile and information form. In this questionnaire we were asked the type of ship we would like to be stationed on board. We were informed, for those finishing in the top 5 percent, the Navy would try to assign the ship-type of their choice. When it was my turn to "select" a ship, I did so through the process of elimination. First, I was completely turned off to a base or land assignment. Likewise, I wasn't interested in serving on board an auxiliary ship (i.e., oiler, ammunition, stores, tender, or supply-type ship) or an aircraft carrier, which operated 300 or 400 miles offshore from any conflict. I was really focused on being stationed on an "in your face" warship. Following the Korean War, all of the battleships had been decommissioned, so I was left with either cruisers or destroyers. After some consideration, I selected the Navy's workhorse, the "greyhound of the sea," the destroyer. It may be worth mentioning, there was minimal demand for radarmen on board a submarine, plus to serve on a submarine I would have had to extend my enlistment by two years. The "selection" was limited to the type of ship; it excluded all other factors such as a coast, specific base, or homeport, etc.

So, the incentive to finish in the top 5 percent was a decent motivator. For me, serving on a warship was equally as important as avoiding other types of naval vessels. The Navy is all about being part of a team; it was teamwork that made us strong. Therefore, while none of us knew where we ranked within our class, if a sailor received orders to report to the type of ship he requested, he assumed he finished in the top 5 percent.

Throughout radar school, my studying habits were as intense as the subject matter. I always felt highly confident after taking a segment test. But following Navy tradition, the results of all testing were classified; the students were simply told if they passed or failed.

Radar class "A" school lasted approximately nine demanding and challenging months. It proved to be so much more than staring at a scope for four hours each watch. We hit topics I never imagined. An example might be the complete functioning of the radar system; from its wiring, through the various vacuum tubes incorporated in its design.

Early on you learned the radarmen's working space is called the "CIC" or "combat information center," and it is part of the OI Division (Operations Intelligence). CIC is the tactical center on all naval warships. Everything that happens while a ship is underway is influenced, evaluated, and monitored within CIC. For this reason, there is a dedicated line between the Bridge (where all surface and air contacts were reported to) and CIC (referred to as "Combat"). Even a basic change in the ship's course is made via a request to CIC. Upon receiving such a request, CIC performs the required calculations and reports back to the Bridge. As an example, let's assume the calculated results required a change of course to 275 degrees. Once calculated, the radarman on the sound-powered headset with the Bridge says, "Bridge, this is Combat [actually shortened to 'Bridge/Combat'], recommend a course change to 275 degrees." The sailor on the Bridge repeats the information and passes it on to whoever is OOD (officer of the deck) or the captain. All calculations from CIC are in the form of a "recommendation." Once the recommendation is received, the captain or OOD decides whether to follow it. Normally within seconds after receiving CIC recommendation, the captain or OOD could be heard saying to the helmsman, "Change course to 275 degrees." While serving on board three different destroyers, I'm unable to recall a single instance when CIC's recommendation failed to be executed.

The interaction between the Bridge and CIC becomes even more critical when operating as part of a task force. A task force is a temporary group of dissimilar ships, usually surrounding one or more aircraft carriers. When operating within a task force, the ship carrying the highest-ranked naval officer is referred to as the "flagship." The flagship controls all the movements of the task force and is normally stationed near the center of the formation.

When operating within such a formation, a destroyer is assigned a specific location on the perimeter of the task force. The assignment comes along with the understanding that the ship is to maintain this position for safety and security purposes. When attached to or operating within such a group, CIC is instructed to constantly monitor the ship's bearing and distance from the flag. If it appears we're drifting off station, CIC will notify the Bridge and include a recommended course or speed change to return to our assigned position.

All task force course and speed changes are controlled by the flagship. As an example, let's assume the flag is on a carrier and is about to launch or recover aircraft. For this type of exercise, to achieve the maximum relative speed across the flight deck, the flag would order a course and speed change directly into the wind. Whenever making a major change, the flag normally gives the task force advanced warning. This notification allows each type of ship to calculate a course and speed to maintain the same relative position within the formation. As an example, after providing advance notice of the pending change, to execute the flag simultaneously communicates the new course and speed to all ships by saying, "Change course to 275 degrees, speed 32 knots in 5–4–3–2–1… change course to 275 degrees, speed 32 knots."

I'm sure you realize, when compared to a destroyer, an aircraft carrier requires considerably more time and distance to complete a course change. During a change in course, all ships are required to maintain the same relative position from the flag. Therefore, calculations will differ from ship to ship. Following the flag's order to execute, CIC continually reports the flag's bearing and range to the Bridge. This reporting continues until all the ships are on station. Ships are positioned on the perimeter to prevent enemy submarines or aircraft from entering the interior circle of the task force.

Before returning to radar school, it may be a good time to mention that when an aircraft carrier changes course to either launch or recover aircraft, a destroyer is selected to leave its perimeter station and take up a position aft of the carrier's stern. This position is on the port side of the carrier, and the ship is referred to as a "plane guard." The purpose of a plane guard is one of safety. In the event an aircraft is ditched or crashes, the destroyer's duty is to rescue the crew. When a destroyer receives this assignment, CIC calculates the fastest course and speed to assume the position of plane guard. Of course, the maneuver (course and speed) to assume this position is solely the responsibility of the destroyer. The change in course or speed takes into consideration the closest point of approach (CPA) to any other ship, following the Navy's strict protocol. This is to avoid compromising safety and reducing the danger of collision.

When operating within a task force, the flag monitors the performance and ability of all ships to execute their orders in a competent, efficient, and timely manner. If you ever want to visually witness or feel the definition of a "shit-fit," just let your captain be reprimanded by the flag for failing to have his ship maintain its relative position. I was fortunate, as none of the captains I served under were ever dressed down by the flag. If such a dress down were ever necessary, I understand a public flogging is much less painful.

Returning once again to radar school, below is a brief summary of the major segments related to the duties of a radarman. We'll start with the area most people think of when it comes to being a radarman, looking for blips or contacts on a surface scope or on an air search radar scope.

Surface Search Radar

The type and model of the surface search radar (SPS-10) presented during school was used almost exclusively on all warships of the Vietnam War era. It was a medium-range and extremely reliable radar system.

The air search and surface search radars were retrofitted or updated from systems employed during World War II and the Korean War and had a range from 10 to 12 miles. When at sea, CIC manned the surface and air search radars 24/7. CIC was accountable for monitoring, interpreting, and reporting all activity appearing on the scopes. When sailing within 50 miles of land, it was normal to track multiple contacts simultaneously. The farther we were from land, fewer contacts appeared on the scopes. While cruising to or from the Far East, there were four-hour watches when neither a single air nor surface contact would appear on radar scopes.

Whenever a blip or surface contact was observed, the Bridge was immediately notified. Talking into a sound-powered phone, the radarman would begin with "Bridge/Combat, we have skunk alpha [a 'skunk' is an unidentified surface contact and alpha (A) would indicate it was the first surface contact on the watch] bearing 281 degrees, range 20,000 yards." Upon receiving notification from CIC, the sailor on the Bridge would inform the captain or officer of the deck about the contact.

As a point of interest, the sailor on the Bridge would simultaneously notify the Bridge, as he repeated the information into the sound-powered phone connected to CIC. This was the case with all communications between CIC and the Bridge. Repeating information was the Navy's way of ensuring the accuracy of the data being conveyed. Normal protocol was for the Bridge to acknowledge the contact and request we track the skunk. Using a grease pencil on the radar scope, a radarman would mark the skunk's track once every minute and feed the skunk's bearing and range to the CIC watch supervisor. The watch supervisor would plot the data on a "maneuvering board" sheet and, after three or four minutes, would calculate the skunk's course, speed, and CPA (closest point of approach). The information was reported to the Bridge with the radarman saying, "Bridge/Combat, Skunk Alpha is on course 143 degrees, speed 8 knots, CPA 6,200 yards."

If the CPA was 4,000 yards or less (I believe that was the minimum criteria) the Bridge would request an update every three or four minutes, or if there was any change in the CPA. If the CPA was greater than 4,000 yards the Bridge would say, "Continue tracking and report any changes." If the CPA was less than 2,000 yards (there are 2,000 yards or 6,000 feet in a nautical mile), the Bridge would request a course or speed change to increase the distance of the CPA, reducing any concern or danger of a collision.

CIC would constantly track all skunks until they were no longer on the radar scope. Once a skunk reached its CPA, CIC would report: "Bridge/Combat, Skunk Alpha has passed its CPA and is no longer closing" (meaning it has reached its closest point of approach and the distance between the ships has begun to increase). Of course, whenever a skunk made a course or speed change, one that could or would affect its CPA, the Bridge was notified immediately. Unlike air search radar, the blip on a radar scope only identified it as skunk or contact. There wasn't a means of identifying if it was a commercial or military vessel, its country of origin, destination, or any other characteristics. The only way these could be determined was by means of visual contact.

Air Search Radar

When underway our Air Search (SPS-6) was also manned 24/7. Depending upon altitude, the radar had a range exceeding 75 miles. When an aircraft was picked up on radar, it was immediately reported to the Bridge. Again, using a sound-powered phone, the radarman would say, "Bridge/Combat, we have Bogey Charlie ['bogey' being a term for an unidentified aircraft, 'Charlie' meaning the third air contact of the watch] bearing 184 degrees, 42,000 yards, altitude 35,000 feet, and closing; not squawking."

As with a surface contact, the norm was for the Bridge to request CIC track and report on the contact. The reference to "squawking" meant, at the time of the report, we were unable to determine if the contact was a friend or foe. All planes (commercial and military) from the United States and our allies had IFF equipment on board (identification friend or foe). This equipment contained receivers and transponders to receive and respond automatically concerning their identity. Within a few sweeps of the radar, the IFF equipment would have been activated and automatically responded, thus showing if the aircraft was a friend. If the aircraft was a friend, an image would appear above the blip (somewhat like a stack of arcs). CIC would then notify the Bridge by saying, "Bridge/Combat, Bogey Charlie's course is 230 degrees, speed 320 knots, CPA 11,000 yards, altitude 35,000 feet, and squawking friendly." While CIC continued tracking the aircraft, unless there was a significant change, no further information was exchanged between CIC and the Bridge.

Generally, most seagoing ships and aircraft used virtually the same routes when sailing between the United States and the Far East. Naturally, our adversaries were aware of these routes and we repeatedly encountered their presence with frequent flyovers. Far and away, Russian reconnaissance planes were our most frequent "visitors." An aircraft that did not squawk friendly was reported to the Bridge as a "bandit." The Bridge would request a constant update of a bandit's position, including any course, speed, altitude, or CPA changes.

As we were in international waters, it was perfectly acceptable for our adversaries to fly in this international air space. I should also mention, it was relatively common to encounter Russian trawlers as well. Trawlers were relatively small vessels, usually disguised as being fishing boats, but crammed with every imaginable size and type of antenna known to man. For the most part they were involved in monitoring electronic signals, referred to as electronic warfare. It was an activity the United States also conducted on a regular basis.

Navigation

Navigating is much like driving a car between point A and point B. To travel between two points, a driver would plan a route using maps of the area. On water or at sea, rather than utilizing maps, a ship navigates by means of laying out a route on navigational charts.

Navigating becomes more challenging when a land mass no longer appears on a radar scope; everything looks the same. Frequently the ship would be hundreds of miles from the closest land, a condition that may last for days on end. During such times, CIC maintained the ship's position using a technique called "dead reckoning." This method of tracking the ship's movement or position was greatly enhanced with the use of an ancient mariner instrument called a sextant. This instrument has been used by mariners since the 1700s to perform "celestial navigation" by measuring the angle between an astronomical object and the horizon. It provided superb precision and was still used in the 1960s as an excellent navigational tool on board ships.

Dead reckoning involved drawing a planned route on a chart. The lines represented the courses necessary to sail between two points or ports. As long as land appeared on the radar scope, the supervisor of the watch (aka, petty officer of the watch) accurately tracked the ship's location. He did so by plotting the bearing of three known land points, points he identified on the radar scope. He would plot the bearing from three of these points on the navigational chart; the point where the lines intersected would be the ship's present location.

Once we were out of range of land, we began using the dead-reckoning method of navigating. Using this method, the ship's position was estimated by plotting the actual course and speed of the ship relative to time. However, as time passed, the effects of "set" and "drift" on dead-reckoning projections or positions decreased in their reliability and accuracy regarding the ship's location.

The term "set and drift" represents the impact external forces have on the ship's ability to remain on the intended course. These external forces are represented by the ocean current, winds, and other meteorological conditions (i.e., rain, thunderstorms, even temperatures) that could cause a deviation in a ship's course or speed.

Set refers to the ocean's current direction, as expressed in degrees; whereas drift applies to the current's speed measured in knots. The impact of a 1- or 2-degree variance, and possibly an increase or decrease in a few knots of wind, could have a major impact on a ship's projected path and position. To offset the effects of set and drift, the ship employs the sextant. The sextant's accuracy is approximately 0.1 nautical miles, a variance well within the acceptable range for ships at sea.

I'm sure today's Global Positioning System (GPS) technology has tightened up this range, but at the time, I believe a deviation of several nautical miles was not uncommon. Inasmuch as celestial bodies were necessary in sextant calculations, the measurements are taken during evening hours and require a virtually clear sky. The sextant's data was provided to and recorded by CIC on a chart. Once plotted, CIC provided the Bridge with recommendations to correct any deviations caused by set and drift. After plotting, the dead-reckoning process begins once again.

Navigating Into or Out of Port

CIC had minimal input when navigating into or out of port. This type of navigating was performed visually from the Bridge; generally, with the captain as the OOD. It was one of the few times that, when the ship was underway, CIC played a relatively minor role. Surface search radars were less sensitive monitoring the area immediately around the ship.

However, CIC did track the ship's position and recommended course changes to remain within the channel. Navigating within a channel is never a straight line between two points. Also, the deepest part of the channel may not be in the middle of the waterway. As a point of reference, the draft (or draught) of a Fletcher-class destroyer was almost 18 feet. The draft is defined as the distance between the lowest part of the ship's keel and the waterline of the vessel. The Fletcher-class destroyer had a displacement of 2,100 tons.

Tracking the ship's progress, as it enters or departs port, is the least challenging navigational activity. The most challenging element is dealing with small boat traffic within the harbor. As ridiculous as it may sound, many small craft operators felt it was imperative to get close to a warship as it navigated the harbor. Visual navigation was absolutely essential in managing small craft traffic. This form of navigation required sailors stationed along the port and starboard sides of the ship. The sailors were equipped with sound-powered phones connected directly with the Bridge. Their job was to report any obstacle that could impede the ship's ability to safely navigate through the channel. The reporting sailor would be accountable for tracking and reporting any changes. This would continue until the obstacle was no longer a threat or was transferred to another shipmate with a better view.

While I never understood it, in many U.S. ports, small craft owners continually showed this overwhelming propensity to get as close as possible to military ships. This included all warships, regardless of their size or type. The most positive thing I can say about these dangerous boaters is that their actions were negligent and beyond reckless. I've always been amazed that people are allowed to purchase and operate small craft without being licensed or having any training or basic understanding of seamanship. Many small boat operators haven't a clue on how to safely navigate a waterway or, more importantly, how treacherous the sea may become. They sail in much the same manner as they'd drive a car. Most were unaware of the forces associated with tides, winds, water depths, or currents. They were completely ignorant of how irresponsibly they operated their watercraft, and unaware they were compromising the safety of themselves and their passengers.

Lacking any navigational training, if an emergency occurred, many small boat owners believed simply shifting into neutral or turning the engine off would result in the boat coming to a full and safe stop. This was especially true with many sailboat operators: it seems sailboat operators have a greater number of those who are inexperienced and lack good navigational skills amongst them. Because wind is their only source of power, sailboats have the "right of way" over any and all power boats, craft, or ships. Let me provide you with an example, so you fully understand the danger many sailboats unknowingly create. This particular event involved our ship as part of a rather large task force. The task force included an aircraft carrier, a few cruisers, and a dozen or more destroyers.

The home port, for most 7th Fleet destroyers, was the 32nd Street Naval Station. This base is located several miles from the inlet to San Diego Bay. In contrast, the aircraft carriers and cruisers tied up at the North Island Naval Air Station (NAS), located at the northern end of Coronado, close to the mouth of San Diego Bay. This was an ideal location for these huge ships, making it easy to navigate in and out of port. In some ports, navigating a channel is so difficult a harbor master is brought on board. A harbor master is an official with full understanding, experience, and responsibility for assisting ships navigating into or out of a particular harbor.

As this convoy of warships began navigating through San Diego Bay, a small sailboat decided it was necessary to get a close-up view of the aircraft carrier. Fortunately, the sailors on board the carrier realized this "loon-a-sea" was on a collision course with this 1,100-foot vessel. It became obvious the wind was negatively affecting the sailboat's movements. Worst of all, it appeared the sailboat's operator was unaware he (or she) lacked control of his boat. Likewise, the operator was ignorant of the danger they had created for the passengers. Being aware of the situation, it was up to the carrier's captain to take evasive action to avoid a collision and possible injury to those on the sailboat. The captain responded to the emergency by ordering this massive vessel to reverse its engines. As the "cockroach" passed, the operator waved to the captain, more or less as a gesture of thanking him for preventing the collision. As we were leaving the harbor, we noticed the Harbor Police had stopped the small sailboat and began towing it to safety. How I hoped this moron was penalized to the full extent of the law. There had to be consequences for operating a watercraft in such a dangerous manner and putting six or seven lives unnecessarily at risk.

Officer of the Deck (OOD)

An OOD is either the captain or a direct representative of the captain. Being thoroughly aware of who is in command is essential for the safe operation and security of the ship. At any given time, there can only be one OOD and there can be absolutely no ambiguity or confusion over who holds that position. For that reason, the position of OOD is formally passed at the end of watches, during general quarters, and whenever the captain takes command.

There is a formal procedure when changing the position of OOD. It begins with the OOD on duty checking with CIC to determine if there are any upcoming actions or events scheduled to take place, confirm the navigational track, review any and all orders, as well as report the position of all nearby ships and aircraft. Once the review is completed and understood, the current OOD verbally states his name and rank, and completes the transfer by saying the name and rank of the new OOD, followed by the words, "has the Deck and Conn." The meaning of this phrase states who has the sole responsibility of commanding and directing the ship.

The new OOD assumes command by stating his name and rank, followed by, "I have the Deck and Conn." Only orders that are given by the OOD are accepted and executed. An example would be, if Lieutenant J. G. Chase Donnelly was passing command over to Lieutenant Nathan John, he would state for all within earshot, "This is Lieutenant J. G. Donnelly; Lieutenant John has the Deck and the Conn." In return, Lt. Nathan John would say, "This is Lieutenant John, I have the Deck and Conn," and the transfer of command is complete.

ECM Equipment (Electronic Counter Measures)

ECM equipment was among the highest technology at the time. It was used to listen for and record on tape electronic signals (frequency, wavelength, duration, etc.).

This "listening" device was usually operated while at sea, most frequently along the coast of non-allied countries.

It was a superheterodyne receiver (aka a sophisticated radio), with the capability of constantly scanning a wide band of frequencies. It stopped whenever it sensed any signal, whether it was radar, radio, or any transmitting electronic device, and began recording.

It wasn't uncommon to forward a recorded tape onto Washington for evaluation and analysis. There was an instance when, after forwarding a recorded tape to Washington, a representative from one of our intelligence agencies came on board for a few days. His assignment was to observe the signal and its location. For the record, with this one exception, once we forwarded a tape there wasn't any further communication regarding the signal.

With radar systems (**RA**dio **D**etection **A**nd **R**anging) the antenna transmits a signal and, when the signal strikes an object, it "bounces" off and returns to the transmitting–receiving antenna. This returned signal is projected as a blip on a scope in CIC. The direction, and time it takes for the signal to make this roundtrip, is measured and converted into the object's bearing and range.

However, in the proper setting the transmitted signal can be picked up 1½ times beyond the range of the original signal. So, if the transmitting radar has an effective range of 20 miles, the ECM equipment could receive the radar signal approximately 30 miles away.

I have to veer off course for a moment. Earlier, I referred to the ECM equipment as a superheterodyne receiver used to record signals emanating from adversaries' equipment. I must admit, when in port I used this sophisticated piece of equipment to listen to local rock and roll stations. Frequently, during my off-hours, I would sit in CIC with a headset on and tune in to a local rock and roll station. I'm hoping you're creative enough to know where this is going. Yup, using old or dated tapes, measuring 10 or 12 inches in diameter, I could record this precious music, almost endlessly. Within a short time, I was recording my favorite DJs' shows from a number of different San Diego stations.

And rather than taping the shows on the highest-quality settings, to get as much content as possible, I taped at a lower quality. Because the equipment was so sophisticated, recording at a lower-quality level had no impact on the sound. If I recall correctly, I could record days of music on just one tape; it was absolutely gold when on a six-month WestPac cruise (a WestPac cruise being a Western Pacific cruise, referring to a naval ship getting underway for an extended cruise to the Far East).

It didn't take long before my OI Division shipmates heard about the recordings. By the way, it was an idea many others thought of but, in all honesty, they just couldn't be bothered to set up the equipment. And it really didn't matter; I was more than happy to share the tapes with them. They were of special value when we were out at sea and beyond listening range of San Diego. You can be assured, listening to the tapes never interfered with our shipboard duties. It goes without saying, the highest priority was to use the equipment for electronic surveillance purposes.

When we were on such assignments, the music tapes were securely locked in the radar equipment room. But their best use was during our 1965 deployment to Vietnam. To build on that, it became interesting when the captain caught wind of the little treasure. One day, while en route to the Far East, I was stopped by the chief radarman. He began the conversation by making reference to the tapes. I immediately thought I had somehow screwed up. But instead, he was rather pleased and joked about its creativity. In the end, he asked me to speak with Burl Roads, an ET, to see if the tapes could be played on the mess deck. Burl, being an electronic genius, rigged up a system to play the music as desired. He arranged for the music to be overridden by any and all announcements from the Bridge. Burl was always the person you'd go to for this type of expertise. As funny as this may sound, initially the music included all the commercial ads, which created a bit of confusion. The crew couldn't understand how we could pick up a radio station from the United States when we were thousands of miles from there. By the time we reached the coast of Vietnam, the crew became used and accustomed to this condition; in fact, it increased their listening pleasure. This was especially the case as it was basically the only form of entertainment when we arrived in Vietnam. The exception being the frequent replaying of the same Super 8-millimeter movies we had on board.

DRT (Dead-Reckoning Tracer)

The DRT was a device designed primarily for ASW (antisubmarine warfare). The plotting surface of the DRT was about waist high, and approximately the size of a desk. It automatically projected the movement (course and speed) of the ship as we tracked a submarine. Sonar provided the submarine data, and it was manually plotted on the DRT. In addition to ASW operations, the DRT was also used for man overboard drills. During the second half of my enlistment, the DRT became obsolete technology and was no longer used. The top of the "retired" DRT was used as a desk or work surface.

Naval Gunfire Support (Shore Bombardment)

Naval gunfire support (NGFS), aka shore bombardment, is one of the destroyer's most important and primary roles. This was especially the case when it came to the Vietnam War.

Once general quarters was ordered and the captain authorized "firing to commence," all communications, calculations, and instructions to direct the fire of our main armament was controlled within CIC. This became my specialty, assignment, and primary duty during general quarters.

Before the captain gave the orders to "commence firing," an extensive sequence of events had to happen. This sequence impacted every sailor on board and not in a small way. While the captain may delegate the firing responsibility to his professionally trained staff, he remained in total control and responsible for his command.

It's important to know that while CIC is interacting with a Marine spotter and preparing to commence firing, the captain is dedicated to many equally important activities. These include:

- Keeping our ship safe by taking evasive action if, or when, fired upon. This includes frequent and random course (zigzag) and speed changes. By doing so, he lessens the risk of being hit by return fire from the enemy's shore batteries.
- Maintaining a broadside profile, ensuring all four 5-inch guns are trained on and available to engage the enemy.
- Always being cognizant of the depth of the waters, both under the ship and those ahead.
- Maintaining contact with all the various departments to ensure the crew operates at the highest levels throughout the mission.

Not unlike a well-trained and experienced symphony, sailors on board are assigned a very specific duty during general quarters. With the captain as "maestro," he ensures the entire ship is operating like a finely tuned orchestra.

As commanding officer, he is accountable for the ship's performance, while remaining vigilant for the safety of his crew and ship. During my tour in Vietnam, I was so fortunate to have served under two extraordinarily experienced and professional captains. There isn't any way of defining the amount of respect and admiration most sailors had for their captain. If called upon, most would sail into hell with their captain; and, as you'll see, that's exactly what we did. This high degree of respect came from his almost obsession with perfection; this was an obsession that would only be satisfied through constant and repetitive training. While conducting training exercises, if there was a weakness, a slow response, or if the captain observed a group's lackluster performance, he'd immediately address the issue. Let me offer up an example.

During an exercise, a gun mount fell behind the other three mounts. They took too long to "reload and fire" (simulated). After the exercise was completed, the captain called the officer involved on the carpet and expressed his view in a very descriptive manner. Let's just say, sticking an ice pick in one's eye would be much less painful than having a captain feel your performance, or that of your team, was less than stellar. In this particular case, the gun crew was required to train hour after hour, over multiple days, until they proved they were proficient in their function. I can assure you, every man in that gun mount understood the captain's goal was perfection. At the end of the training, they excelled as a gun mount crew.

This is just the way it was throughout the Navy. I'll offer up another example of the Navy's demand for excellence. When we were assigned as Da Nang harbor defense ship, the Navy also assigned a team of UDTs to use our ship as a platform from which to operate. For the most part, the UDTs acted, trained, ate, and slept completely independent of the ship's crew. Shortly after their arrival, one of their team members must not have lived up to their performance standards. I mention this because this UDT sailor sat on the deck, with a mask covering his eyes, as he continually disassembled and reassembled his weapon. Blindfolded. He continued this exercise for most of the day, rarely stopping or getting up.

While this type of training may appear to be over the top, I can assure you, every battle-hardened sailor understood its meaning; it was essential to have this degree of perfection in executing one's duties. I suspect that it was from this intense training came the phrase, "War is hell, but peacetime is worse!"

NGFS or shore bombardment is usually a coordinated effort between a naval warship and a Marine spotter. The maps used for NGFS missions contained incredible detail; enough detail that would allow a ship to fire on a fixed target, without input from a spotter. The concern surrounding such blind firing (called "direct firing") involves the high probability of collateral damage, especially as it applied to civilians. In the case of the Vietnam War, when President Johnson approved the use of NGFS, he did so with an important caveat. All NGFS missions had to be directed by a U.S.-trained specialist, from either the Navy or Marines. As you will see, with the exception of the UDTs, every spotter I communicated with was a Marine.

***

Throughout the weeks of radar school, one or more of the students would ask how the class was going. Referring of course to the top 5 percent. Most sailors hoped to be assigned to a specific type of ship, and it varied greatly. Therefore, we were frequently reminded the test scores were "classified." As mentioned, at the conclusion of every segment we were given a comprehensive test. Approximately an hour following the test, a list was posted showing the sailor's name, service identification number, and a single word next to his name: "passed" or "failed."

In the beginning, the dropout rate was moderate; however, as time passed this rate continually fell. Thinking back, I'm unable to recall anyone failing a test after week 20. Personally, I was highly confident that I had done very well. I can remember only one segment that gave me a scare. I was confident I passed the segment test but unsure if I scored in the top 5 percent. When I had the opportunity I asked an instructor, who was not only a great instructor but generally a good guy, about my test score. I recall his reply was, "You passed, now move on."

Greyhound of the Sea

Shortly after passing the final exam, we received our orders. The anxiety associated with opening the orders bordered on overwhelming. While opening the envelope, I thought, "And the winner is?" Carefully, I read the papers until I finally came to it; I was to report to the *McDermut* whose home port was San Diego, CA. Thank God, I was assigned to a destroyer! My first course of action was heading over to the base library to research the history of this ship.

The *McDermut* was a Fletcher-class destroyer; named after Lieutenant Commander David A. McDermut, an officer in the Union Navy during the American Civil War. He was killed in battle on April 18, 1863. The ship was laid down on June 14, 1943, at the Federal Shipbuilding & Dry Dock Co., in Kearny, NJ. Could this be true? I was born on April 20, 1943, in Kearny, NJ. It was commissioned by Mrs. Woodrow Wilson on November 19, 1943. During its entire construction, we were but a few miles apart.

After its "shakedown cruise," it was assigned to the Pacific Fleet. The ship participated in numerous battles; once it came under heavy attack from Japanese planes, as it was conducting shore bombardment. Its most recognized battle was

Photo of the USS *McDermut* (DD-677), estimated to have been taken pre-1960 given the radar antennae on the mast. (U.S. Navy, Wikimedia Commons)

the battle of Leyte Gulf in the Philippine Islands. Another coincidence: my Uncle John was on a ship that participated in the battle of Leyte Gulf.

Following World War II, it was decommissioned on January 15, 1947, and recommissioned in early June 1951, to participate in the Korean War. Like all Fletcher-class destroyers, *McDermut* was a well-constructed warship and outfitted as follows:

Characteristics

Category	*Specification*
Displacement	2,050 tn
Length	376'6"
Beam	39'8"
Draft	17'9"
Propulsion	60,000 shp, geared turbines, 2 propellers
Published speed	35 kt (40 mph)
Range	6,500 nm at 15 kn
Complement	319 (officers and enlisted)
Armament	• Five 5", .38-caliber dual-purpose guns • Ten 40 mm antiaircraft guns • Seven 20 mm antiaircraft guns • Two depth-charge tracks • Two 21" torpedo tubes (removed when recommissioned during the Korean War)

During its service, the *McDermut* received 10 battle stars for World War II, and five battle stars for its service during the Korean War. While it was a superb fighting ship, its end was sudden, tragic, and unfortunate.

***

Along with my orders came a 14-day leave. After approximately nine months of intense studying, I was looking forward to some time off. I must say, knowing it was likely that the "playing field" at home was the same as when I left made my leave much more pleasant. All remained virtually unchanged since my last leave. Once again, it was like going from Friday to Saturday, except nine months into the future. All the same, I had a great time on leave, especially talking with my Uncle John, all the while wondering what life on board a destroyer would be like.

One interesting development came from a neighbor but grew throughout my leave. Shortly after my arrival home, I learned the majority of my relatives, neighbors, and former teachers had been interviewed by the FBI. The interviews were focused on my behavior; they were asked to share opinions and experiences about my character. I learned it was part of a background investigation initiated by the Navy. This background investigation was necessary because I would be handling and operating highly classified information, documents, and devices.

At the start of radar classes, the students were advised the training documents, books, and equipment, used in every segment of the school were classified "confidential or secret." So, from the onset, we were well schooled in dealing with and handling classified information. The Navy worked on a strict "need to know" basis ("loose lips sink ships"). Whenever we left port, only a handful of people knew of our destination and even fewer about our overall schedule. The only known information was whether it was a training exercise or a longer deployment. Once the ship was underway, the crew was notified about the current day's schedule, activities, and possibly our next port of call. But at no time was the crew aware of the ship's overall agenda; in fact, most learned of our assignment as we were arriving on station.

Getting back to my leave, I must say it felt great to spend a few weeks in civvies, although my friends and family continually encouraged me to wear my uniform. Much to their disappointment, they saw me in it when I arrived home and again the day I headed out. No one could be prouder of his uniform than me, but the change of scenery and duds felt awfully good.

CHAPTER 4

Anchors Aweigh

> The pessimist complains about the wind; the optimist expects it to change; the realist adjusts the sails.
>
> WILLIAM ARTHUR WARD

Following my respite, my flight from Newark Airport to San Diego was exciting for a number of reasons. It was my first trip west of the Mississippi, my first time flying on a jet aircraft (Boeing 707), and once again I almost felt like a celebrity. People at the terminal and on the aircraft were asking me about life as a sailor. Unlike Chicago or Milwaukee, where sailors were abundant, it was rare to see sailors on the streets in either New York or New Jersey.

Following an uneventful flight, we landed at the San Diego airport. If you've ever taken off or landed in San Diego, you know it can be a memorable event. This downtown airport is considered one of the more challenging to fly in or out of. With mountains to the north and east, the pilot must contend with a steep approach path, one that brings the plane directly over the city, coupled with strong tailwinds blowing in off the Pacific.

Upon arriving in San Diego, I entered the terminal and, unlike Newark, there were sailors everywhere; some were arriving, others departing. The airport processed so many arriving sailors, there were overhead signs and arrows directing them to the "Naval Information Booth." After checking in at the booth, I was pointed in the direction of a line of Navy buses going to various locations. As instructed, I boarded a bus heading to the "32nd Street Naval Station." I thought, "Can this really be correct?" The 32nd Street Naval Station sounded more like a bus or railway depot. Realizing I was early, with eight hours to find my ship, I was confident I had plenty of time, even if the instructions were misleading or I arrived at the wrong location.

As it turned out, the 32nd Street Naval Station was the second-largest surface ship base in the United States, with Norfolk Naval Station being the largest. The base consisted of 13 piers, stretched over 977 acres of land and 326 acres of water. It was the home to more than 50 ships of every type and designation. As the bus passed through gate security, the sheer size of the base became apparent. Following a 10-minute ride from the main gate, we arrived at a pier. I was told the *McDermut* was the third ship in from the pier. I couldn't believe my eyes; four similar destroyers tied up alongside one another, and I was about to cross two to board the "Mighty Mac."

As I left the bus, I mentally rehearsed the proper protocol for crossing and boarding a naval vessel. As a sailor crosses the gangway and steps onto a ship's quarterdeck, he salutes and says to the OOD, "Sir, request permission to cross." The OOD returns the salute and responds with, "Permission granted." The same ritual is followed as he crosses each ship. As a sailor steps onto his duty ship, he salutes and says to the OOD, "Sir, request permission to come aboard," and the OOD salutes and responds with "permission granted." When a sailor reports for duty and boards for the first time, he salutes and says to the OOD, "Sir, John Calder, reporting for duty, request permission to board." The OOD returns the salute and replies with, "Permission granted, welcome aboard."

As a point of interest, in port the quarterdeck watch usually consists of an officer (OOD), a petty officer of the watch (POOW), and a lower-ranked sailor who performs miscellaneous tasks. In some locations the OOD and POOW are armed with an unloaded .45-caliber handgun. When boarding a ship for the first time, sailors quickly learn weapons on board warships are as common as forks and knives. After I was welcomed on board, the POOW directed the junior sailor to escort me to OI Division (Operations Intelligence) living quarters.

On all Fletcher-class destroyers, OI Division living quarters are located just below a 5-inch gun mount near the stern of the ship. On the other hand, CIC is located closer to the bow, below the Bridge and abutting the wardroom (the officer's mess and conference room). This arrangement was well-thought-out; if the ship was struck by enemy fire in the forward or aft sections of the ship, there was a high likelihood some of the sailors in OI Division would survive. This philosophy generally applied to many of the critical classifications; the design generally separated crew quarters from their workspace.

As I carried my duffel bag down the ladder (not stairs) to the OI Division, I was greeted and welcomed on board by a number of radarmen and ETs. It was customary to welcome all new sailors, regardless of rank, into the division. Not knowing what to expect, it felt great to be welcomed into the inner circle by those who would become my closest shipmates. Almost immediately I began feeling at home. As I was being assigned a bunk and locker, I began to realize just how little personal space I had to store all my worldly belongings. By worldly belongings, I'm referring to my Navy-issued clothing; no civilian clothing whatsoever was allowed on board. Any and all civilian clothing would have to be stored in rented lockers off the base. As I looked around, I realized every other sailor, regardless of rank, had the same size locker and bunk. I had at least twice as much personal storage space in both boot camp and radar school. After assessing the situation, I realized there wasn't any sense in complaining.

And if that wasn't bad enough, I took a close look at my bunk. These weren't bunks but rather cots suspended in "pancake" layers of three high. I'll take a stab at describing the sleeping arrangements. You can be assured that whatever you might imagine, it was far worse and even more cramped.

Remember what H. G. Wells said about sailors' living conditions: "Sailors ought never go to church; they ought to go to hell, where it is much more comfortable." He wasn't exaggerating. There were stack after stack of columns, with three cots suspended from overhead I-beams. Each cot had a canvas bottom with a group of springs attached to an aluminum tubular frame. The back of the tubular frame rested on a hook welded to a vertical beam. The front was connected to the cot above and below by means of a hook and chain link system, with the upper cot supporting the lower. I'd estimate there were about 18 inches between bunks. The "mattresses" were well used and less than 1½ inches thick; the pillows were even smaller. In order to get into the footlockers, sailors lifted the lower bunk and suspended it using the hook and chain arrangement (see below). This was extremely annoying to the occupant of the lower bunk, especially when he had just come off the midnight watch. Sailors having the 0000 to 0400 watches were allowed to sleep in until 0700. As one would expect, the junior sailors were assigned to the lower bunks.

Seeing the bunks for the first time, I wondered what kind of sadistic, perverted, vicious, cruel, barbaric, savage son of a bitch could ever expect a group of humans

OI Division quarters on the *Stoddard*. This photo shows how close the bunks were mounted and the lack of any form of mattresses. (Author's collection)

to live in such deplorable conditions. But after a week or so, I found it wasn't all that bad; maybe misery does like company! With that said, whenever the galley decided to serve Navy beans or anything containing cabbage, the look of misery and pending sorrow was projected on the face of most sailors. As you would expect from a bunch of guys, and in the true spirit of the Navy, let the competitions begin! The only air conditioners or air handling systems were used to cool the electronic equipment; there was minimal movement of air within the sleeping quarters. There were times when walking into the crew's quarters, following the serving of one of these gaseous delights, could make your eyes water; and God forbid the thought of striking a match. After being exposed to the living conditions, I was reminded it wasn't a cruise liner; it was a warship. When designing a warship, the architects' focus certainly wasn't on luxury or comfort. Instead, their focus had to be on designing the most powerful, fierce, and effective seagoing war machine.

Within hours after reporting for duty, several of the radarmen took me on a tour of the ship. We visited the most important areas; the tour included an introduction to other crew members. Our journey ended up just outside CIC; I was about to see a ship's CIC firsthand. The first unusual feature I noticed was the door. Rather than a hatch, there was a pocket door that slid into the bulkhead, leading into CIC. It was both breathtaking and magical as we entered. I had imagined this moment for the better part of a year, and I wasn't the least bit disappointed.

While the space may have been tighter than expected, I immediately identified every device or instrument within sight. It was absolutely amazing. The darkness of CIC gave way to an aura of beauty; it was all there. The first object I noticed was a backlit board, listing all the ships and their call signs for the upcoming operations. The radar scopes (referred to as repeaters) were being inspected and tested. It was apparent, even to the untrained eye, we'd be getting underway in the near future and operating as part of a task force. Most amazingly, I connected with all of it. What an incredible day it turned out to be. Welcome on board, John, welcome aboard, sailor!

The following morning, during our "gourmet" breakfast, I asked one of the other radarmen, "What's next?" He replied, "OI Division musters at 0800 hours on the starboard side of the 01 Level." I remember thinking, "What in God's name did he just say?" Rather than asking him to repeat what he said and confusing the matter even more, I thought I'd take a different approach. I asked, "OK, I'm new on board. Could you point me in the right direction?" I was hip, so I threw in a few choice strategically placed expletives for effect. This was intended to show him that although I was new on board and green, I was also a cool salt. With a smile on his face, he said, "OK, as you leave the crew's mess, there will be a ladder leading up to the main deck. At the top of the ladder will be the passageway just outside CIC. Continue going forward and exit through the hatch leading onto the main deck. Stay on the starboard side and you'll see a ladder a few feet aft of the hatch;

this hatch leads up to the 01 Level. Climb this ladder and when you reach the top, remain on the starboard side; just hang around the area near the bulkhead, that's where we muster. It's that simple."

OK, now I'm beginning to understand what's happening here; sailors are known for playing practical jokes on "green" apprentices; especially those assigned to their first ship. I was confident I was in the process of being pranked. So, what's next? Maybe I'll be asked to fetch a bucket of steam or better yet, sent to a neighboring ship to borrow 100 feet of chow line. I continued, "Very cute, OK you got me; now can we get serious?" He laughed, I mean really laughed, and said, "Aye, aye, and if you think I'm pranking you, well just follow me." As we moved along, he pointed out the various markers along the route. I didn't realize it at the time, but I'd be speaking this gibberish fluently within a week or so.

At 0800, OI Division mustered on the 01 Level, and the size of the group had more than doubled. Turns out the married men, or men with families in the area, had been away for the weekend but had now returned. Much like a regular civilian job, when in our home port and unless a married man had duty, he would leave the ship at 1600 on weekdays, head home, and return by 0800 the following morning. Also worth mentioning, when tied up in our home port, if a married or family man had a watch, he frequently traded it with one of the single sailors from the same division. His "debt" would be repaid when we were away domestically or internationally; it worked out well for everyone.

During muster, after the division officer had verified all the sailors were present and accounted for and had gone over the "Plan of the Day," the division was released to commence daily operations. At this point you're probably wondering what a typical day was like for a sailor assigned to a destroyer. Let me begin with saying, when operating in the San Diego area, the ship averaged the same amount of time in port as at sea; usually a week or two at a time.

A typical day in port versus at sea couldn't be more different. There may be even a third variable: when the ship was operating in foreign waters. But let's focus on being in port or at sea while operating off the West Coast of the United States.

In port, the crew participated in numerous simulated training exercises. A major portion of their time was also focused on maintenance. This maintenance could be either routine or preventative maintenance.

Routine maintenance included activities such as the testing of all instruments and systems, inspecting the radar antennas, and ensuring CIC was neat, clean, and prepared for the next time we got underway. It also meant making sure all of the charts for navigating the harbor and offshore were in top condition and up to date. In addition, we kept our living quarters clean and tidy, as well as our area on the 01 Level.

Preventative maintenance (PM) was based upon time and operating hours. PM was scheduled and performed to reduce the likelihood of failure or malfunction while underway or conducting training exercises. PM was based upon detailed data logs. These logs were kept and posted on a daily, weekly, monthly, or annual basis. The objective was to maintain, remove, or replace aging system components before they failed. A good example is the vacuum tube used to operate the surface and air radar systems. Before going any further, let me mention, although we were introduced to transistors, diodes, and integrated circuits in radar school, our radar systems were not upgraded with these components during my enlistment. However, new designs or upgrades installed on the ship contained this new technology.

While in port, the crew stood watch, but much less frequently than at sea. In port, the OI Division crew generally stood four-hour watches on the quarterdeck with the OOD. The OI and OC Divisions (Operations Communication) normally provided the POOW and the junior sailor for this watch. As mentioned, this watch was required to acknowledge sailors as they arrived, departed, or crossed the ship. While in port, the quarterdeck was manned 24 hours a day. It was also the duty of the junior sailor on watch to wake up the replacements for the midnight watches (0000 to 0400) and mid-watches (0400 to 0800).

At sea, maintenance was performed only on an emergency basis. The crew was more focused on operational tasks and duties. With the exception of training exercises, while in port relatively few people were ever in CIC. With CIC containing numerous classified documents and devices, only officers, radarmen, and ETs had access to or could enter this space. While at sea it was manned around the clock. Under normal running conditions CIC was staffed with an officer of the watch, a relatively senior radar petty officer (watch supervisor), and several junior radarmen. The petty officer normally assigned one of the junior sailors to the surface scope to watch, track, and report all surface contacts.

There were times when the air search radar scope was manned by the officer (or chief radarman) assigned to CIC. It was a voluntary assignment; it gave them something to do and allowed time to pass a bit faster. All other times, it was manned by a junior radarman or the petty officer on watch. Sailors on both scopes wore sound-powered phones connected to the Bridge. As mentioned, if a surface or air contact was observed, the sailor on the scope would first report it to the petty officer of the watch or officer on duty. With the acknowledgment of the POOW, the contact would be reported to the Bridge. CIC would track the contact until it no longer posed a concern or threat. Under normal conditions, each crew member was assigned two four-hour watches per day. For clarity, the two watches are over and above the sailor's normal duties and expected participation in training exercises. With few exceptions, the majority of exercises are conducted while at general quarters.

While at sea, GQ was generally called once a day. By having these frequent drills, the crew was able to maintain the highest degree of readiness. This was the Navy's primary objective for the entire fleet. It wasn't until we were in actual battle situations that we fully appreciated the meticulous, exhaustive, repetitive, and thorough training.

In a combat situation, second best doesn't cut it. Being other than the best equates to failure or possibly disaster. Our successes in Vietnam were 100 percent attributable to the intense and repetitive training demanded by the Navy.

***

Following my first morning muster, I mentioned to a senior petty officer that I hadn't been given an assignment. I barely finished the sentence when he said, "Sorry, I forgot to mention, the chief wants to meet with you in CIC at 0900, at which time you will be given your first assignment." The chief, the highest-ranking radarman on board, wanted to meet with me. The excitement was palpable. I was about to receive my first shipboard assignment. I spent the better part of the last year studying and busting my balls leading up to this very moment.

I was practically out of breath when I arrived in CIC. The chief introduced himself, welcomed me on board, and we chatted for a few minutes. He informed me we would be getting underway later in the day. Our agenda included conducting a number of exercises just north of San Diego. He also mentioned there was a large area off the coast with waters that were restricted to use by only military ships and aircraft. The Navy uses these restricted waters to conduct exercises, many of which involve the firing of live ammunition. Can you imagine a rubbernecking sailboat crossing the path of an aircraft carrier as the ship was conducting flight operations, or a destroyer firing its main armament?

I thought that he must be telling me the ship's agenda because I had a vital role in the success of the exercise. It must be a test of sorts; he intends to observe the skills of the latest addition to the radar squad. I was ready for my first assignment; I couldn't have been any more prepared! Following a few more details about the upcoming exercise, the chief "hits" me with my first assignment: "Starting immediately, you'll be working in the galley as a mess cook!" He continued "You'll report to the master cook immediately and, for the next week or so, you'll report to the galley for duty at 0400. You'll perform your assigned duties until dismissed by the chief or master cook."

Really? Mess cooking? I thought, "I'm a radarman, not a culinary specialist." Was this in some way associated with my past experience of being a short order cook? If so, how did the Navy find out I had such a skill? I'll bet those friggin' FBI agents learned of my kitchen skills when conducting my background investigation. The most positive thing that came to mind was shock and disappointment. Here I was anticipating the chief was about to tell me how my arrival may have saved the ship. Or maybe he was about to ask me to share my extensive radar class "A" school knowledge with the entire radar staff. Instead, I'm being sent to the galley? No way, it just can't be true, it must be a mistake!

This must be a prank. I look around, anticipating seeing people pointing, laughing, and slapping their thighs, as they enjoy the entertainment; but there's no one within sight. Still, being a nonbeliever, I thought perhaps a more rational approach may turn this toxic red tide. I suggested the chief relax a bit and reconsider this illogical decision.

From his reply, he "definitely" understood my guidance; his reply was immediate and definitive. Before I was able to answer, and knowing he was aware I was less than a "happy camper," he relieved my pain by adding, "When boarding a ship for the first time, every new OI Division seaman apprentice is assigned to work in the mess for a week, and you're no exception!" Continuing, "If you resist, show any signs of unwillingness to follow my orders, or cause even the slightest amount of trouble, the week or so will be extended to four weeks or more! Do you understand?"

Minutes later I reported to the chief cook, who turned out to be a really great guy. In fact, we remained friends as long as both of us were on board the *McDermut*. Surprisingly, we were transferred within a day of one another. My assignment would be limited to peeling potatoes. Later, I felt it was a great assignment; not only was it a walk in the park, it was also a remarkably rewarding experience.

My workstation or workspace was an infrequently used hatch, leading from the galley onto the main deck. As I was receiving my assignment, I noticed a rather unsophisticated-looking machine a few feet from the hatch. The machine was designed to remove most of the peel from the potatoes. The capacity of the machine was about 10 pounds of unpeeled potatoes. It had an internal rotating drum, which looked much like a hand-held grater, along with an on-off switch. When activated, the drum rotated and removed more than 95 percent of the potato peel. My assignment was to turn the machine on, remove most of the potato peel, and toss the partially peeled spuds into a large bucket of fresh water. Once this phase was completed, the machine was reloaded and the sequence repeated. When all the potatoes were processed, the machine was cleaned in preparation for the next meal. The next step was to carry the buckets over to the infrequently used hatch, where I had placed a bucket of clean water. Of course, with a crew over 300, this cycle was repeated numerous times.

I sat on the hatch opening, facing the starboard side of the ship. From this vantage point, I had a clear view of the Pacific Ocean. Once seated, I began removing any remaining potato peel, along with the potato eyes, using a hand-held potato peeler. I did this for all three meals, with potatoes being a staple for most meals. The assignment would take me about one and a half to two hours per meal. Once the potatoes were ready for the galley, I was on my own; free to do whatever I'd like. I worked a little more than six hours a day, the evening meal came along with a few more spuds, yet I was excused from standing any watches. The only drawback was my day began at 0330. As I said, while the assignment was a walk in the park, the best was yet to come.

CHAPTER 5

Underway, Shift Colors

I finished my first mess assignment as we started the process of getting underway. When departing or arriving in port, the "Special Sea Detail" is called. The Special Sea Detail involved most of the crew. Every crew member was assigned a station entering or departing port. For the radarmen, our duty station was CIC. Once the Special Sea Detail was mobilized, it was shortly followed by an announcement over the 1MC, "Underway, shift colors!" The 1MC was a general communication system, with speakers in every compartment and space throughout the ship. The phrase "underway, shift colors" meant the final line, securing us to the pier, had been dropped. Upon announcing we were underway, our country's flag was lowered from the fantail and raised up the main mast. It was at this time that the unfathomable occurred to me: "Am I going to get seasick?"

As we drifted away from the dock, I was in CIC hoping to be assigned a task. Lacking any experience, I became an observer rather than a participant. This being my first time getting underway, I was amazed and impressed with the professionalism shown by the entire CIC team. This group of fun-loving, women-chasing, hell-raising sailors was uniformly focused on navigating out of San Diego Bay. It was like being in an ER, watching doctors and nurses caring for a heart attack patient. Even though we had minimal input to the navigational task, there was no fooling or joking, just the complete focus and commitment to the safe operation of the ship. People only spoke to communicate information and data related to the navigation process. As a reminder, navigating into or out of port can be challenging and involves numerous potential distractions.

At 376 feet, a destroyer may be considered a small ship; however, when 10 or more are part of a convoy, it becomes a breathtaking display of America's firepower. It not only draws attention from small civilian boaters, but people stopped and lined the docks and bulkheads along the route. Others could be seen standing by the windows in the high rises or skyscrapers; people will watch in awe as this fleet of magnificent warships heads out to sea.

As we neared the mouth of the harbor, I realized our maximum speed was about 3 knots. This was the reason it took so long to reach the open seas. Finally, we exited the harbor and, with the chief's permission, I stepped outside and saw the swells a few hundred yards ahead. Once again, the thought of being seasick returned.

As we passed the one-mile buoy, I noticed the ground swells were causing the ship to roll. It was at this moment I realized all was well; the motion of the ship wasn't bothering me in the least.

When we were about five miles out and the small boat traffic had begun to dwindle, an announcement came over the 1MC for the Special Sea Detail to "stand down and carry on," as the captain increased speed to about 15 knots and I headed back to the galley. With all the challenges associated with leaving port, only about 75 percent of the task force ships made it to the rendezvous point by late afternoon. Some 30 miles off the coast, we reduced speed and waited for the balance of ships to arrive. Once all the ships were on station, a task force would be formed and exercises would commence.

As a reminder, in naval terms, a task force is a temporary organization of different types, divisions, and squadrons of ships, not requiring a formal and permanent fleet organization. Task forces are normally dissolved following completion of an exercise or mission. But today, the formation of the task force wouldn't take place until well after sunset.

An hour or so out of port the sea begins to kick up; whitecaps can be seen in all directions. OK, now you're wondering whether I'm about to get nauseous, hang my head overboard, and begin calling for the "one fin shark O'Rourke" (aka hurling, tossing my cookies, or up chucking; all perfectly good naval terms for defining seasickness). Well, maybe I didn't get sick because of a conversation I had in boot camp with a chief boatswain. It involved how it feels to get seasick and someday may be helpful to you. He began to explain getting seasick does funny things to people; it can even make a man wish he was dead. This is especially true if he enters the phase commonly referred to as the "dry heaves." Just a few minutes after the dry heaves commence, it's normal to feel an object similar to a ring in your throat. If this happens, immediately swallow as hard as you can, as that "ring" is probably your butthole!

As I was nearing the completion of my assignment for the evening meal, I was unaware Mother Nature was about to formally indoctrinate me on who was in charge. It's a lesson every seaman is taught, the ocean's way of demanding the upmost respect from every sailor. The ocean or sea (a sea being part of an ocean usually around where it meets land) is unpredictable. At times, it can appear to be calm, peaceful, and tranquil. It can be as smooth as a sheet of glass and, at the snap of a finger, suddenly transform into a violent and angry rant. To this day, I'm amazed by the complete lack of respect the average boat owner shows toward the sea and by how they treat it. Those who disrespect the "lady of the sea," eventually witness her wrath at one time or another; and her wrath can be deadly! I think I'd rather sword fight with Zorro, or throw rocks at Superman, than disrespect and witness the fury of the sea. The oceans have withstood volcanos, earthquakes, hurricanes (cyclones in the Pacific), and nuclear explosions. The ocean is far and away the most powerful force on earth.

Back to my indoctrination. Later in the afternoon, as we awaited the arrival of the remaining ships, I was sitting on the ledge of a galley hatch just peeling my spuds. I hadn't been at sea long enough to get my "sea legs," when the ocean began to kick up. Without warning the unexpected happened; suddenly I was "sea schooled" with the introduction of a "greenie."

I was rather relaxed, minding my own business. I was just sitting on the galley hatch enjoying the boat ride (any former sailor reading this just cringed at the phrase "boat ride"), when suddenly, and without any warning whatsoever, a rogue wave unceremoniously broke over the side of the ship and completely drenched me. This wasn't like getting hit with a little sea spray. I could not have gotten any wetter if I jumped, fully clothed, into the deep end of a swimming pool. Before the wave hit, the pail of fresh water was less than half full; when the rogue wave receded, the pail was overflowing. The chief cook thought it best that he seasoned the potatoes, so I dumped the brine solution overboard and refilled the pail with fresh water. It was my first introduction into respecting the sea. Just when you get a little cocky, confident, or overly comfortable, the sea leaps up and reminds you who is in charge. While it may have been the first time I was schooled by the sea, it certainly wouldn't be my last.

Being on mess duty, I hit the rack a few minutes after sunset. After all, 0330 comes very early. There wasn't a need to set an alarm, the Navy takes care of that for you (another example of how the Navy owns your ass). For mess duty, it was the responsibility of one of the line cooks to wake up the galley crew.

My first day of getting underway was pretty good; there were no complaints including the greenie. The greenie was a frequently reoccurring event, a normal part of life at sea. I don't believe I mentioned it, but a Fletcher-class destroyer lacked indoor passageways. The route between our sleeping quarters and any stations forward (the galley, mess deck, CIC, etc.) was open to the elements. When commuting bow to stern or vice versa, every sailor became a target for the greenie, as well as any other weather condition.

I woke at 0330, and by 0400 reported to the galley for duty. You can rest assured, starting off my day before sunrise wasn't one of my favorite activities. With a minimum amount of light, it was a bit challenging making my way forward to the galley. However, it was an activity I'd eventually master. The early morning hour was one thing but lacking an indoor passageway, coupled with a moderately choppy sea, left me concerned about falling overboard. Hitting the main deck, I took a firm grip on the life rail and headed up to the galley. The moon was up, which made my commute a bit easier.

The moon actually served a dual purpose; at sea it was indescribably beautiful and also served as a dim nightlight. This first morning at sea introduced me to the unbelievable reality of the number of stars visible to the naked eye. With almost complete darkness (void of the light pollution present on land) the sky appeared darker, clearer, and even closer.

As with the previous day, after the machine removed the potato skins, I cleaned up the area, picked up the buckets of spuds, and headed over to the galley hatch. The temperature was comfortable, as I positioned myself on the hatch and looked out toward the horizon. It being pre-dawn, there was little to see; however, as I scanned the horizon, I could see what appeared to be numerous lights off in the distance. Although they appeared dim, the sheer volume made me wonder if we were close to land.

As dawn began to break, I was amazed to see silhouettes of different types of ships on the horizon. These silhouettes extended from bow to stern. As the sun rose, so did my heart rate. Before long, I was completely in awe witnessing the spectacular view. Off in the distance was a fleet of destroyers of every type, DDs, DEs, DLGs, etc. Toward the center of the task force were several cruisers, and directly in the center was the USS *Enterprise* (CVN-65, but known to the fleet as "The Big E"), the first nuclear-powered aircraft carrier.

With a quick stop in CIC, I learned there were two submarines operating inside the perimeter of the task force. As unreal as this may sound, I was informed this display of military strength would become my new norm. Such formations are frequently the foundation for most naval exercises. Still, I wrestled with the idea of characterizing this magnificent display of firepower as anything other than normal or routine. Being so awestruck, I was still struggling to believe I avoided cutting off one of my fingers. Unquestionably, this far exceeded anything I could have imagined or envisioned standing watch in CIC. When on duty in CIC, the task force ships had appeared as nothing more than a circle of blips on the radar scope. I thought to myself, maybe I should tell the chief radarman to go shit in his flat hat and pull it down over his ears, because he looks good in brown. That certainly would earn me at least another four months of mess duty. But then I thought, perhaps I should be thanking him for the opportunity to personally witness this magnificent armada of ships; with each ship sailing independently in its entire breathtaking splendor. I was hoping this spectacular view would continue until we returned to port.

Over my four and a half years in the Navy, I was always impressed when we were called upon to sail as part of a task force formation. The sight of 15 or 20 heavily armed warships in the open waters, all operating in perfect unison, is just a breathtaking sight. Suddenly it hit me: how could any country dare confront such an awesome display of firepower and military might? It was one of those times I was not only excited but pleased and thankful I enlisted in the U.S. Navy. It was turning out to be so much more than I ever imagined. Sailing as part of a task force formation gave a whole new meaning to the phrase, "Don't tread on me!"

Plane Guard

If sailing with a task force wasn't heart pounding enough, our first exercise was being assigned "plane guard" duty. Earlier, I mentioned the purpose of a plane guard was one of safety. In the event of an aircraft incident, during either takeoff or landing, the plane guard's role is to rescue the flight crew as expeditiously as possible. Another element of the assignment was to ensure the plane fuselage and instruments were rendered inoperable or unrecoverable, while making certain any classified documents were either recovered or destroyed.

The launch and recovery of carrier-based aircraft always presented an element of danger. This danger is substantially higher than taking off from or landing at a land-based airport. For starters, while an aircraft carrier is more than 1,000 feet in length, the runway for takeoff is slightly more than 300 feet and angled off the port side of the vessel. In the event of a mishap, this angle prevents the ship from running over a downed aircraft.

To safely take off from an aircraft carrier, a 24-ton aircraft is required to accelerate from 0 to a relative speed of 150 knots (170 miles per hour) in just 2 seconds.

Returning a shipmate following a brief visit to the carrier. Believed to have been taken in September or October 1965 when operating with an aircraft carrier. This sailor was probably injured and in need of medical attention. The *Stoddard*, like other destroyers, only carried one corpsman to provide essential medical care to the sailors and Marines, whereas an aircraft carrier had doctors and even operating rooms. (Author's collection)

Remember, this is relative speed, so it's the combination of four elements to meet this requirement. These elements include the speed of the wind, the speed of the ship, the thrust of the jet engines, and the propulsion created by four steam-powered catapults.

Prior to commencing flight operations, the task force commander (TFC) notifies every ship in the group of his intention to begin flight operations. This notification normally includes a change in course and speed, as well as detailing when the change will occur. The course change is necessary to allow the carrier to take full advantage of wind speed. With the thrust created by the aircraft engines and steam catapult being a constant, a higher wind speed allows the ships, within the task force, to cruise at a slower speed during the launch or recovery of aircraft. During flight operations, the aircraft carrier normally remained in the center of the task force. In order to maintain the same perimeter defense and relative position from the carrier, all ships must cruise on the same course and speed as the carrier.

Here is an example of how the commencement of flight operations would begin: when the task force was formed, the TFC would provide all the ships with a call sign. This call sign would allow him to communicate simultaneously with every ship. Let's assume this call sign was "Poseidon." As mentioned earlier, Poseidon (the TFC) would likely be stationed aboard the *Enterprise* (call sign "Climax"). Communicating a course change to all ships, the TFC message would sound something like: "Poseidon, this is Climax, change course to 183 degrees, 33 knots, in 5, 4, 3, 2, 1; change course to 183 degrees, speed 33 knots."

As this course change was being executed, the CIC on every ship would be in constant communication with their Bridge. Until the ship reached its new course, speed, and position, CIC would frequently feed the Bridge the bearing and range from the carrier. A preplanned course and speed change would have been calculated and adjusted as necessary during the execution of the maneuver. Normally during such operations, the captain assumes the role of OOD. The progress of the change is also closely monitored by the TFC. As mentioned earlier, if a ship veers off its relative position from the flagship, the captain will hear about it in very detailed and somewhat stern terms.

While the above dealt with a carrier launching aircraft, recovering them was equally challenging. The term "landing" has such a different definition when landing at an airfield versus the flight deck of an aircraft carrier. Landing on a carrier deck can better be described as a controlled crash. When returning to a carrier, rather than landing on the angled runway, the pilot lands on the flight deck that runs from the stern forward, the longest dimension of the carrier's deck. This dimension is but a fraction of the distance of a runway on a land-based airfield. However, unlike taking off, the pilot has to deal with a landing platform that is rolling port to starboard and pitching bow to stern (left to right as well as up and down). As a pilot is making his final approach, he is instructed to "call the ball," which means he sees what appears to be a beam of light reflecting the glide path onto the flight deck.

All Navy aircraft are equipped with arresting hooks directly below their tail wings. As the aircraft touches down on the flight deck, the hook engages with one of three arresting cables strung across the width of the flight deck. This arresting gear has but one function, to bring the landing aircraft to a full stop in a very short distance. If a problem develops while landing, the pilot is notified by a red flashing light that appears on his optical landing system (OLS). This flashing light instructs the pilot to abort the landing and go around (re-enter the landing pattern and attempt the landing again). When a pilot receives an instruction to abort a landing, he must be able to take off under his own power; the thrust provided by the catapult is unavailable. To prepare for such an event, just before engaging the arresting gear, the pilot increases the jet's engine (or engine's) power to full thrust. If the landing is aborted or if he misses the arresting gear, this allows him sufficient thrust to take off under his own power. As a point of interest, when a 24-ton aircraft engages the arresting gear at full throttle, it goes from 150 to 0 knots in less than 3 seconds, and under 150 feet; I guarantee that'll rattle your teeth!

While we're on the topic, I'll mention a few other interesting bits of information about aircraft carriers:

When an aircraft carrier is in port, the only aircraft on board are those that are unable to fly. Prior to arriving in port, carriers launch their air wings or flight squadrons for return to their assigned airfields. If they should fail to do this, every aircraft on the ship would be rendered unavailable should an emergency arise. Likewise, once a carrier leaves port and is away from public boat traffic, the air wings return from their land base to the ship.

Flight operation may last for hours or most of a day. Part of the training includes an exercise called "touch and go." This involves a pilot going through the routine of landing on and taking off of a carrier's flight deck. During this exercise the arresting gear is deactivated. After "calling the ball," the pilot touches the carrier's deck, where the arresting hook would normally be engaged and, with the power of his engines, is able to take off. An air wing may conduct this training for hours on end. It was always an adrenaline-charged activity to watch, especially when operating as the plane guard.

Being such a large vessel, an aircraft carrier takes a greater distance to make a turn compared to smaller ships. To give you an idea, for a carrier to make a 180-degree turn takes about 3 miles at 30 knots. A destroyer could make the same turn in under a mile.

In combat situations a carrier usually operates more than 100 miles offshore. When your primary weapons are sound barrier-breaking jet aircraft, there is no reason to put a $10 billion-plus asset in harm's way.

Aircraft carriers have air wings assigned to their vessel; frequently as many as 70 aircraft were attached to a single carrier.

The example I used above involved a temporary assembly of ships, referred to as a task force. Another form is called a carrier strike group (CSG). It is composed of an aircraft carrier, at least one cruiser, a destroyer squadron with at least two frigates, and a carrier air wing. Both formations are similar in nature; however, the task force is much larger and may include multiple aircraft carriers.

Plane guarding during air operations. (Author's collection)

Being designated as a plane guard was an assignment I always enjoyed, especially during touch and go exercises. Beside the excitement of watching fighter jets taking off and landing, it usually involved operating the ship at high speed. This high speed causes the screws to kick up a turbulent wake; a wake commonly referred to by sailors as a "rooster tail."

I can vividly recall my first plane guard experience, as if it were yesterday. Although we were significantly lower down than the flight deck, I still had an excellent view of the aircraft as they prepared to take off. The flight deck, angling off the port side of the carrier, provided me with an unobstructed view of launching operations. Likewise, when aircraft were landing, I was close enough to clearly see the pilot during his final approach. Shortly after being assigned as plane guard, and after we reported being on station, the carrier began to launch aircraft. I heard the roar of the jet engines at full throttle, and watched as the aircraft was catapulted off the flight deck. As the plane left the end of the runway, it suddenly dropped slightly from the elevation of the flight deck. With this being my first experience, my mind began to race. Would my first experience with flight operations end with a downed aircraft? Just as quickly, the jet recovered and began to increase altitude at a mind-boggling rate of speed. That unexpected event was quickly repeated over and over again, until all the planes involved in the exercise were airborne. Yet another occasion on which I couldn't believe I didn't amputate a finger.

This experience also included touch and go exercises. I was completely baffled to hear the pilot increase the engines to full power as he approached, touched down, and immediately took off from the flight deck. I honestly didn't know what to think; would he run out of fuel? I'd heard a plane dumps its fuel tanks before landing. When I instinctively stood up showing concern, the old salt of a chief cook told me, "Relax, it's just part of a pilot's training."

What a first day of exercises; I was exhausted as I was lying in my bunk replaying this incredible, educational day over in my mind. It was so much for a 20-year-old to absorb and process. As I closed my eyes, I wondered what tomorrow may bring; could it in any way match or live up to this extraordinary day?

As morning broke (just an expression as sunrise was still hours away), I reported to my galley hatch and noticed we had returned to our perimeter station; the ships were still in formation and cruising at about 10 knots. I wondered how many miles from land we might be, as if it really mattered. The only objects between us and the horizon were this impressive, lethal group of warships and a large body of water. A body of water that seemed rather cantankerous at the time. As I began my day, I was rather pleased and happy I had gotten a good night's sleep.

Naval Gunfire Support (NGFS)

Shortly after sunrise, we changed course and broke away from the task force. An hour or so later, I noticed land coming into view. I began wondered if we were close to the California coast and preparing to return to San Diego. As we got closer, I began to realize it wasn't the coast of California, but rather an island. I told the chief cook I had to "hit the head" but instead made a beeline up to CIC. As I entered CIC, I learned we were preparing for our next exercise, which happened to be NGFS (shore bombardment). I'd returned to my workstation and completed my spud duty when I noticed we were about a mile from land. Finishing my task, I immediately returned to CIC.

I asked the POOW what was going on. What were the specifics associated with the upcoming training exercise? Anytime a "striker" asks a petty officer a legitimate question, he could expect a detailed answer, or an "I'll check and get back to you." As a reminder, a striker is a lower-ranked sailor who has been designated as being technically qualified in a particular classification. The petty officer said we would be conducting shore bombardment in conjunction with a Marine spotter that was located on San Clemente Island.

Shortly following lunch, while peeling my starchy little buddies and admiring the view, the 1MC comes alive: "Now hear this, now hear this, *general quarters, general quarters, all hands man your battle stations.* This is a drill, only a drill. *Man your battle stations*, general quarters!" It's the exact same announcement used on every naval vessel when being called to general quarters or battle stations. In actual combat situations, the words are very similar: "Now hear this, now hear this, general quarters, general quarters, all hands man your battle stations; this is not a drill, I repeat this is not a drill, man your battle stations, general quarters!"

Long before boarding a warship, every sailor is taught the most important command or duty on a ship is the call to general quarters (GQ). When GQ is called, you immediately stop whatever you're doing and report to your preassigned battle station. It's important you arrive there as expeditiously as possible. To avoid confusion, sailors heading aft (bow to stern) move along the port side of the ship, whereas those heading forward (stern to bow) move along the starboard side. A senior petty officer or commissioned officer keeps a head count for his station. He notifies the Bridge when all personnel have arrived and are accounted for. The report also included confirmation all hatches had been dogged or battened down (meaning the exterior of the ship was sealed, along with each individual compartment). The reason for sealing the hatches between compartments was to limit the impact an enemy's ordinance would have on the ship. The sealed hatches would "contain" the damage to the one compartment and allow the ship to continue its mission.

If the captain felt a station took too long to report "all hands present and accounted for," they spent extra hours practicing techniques to improve their response time. And, I may add, I can only recall one instance when that actually occurred. The crew's response or commitment to GQ must be just that passionate and intense.

As the last sailor arrived, I heard the chief report our status to the Bridge by saying, "Bridge/Combat, all men are present and accounted for." Being donned in my galley whites and apron, I felt completely out of place with my peers. They were ready for battle and I was prepared to rumble with an evil mashed or French-fry potato. In order to gain some dignity, I removed my apron and hat. Ah yes, I felt so much more presentable! This being my first GQ drill, I was relegated to the role of being an observer; aka, to staying out of the way.

Next, I heard one of the speakers come alive with exercise instructions in another language: "Gatekeeper [the *McDermut*'s call sign], this is Ceremony Two Six Charlie, coordinates X-1234, Y-5678 …," and a list of other instructions.

I recall the chief mentioned that the spotter provides coordinates based upon a magnetic bearing, and for reasons related to the gyroscope technology, they must be converted to true bearings. I should probably try to explain why gyroscope technology played such an important role in NGFS, as well as the differences between magnetic and true bearing.

The purpose of gyroscope technology is to compensate or stabilize the rolling motions of the ship. This technology is used on the main armament and plays a vital role when conducting NGFS exercises or missions. During such exercises the ship's movements are influenced by a number of factors including ocean currents, surface winds, weather, and general sea conditions. Gyroscope technology was employed to mitigate these movements. During gunfire exercises, when the guns are locked on target, you get the sense their movements are erratic, or better yet, completely out of control. In reality, the gun barrels remain stationary and locked on target; it's actually the ship that rolls and pitches with the movement of the sea.

As far as magnetic and true bearing, the geographic North Pole or true north is fixed and located at the top center of the Earth. On the other hand, magnetic north lies to one side of true north. The exact position of the magnetic north moves over time, and this movement is shown on maps. The north magnetic pole moves according to magnetic changes and flux lobe elongation in the Earth's outer core. It moves at a speed of about 55 kilometers every year; just over 34 miles. True north and magnetic north bearings may differ depending on where you are located on the globe; however, in some cases they may align. The Marine spotter always uses a magnetic bearing when presenting a target's coordinates and must be converted to true bearing in order to meet the requirements of our FCS.

Back to the exercise. After the data is entered into the FCS and a "solution" is calculated, the radarman trained as the NGFS Coordinator notifies the spotter we are ready to fire. The spotter, in turn, gives him the release to "Fire." Remember, this is my first experience involving naval gunfire, an exercise when a live round is being fired.

The instruction to "fire" is passed on to the gun mount and a moment later (no, a half a moment later), the gun is fired. OK, the sound isn't anything like the sound when a pistol or rifle is fired. No, this was an explosion; an explosion that caused the ship to shudder. At first, it led me to question whether the shell may have exploded prematurely in the gun turret or barrel. To give you an idea of the force behind the recoil, I was told when firing all four guns broadside, the recoil would move this 2,100-ton destroyer 12 to 18 inches in the opposite direction of the target. Upon hearing or feeling the gun firing, the NGFS coordinator notifies the spotter of an incoming round by broadcasting "SHOT" into his microphone.

During boot camp the largest gun we fired was a .50-caliber machine gun. Comparing the sound of a .50-caliber being fired to that of a 5-inch, 38-caliber cannon, is like comparing the noise a cap gun makes versus a stick of dynamite. Let me put it another way, it's like comparing someone coughing in a movie theater versus a cherry bomb exploding. I loved it, load another round.

Here, though I never operated them, I'm admiring one of the .50-caliber machine guns mounted along the main deck of the *McDermut*. (Author's collection)

Remember, at this juncture, I was nothing more than a mess cook and part-time observer, so I asked the chief for permission to go outside to witness the gun firing firsthand. After being granted permission, I left CIC and took up a position about 10 yards from the gun mount that was firing. I was close enough to CIC to hear the NGFS coordinator say, "Fire out." A fraction of a second later, a huge fireball projected from the gun barrel, followed by a smoke ring that was more than 10 feet in diameter. But most impressive was the noise it created. It was a percussion that just pounded into your chest; it was just surreal. The warhead being fired, weighing in at 55 pounds, was so large it could easily be photographed exiting the gun barrel.

Naval gun fire-control drills last less than an hour, with maybe two or a maximum of three rounds being fired. With the cost of each round exceeding $1,500, I'm sure the number of rounds fired was directly related to cost. After a successful exercise, the 1MC comes to life, advises the crew to stand down from GQ, and to return to their normal duties. I was in another world as I returned to my galley hatch, where the potatoes patiently awaited. I can assure you, the taters and I just sat back and mentally replayed the last hour or so over and over in my mind. The day before, there were planes taking off and landing (at close range). On this day, it was shore bombardment. I began to wonder what tomorrow may bring. While I may not have had a clue, regardless I couldn't wait.

Antisubmarine Warfare (ASW)

The following morning, I was disappointed as I made my way up to the galley. Rather than seeing the awesome display of warships, I could only see the Pacific Ocean. After running the potatoes through the machine, I perched myself on the hatch facing the ocean. As I scanned the horizon, I noticed lights on what appeared to be another ship. After about 30 minutes, I realized the relative position of the ship hadn't changed. It seemed both ships were sailing in some sort of a formation.

Shortly after daybreak, I realized the other ship was a destroyer and the distance between the two ships was decreasing rather rapidly. This continued until we were sailing on the same course with about 2,000 yards (a nautical mile) between ships. Being unaccustomed to the sight of warships, I thoroughly enjoyed this view and hoped it would remain the entire day. As I tended to my spuds, I kept an eye on the other ship. Unexpectedly, I noticed a rod or object rising from the sea. Seconds later, a submarine began to surface between the *McDermut* and our companion destroyer. I couldn't believe my eyes; this huge metal structure, longer in length than our destroyer, had just emerged from the ocean. Then a thought struck me: I hope it's ours. The captain hadn't called GQ, so it must be friendly. Shortly thereafter, a small craft from the other destroyer was lowered and began heading toward the submarine. From my observation, they delivered or exchanged somebody or something. Having completed their transfer, and after the small craft was at a safe distance, the submarine began to submerge: an unbelievable sight!

This was just another jaw-dropping experience, and I had years of similar events coming my way. Thank God they didn't ask me to "ship over" (extend my enlistment for an additional four years), because I would have asked, "Where do I sign." I asked one of the senior radarman who happened to be passing, "What's this all about?" He replied, "We'll be conducting ASW exercises in an hour or so."

I finished my morning assignment, turned the finished product over to the chief mess cook, and headed up to the 01 Level. I was just sitting up against the bulkhead, puffing on a cigarette, waiting for the next unexpected event. Perhaps a mermaid would emerge and wave as she passes by. With everything that I'd witnessed over the last three days, I probably would have simply waved back.

As I tried to continue enjoying my mindfulness time, the 1MC interrupted the moment with the call to general quarters. In accordance with naval standards, I dashed to CIC to continue my role as an "observer" from the galley. As I entered CIC, I learnt we were about to conduct ASW operations. Sonar confirmed the ping they picked up was moving and likely to be a submarine.

From radar school, I was aware ASW was normally performed by two destroyers, operating in extremely close quarters, with the ultimate goal of "sinking or neutralizing" the submarine. This was accomplished by dropping depth charges, set to detonate at predetermined depths, as they passed over the submarine's location. The purpose of the depth charge was to create a violent and damaging hydraulic shock; a shock powerful enough to sink or cripple the submarine. To improve the likelihood of a "kill," they were most frequently dropped simultaneously by two destroyers, as they crossed each other's wake, in an "X"-like pattern. Because the two ships were operating at such close quarters, it made ASW an extraordinarily dangerous exercise.

Like all shipboard operations, ASW is monitored, tracked, and executed in the ship's nerve center or "war room," CIC. But it's important to mention, not unlike navigating into or out of port, all course and speed changes are controlled from the Bridge. These course and speed changes are strictly based upon visual observations. With the ships operating at high speeds and at such close quarters, it makes it virtually impossible to see or track the other ship on the radar scopes.

Similar to radar, the sonar system ("sound navigation ranging") transmits a signal through the water. When it strikes a large metal structure, it returns a pinging sound to a sonar receiver. When sonar suspects they have picked up what may be a submarine, they simultaneously report the contact to the Bridge and CIC. The sonarman on duty provides data, including the contacts bearing, distance, and depth to CIC. CIC plots the data on the DRT (dead-reckoning tracer) and provides the Bridge with the contact's course and speed.

When requested by the Bridge, CIC would also recommend a course and speed to intercept the contact. Using information provided by sonar, CIC tracks the contact and feeds all information, related to its movements, to the Bridge. CIC immediately notifies the Bridge if the contact makes any maneuvers, especially any appearing hostile or compromising safety. It was almost a given, because of the danger associated with operating at such close quarters, that when conducting ASW exercises, the captain had the "Conn." Obviously, if the captain has the Conn, he alone is responsible for giving all orders and the safety of the ship.

ASW exercises were simulation exercises. While they included actual naval warships, live depth charges were never dropped or fired during the exercise. Instead, if the two destroyers were able to execute the "X" crossover pattern, it was assumed the submarine was neutralized and the exercise considered a success. The ships' goal was to initiate the attack and drop depth charges simultaneously over the port and starboard sides of the submarine. Closely tracking the submarine's course and speed prevented the destroyer from becoming a target. Crossing in front of or providing the submarine with a broadside profile of the ship would likely result in disaster.

Based upon the danger associated with ASW operations, this type of warfare was completely changed before the end of my enlistment. The change eliminated the need for two destroyers to simultaneously attack a submarine. It was replaced with a much safer and more effective means of locating, tracking, and attacking a submarine. In later years, when operating within a task force or carrier group, if a destroyer picked up an unidentified ping, it would document, track, and report its location to the task commander. This tracking would continue until the carrier launched an ASW helicopter. When the chopper arrived on station, it hovered over the subsurface contact, while dropping a listening device below the water's surface. If it became necessary, the helicopter was equipped to engage and neutralize the contact.

From a destroyer's perspective, rather than rolling depth charges, ships were retrofitted with an antisubmarine rocket system known as "ASROC." This unique technology allowed a destroyer to fire an acoustic homing missile at enemy submarines. Most importantly, this system had an effective range of six miles. The ASW helicopter and ASROC technology increased crew and ship safety, as well as the effectiveness and success of such missions. However, the destroyers I served on board were not retrofitted with this technology, therefore we continued to carry as many as 20 depth charges in our arsenal.

No More Messing Around

As we ended our week at sea, I watched as the carrier launched its air squadrons for return to the North Island Naval Air Station. This base is located on the Coronado peninsula near the entrance of San Diego Bay, close to the piers where the aircraft carriers docked.

As I was sitting on my galley perch and bidding farewell to my "tater friends," I attempted to replay the entire week in my mind. Just the process of trying to relive all that had transpired left me pleasantly exhausted. As I saw the mouth of the harbor off in the distance, the chief mess cook joined me, sat down on the bottom of an inverted pail, and we began to chat. I should mention, he stopped by rather frequently during the week, knowing peeling potatoes can get boring and somewhat lonely. This time he thanked me for my help and released me from any further mess cooking duties. He ended our conversation with good news; I had been given weekend liberty, starting immediately after we docked and the gang plank was secured. I thanked him for our many conversations, his advice, and sharing his experiences. I also expressed my sincere desire that we remain friends. I revealed how disappointed I was upon learning I was assigned to the galley. Now I was somewhat sad, as it came to an end. During the remainder of my stay on the *McDermut*, I made it a point to frequently stop in and say hello to this dear and treasured shipmate.

The week turned out to be a great introduction to humility, an experience essential for becoming a good shipmate. Sitting on an exterior hatch also exposed me to many more shipmates, while visually presenting some unbelievable naval sights. Whenever I was away from the potatoes, I spent a good portion of the time in CIC, observing its operation. And may I add, not once did any of those on duty bust or ridicule "the kid dressed in his mess duty whites." I felt better about both myself and my shipmates. I was never more confident in my decision of enlisting in the Navy; I had made the right choice, and it was going to work out just fine.

As we entered port, with Point Loma on our port side and the North Island Naval Air Station to our starboard, my curiosity led me to wonder what my next adventure would be. However, as we closed in on the 32nd Street Naval Base, that thought quickly faded and was replaced with the fact I had weekend liberty. Any future "adventures" would have to wait until Monday.

Within 15 minutes of tying up alongside another destroyer, the bosun's whistle announced the ship had been secured, the gangplank lowered, and the crew could begin departing the ship. There was an unwritten rule that married men and those who had family in the area exited the ship first.

During most weekdays, many of the single sailors remained on the ship or spent time at the Enlisted Men's Club. However, on weekends the crew would head out for a day, and possibly a night, on the town. Being only 20 years old, California laws prevented us from enjoying the local bars (we were old enough to fight, but we weren't old enough to drink). We spent many weekends at the beach flirting with the local ladies. For the most part the ladies loved it, but I can't say the same of their parents.

CHAPTER 6

Transformation from a Mess to a Radarman

Completing my mess cook duties afforded me the opportunity of spending more time with my OI Division peers. With the mess duty assignment behind me and having the weekend off, I had my first "unanticipated" liberty experience. Early Saturday morning I was invited to tag along with five or six other sailors, for a trip to Tijuana, Mexico (aka TJ in Navy slang). TJ is about 17 miles south of the 32nd Street Naval Station. Buses to the Mexican border crossing departed regularly and could be boarded a short walk from the base's main gate. For those of you who have never had the privilege of visiting this southern border town, TJ was an "eye-opening"—bordering on a shocking and crude—experience. TJ had a lot of "class," but unfortunately, it was every degree of low. I'll try to paint you a picture, but whatever you're thinking, it was much worse.

I'm sure you're wondering, "If it was that bad, why did you go?" Well, it did have its advantages, especially for low-income people, such as sailors. As a reminder, I was being paid $99 a month at the time. Another plus was the drinking age in TJ; if you could see over the bar, you could order an alcoholic drink. Rooms in TJ were very cheap and yup, we overnighted many times in this armpit of a border town. Frequently, sailors would share rooms to reduce costs and increase safety. To top it off, the liquor was watered down and cheap. A brief visit would suggest TJ is the odds-on favorite for being the place where the term Montezuma's Revenge originated. I'm confident TJ was infected with many unnamed diseases and viruses just awaiting discovery. With that being said, many of the junior, low-ranked sailors below the age of 21 made TJ a regular stop.

On the other hand, if we were short on cash or wanted to take in a movie, we'd stay in San Diego. And even this beautiful city was much different in the 1960s than in the present day. In the 1960s, San Diego lacked any professional sports teams, and the Navy bases were the city's major source of employment and revenue. In fact, the famous and beautiful Coronado Bridge, crossing San Diego harbor, wasn't even on the drawing board during my stay in "America's Finest City." The downtown area was a fraction of its current size. Instead, it was largely made up of bars, night clubs, burlesque shows, USO store fronts, and businesses that rented lockers to naval personnel, with only a smattering of clothing and similar stores. Bear in mind, this was a Navy town; on any given weekend, as many sailors could be seen on the streets as locals. Practically every resident of San Diego was, in some way, connected to the Navy.

After a week in port, and of participating in numerous striker drills and exercises, I learned we'd be getting underway within a day or so. Of course, this would be the first time I'd be assigned a watch in CIC. Finally, my past training would begin paying off.

As we set sail, I learned the ship would be conducting surface-to-surface exercises, better known as "ship versus ship" warfare exercises. I overheard the chief mention we would be firing our 40-millimeter guns. My only question was, "firing" at what?

Like most green sailors, my first watch was from 0000 to 0400. The sailor whom I was to be relieving woke me up about 20 minutes before midnight. He said, "Get up, Midrats are ready in the galley." Up to this point I had never heard of this term. Knowing I was still green, and seeing the expression on my face, he said, "Midrats are short for midnight rations." They are meals, consisting primarily of leftovers from dinner, for those who have the midnight watch. With CIC located just above the mess deck, I enjoyed a bite to eat before making my way up to CIC. It probably goes without saying, I arrived for my first watch well ahead of time.

As a reminder, CIC was strategically located in a corridor a deck below the Bridge, and aft of the wardroom and officer quarters. It's a location that would be difficult for an enemy to attack without inflicting major damage to the ship. As I entered CIC, I was struck by how dark the interior appeared. This condition was necessary to increase the visibility of radar scopes, tracking devices, as well as the various data and vertical informational boards. The sun never shines in CIC. The boards displayed the names and call signs of every ship in the formation, as well as ships involved in upcoming exercises. It also included the auxiliary or replenishment ships we would be interacting with over the next week (i.e., stores, fuel, etc.), plus our current course and speed. In most cases, when operating off the West Coast of California, the need to replenish supplies or refuel never arises; generally, this period at sea is less than a week. However, as part of the Navy's continual training program, we conducted UNREPS (underway replenishments) on a regular basis.

Within minutes of arriving in CIC, I was assigned to the surface search radar. My assignment was to monitor our bearing and distance from the ship carrying the task force commander (TFC), aka flagship. While all the ships in the formation were visible on the scope, most meaningful was our position relative to the aircraft carrier. With all the blips (radar contacts) being the same size, it was easy to identify the carrier, as it was in the center of the formation. As a reminder, it was our duty to remain within the acceptable distance from the flagship. If we began to drift off our station, the watch supervisor (petty officer of the watch) would be immediately notified. Before falling outside of our assigned station limits, he would notify the Bridge and include a course or speed change for maintaining station. Most destroyers had enough flexibility to easily maintain position, without veering off station; this prevented upsetting the TFC or captain.

In the beginning, when I picked up an unidentified surface contact, a skunk, I would report it to the POOW. He would report it to the Bridge and simultaneously broadcast it to the TFC. The broadcast to the TFC would be over a frequency monitored by all ships within task force. After plotting the skunk for three minutes on the scope and entering the data on a maneuvering board, the POOW calculated and reported the skunk's course, speed, and CPA to the Bridge and the TFC.

By week's end, I was given the sound-powered phone connected to the Bridge and, with the approval of the POOW, communicated the status of surface contacts directly to the Bridge. However, the POOW continued reporting any skunks or bogeys to the TFC.

On the second or third day out at sea, I was informed we would be conducting surface to surface warfare drills. This required the crew to be at GQ for a number of hours, which went over like a lead balloon (remember, war is hell, but peacetime is worse), yet I was thrilled.

I'm sure I had the 0800 to 1200 watch, as I vividly recall the chief telling me about the exercise and repeatedly asking if I saw two blips appear on the screen. These blips would appear to be operating in straight line, on the same course and speed. After the third or fourth inquiry, I thought, "Does he feel I'm incapable of recognizing and reporting such a contact? Does he still think of me as being a mess cook or what?" We were operating in waters restricted to military use; with the exception of the destroyers in our formation, the radar scope was void of any other contacts.

I was informed the contact would be a large rubber scow, towed a mile behind by an ocean-going tugboat. So, we weren't going to sink anything, the shells would simply bounce off the scow like water off a duck's back. Rather than our 40-millimeter guns, we would be firing our 5-inch guns at a distance of six or seven miles. I sure hoped our gunnery crews were accurate. Otherwise, I could see the headlines: "Earlier today the USS *McDermut* successfully sunk an ocean-going tug, while aiming at a scow being towed a mile in the tug's wake."

Being my first exercise after mess duty, after being relieved from the watch and following lunch, I hung out in CIC. Finally, the radarman on the surface search radar reported he had "two skunks traveling in formation." They were about 12 miles out when we made radio contact, which signified the beginning of the exercise. From a training perspective, there were three or four other destroyers, all sailing in a straight-line formation, who would be participating in the same exercise. When the tug was about eight miles out, the 1MC called the crew to GQ, and so it began.

I was assigned to take a position behind a 4 foot by 4 foot illuminated clear plastic vertical board, with the ship being in the center of this 360-degree display. The lighted display was visible to everyone within CIC and was used for tracking unidentified aircraft within the range of our air search radar. While standing behind the board, if an unidentified aircraft appeared, the radarman on the air search radar scope would provide me with the bogey's bearing, range, and speed (i.e., "Bogey at 184 degrees, 35 miles, speed 300 knots"). To allow all within CIC a clear view of the plane's position, using a grease pencil, I would print all the data backwards on the board. Writing backwards was part of the training in radar school. So, what I'm really trying to say is, for this surface-to-surface exercise, I was as useless as tits on a bull. About 10 minutes into the exercise, the chief told me to come around the board and join the team in CIC. From this position, I could observe the mission from a much better perspective.

Using our radars, coupled with visually observing where our rounds landed, would allow us to lock on target, in a minimal amount of time. With the chief's permission, I went outside to visually witness the results of our firing. It turned out to be quite an impressive experience. Using a pair of high-magnification binoculars, not only could I see where our rounds were landing, but it allowed me to observe the accuracy of the other destroyers as well. There were destroyers, both forward and aft of our ship, participating in the same exercise. It was amazing to see how quickly every destroyer was able to find the target. This was one of the reasons our destroyers were so successful when engaging and sinking much larger Japanese warships during World War II.

Following the firing of live ammunition, the chief asked me for my impression of the exercise. I think my response caught him off guard. Rather than expressing excitement over witnessing the firing, I instead suggested a possible change. If the first salvo was 50 yards off target, I suggested that while adjusting the coordinates of the firing mount, we should adjust a second mount to fire 50 yards longer, and a third 50 yards shorter. This way if the target was steering in a zig-zag pattern or was changing speeds, it would increase the probability of a favorable result. While I never saw such an adjustment implemented, his smile, nod, and commitment to "think it over" said it all. I should probably add that allowing a striker to visually observe the various exercises is afforded to every new radarman, but only once per exercise. During all further training exercises, including actual combat situations, when GQ was called, we remained at our assigned CIC post. As with most exercises, the guns were fired for a limited amount of time. This allowed for other drills to be conducted concurrently, covering a variety of scenarios; scenarios which could develop during actual combat situations.

After an hour or so, the order to "stand down from GQ" is announced, hatches are opened, and we returned to our normal duties. Time for a little relaxation, which meant writing letters, playing cards, cribbage, hearts, or poker. It could also involve watching a movie on the mess deck (off a Super 8 projector against the bulkhead or a readymade screen) or just sitting against the bulkhead along the main deck, while throwing the bull with fellow shipmates. The view of the sea always has been a welcome form of entertainment for most sailors. Even the most seasoned sailors are continually mesmerized by the collection of moods presented by the seas. A sea's waves are as diverse and different as snowflake patterns. While they may appear similar, no two waves are identical. It was always entertaining to attempt predicting the sea's next mood; seldom were our forecasts accurate.

Many people are completely unaware what it's like to be at sea for extended periods. They frequently ask, "What happens if someone is injured or becomes ill?" If there is a serious accident or emergency, the affected sailor would be airlifted by helicopter to a carrier or land-based hospital. When it comes to illnesses (colds, flu, etc.), most develop the first three or four days following infection. When this develops, the patient is isolated and cared for in sick bay. (All destroyers carried a trained corpsman. I can assure you, the Navy frowns upon the entire crew becoming infected.) But once you're at sea beyond the incubation period of a disease, the likelihood of a sailor becoming sick is quite low. Think about it: when you are hundreds of miles from land, where the air is the purest and cleanest on earth, what could be a source of a transmitted disease? This may be of interest; when at sea for an extended period, the air is so pure, many times you could actually smell the land miles before entering the harbor. And let me add, it was never a pleasant odor.

***

In actual combat situations, all of our guns would be available for use in surface-to-air attacks. But, during live-fire training exercises, we usually limited firing to our 40-millimeter guns. I'm sure you've watched videos from World War II, where a ship is firing at an attacking enemy aircraft. You probably noticed many small puffs of smoke in the vicinity of the aircraft. More than likely, you questioned the marksmanship of the gun crew. However, these puffs of smoke were actually a series of small explosions that created a field of shrapnel. Rather than striking the aircraft, which would have been a bonus, the objective was to bring the "bandit" down by having the plane fly into this field of shrapnel.

Live antiaircraft drills involved an aircraft towing a target or banner a substantial distance behind a plane. It's the same principle used by advertising aircraft along seaside beaches. Of course, the banner is flown much farther back from the plane and at a much higher rate of speed. To avoid a disaster the planes fly parallel to the ship, never directly toward or away from the vessel. Surface-to-air drills were generally short in nature because of the accuracy of weapons. The 40-millimeter twin mounts were equipped with fire-control radar to lock onto the target. The mounts fired at a rate of 160 rounds per minute per barrel, with an effective range of 4,000 yards or 2 nautical miles. The actual firing of live ammunition was brief and evaluated for its accuracy and effectiveness.

Following surface-to-air drills, the remainder of the week was devoted to exercises with the aircraft carrier, and other ships within the task force. As you would expect, most watches included a variety of simulated drills for the radar strikers. If a striker was on watch when one of these drills was being conducted, he would be relieved from his duties to participate in the drill. Like all new radarmen, within four to six weeks of being exposed to CIC, I became just one of the gang. Before long I was tracking air and surface contacts, reporting them to the Bridge, plotting their movements, and calculating their course, speed, and CPA. When operating with a carrier task force, after receiving approval from the watch supervisor, I was authorized to report the contact to the TFC.

Another part of becoming a seasoned sailor was getting accustomed to the rather strong coffee. While at sea, a pot of coffee was brewing 24/7 in CIC. Initially, I was less than a fan of this black, almost toxic, brew. When I complained, I was reminded the problem was not in the coffee but rather with my cup. The cup was new and wasn't properly broken in or seasoned. By the fifth week, I actually began to enjoy the brew. And they were right, it turns out the cup just needed to be "seasoned." It was simple, but the method of seasoning had to be exact and followed blindly. Seasoning meant you never washed, rinsed, or wiped out the coffee cup. The proper way of cleaning it was, at the end of a watch, to simply step out onto the main deck and toss the remaining contents into the sea. You then returned to CIC and hung it up for the next watch. I kept—no, guarded—the same cup until the day I was discharged. When I finally discarded it, which I truly wish I hadn't, the inside resembled a Jackson Pollock masterpiece. I wouldn't have been surprised if "things" were actually living and thriving inside that old cup.

CHAPTER 7

The Sea Adventures of the "Mighty Mac"

> Sailors, with their built-in sense of order, service, and discipline, should really be running the world.
>
> NICHOLAS MONSARRAT

My time on board the *McDermut* was relatively short. However, throughout my stay I worked hard and gained a substantial amount of knowledge and experience. Before departing, I passed the radarman test to be promoted from "seaman apprentice" to "seamen." This may be a good time to mention the factors leading up to promotion in the Navy. It's so different from civilian life.

In civilian life, competition rules. Competing is the major element between companies within the same industry. It also plays a key role or factor within companies. Employees are frequently encouraged to compete against one another, which often causes a division or rift within the company. Performance lists are published and bonuses awarded to the top performers. This may involve the sales staff, manufacturing department, or others related to productivity. In many cases, it creates a feeling of jealousy or resentment among the employees. The Navy does not encourage competition among its members and avoids any subjectivity when it comes to promotion.

The Navy created "promotion criteria" to avoid or severely limit favoritism, subjectivity, or other forms of bias. To prevent the most common form of prejudice, those of higher rank had little input when it came to a sailor's eligibility for promotion. Rather than selecting or recommending an individual for advancement, their involvement was limited to explaining why the candidate shouldn't be considered for a promotion. Another reason the senior staff had minimal input on a sailor's promotion was the frequency in which crews were rotated. It was highly unusual for a sailor to spend more than a few years in a given assignment. For every type of ship, the Navy defined the number of men, from each specific job classification, necessary to operate the ship. They broke this number down further based upon rank or pay grade. For example, initially the Navy may designate 13 radarmen to be stationed on board a Fletcher-class destroyer. This may be further broken down as one chief, one 1st class petty officer, five 2nd or 3rd class petty officers, and six seaman or seamen apprentices. As each met the conditions for advancement and passed a comprehensive test, they would be either assigned to a higher billet on board the ship or transferred to another assignment; one requiring his new classification and pay level.

There are two primary requirements for promotion. First, a sailor had to have served "time in grade or rank." Regardless of your acquired abilities, knowledge, or assigned duties, a sailor had to serve in their current pay grade, as a prerequisite of eligibility to taking the advancement test. Whether it was fair or not is open for debate; however, I can assure you this approach eliminated any favoritism. You're probably thinking, if that's the case why should a junior sailor obey orders given by someone of higher rank? It's the chain of command, which is the backbone and bible of the Navy. It's essential for the safe and effective operation of a warship. Every sailor was required to respect and follow the chain of command, period. You can rest assured, the Navy reacted swiftly when an individual did not listen to or failed to obey an order. While someone of higher rank may be less involved in the promotion process, he had considerable power when it came to the sailor following orders. If a sailor failed to obey or execute a valid order, the individual would be written up and the incident reported to the chief or division officer. If it was deemed serious enough, it would be brought to the attention of the captain. If the offense required legal action, it was given to a higher military body, with the sailor being immediately transferred off the ship.

For less serious matters, the command was authorized to administer a nonjudicial punishment. This punishment could be as simple as having liberty taken away, thus confining the sailor to the ship for a defined period of time. However, it could also result in the sailor being "busted" or reduced in pay grade or rank. If busted, his monthly salary was reduced to the lower pay scale. Furthermore, it required him to remain in the lower pay grade until he became eligible (time in grade) for retaking the advancement test. In my 4½-year enlistment, I can recall only one radarman being busted. He got drunk, ended up being arrested for disorderly conduct, and missed the ship getting underway.

Getting back to the process for advancement, I'll offer up this example: a 3rd class petty officer may possess the knowledge, and possibly the experience, to pass a test three or more pay grades higher. However, the time in grade prevented the sailor from taking a test more than one pay grade higher. To build upon this, near the end of my enlistment, as a 3rd class petty officer, I'm confident I could have taken the exam for senior chief radarman and easily passed. But time in grade prevented me from taking anything other than a 2nd class radarman examination. I should also mention, the pay scale for the specific rank was the same for every position classification. Regardless of whether you were in the military for 4 years or 15 years, if you were a 3rd class petty officer, you were both paid the exact same amount. I understand that it has changed and there is now a pay scale based upon time in a particular pay grade.

While standing watches, all radarmen are exposed to and learn every possible scenario that could possibly come up while underway. Regardless of rank, every radarman is taught and learns through constant and repeated in-your-face experiences. But there is one final element involving a promotion: a sailor not only had to pass the test but may have to fall within the top percentile of those tested. This percentile was based upon the number of individuals being tested within a specific position's classification. The more critical the classification, meaning there were fewer candidates being tested versus openings in the Navy, the more likely the sailor would be promoted. For instance, for a radarman to be promoted he simply had to pass the written test; whereas for a boatswain's mate to be promoted, he would have to pass the exam and score in the top 5 percent of those being tested.

One final comment about promotions: when we were deployed to Vietnam and operating within a combat zone, all tests and promotions were more or less delayed or put on hold. The Navy, and rightfully so, wanted the ship crews to focus on their present duties or assignments, rather than worrying about studying and passing a test. From a money perspective, combat pay more than compensated for any pay increase resulting from a promotion.

***

The *McDermut* had just completed her WestPac cruise (operating in the Far East), less than a month before I reported on board. Most WestPac cruises were approximately six months in duration and scheduled at 18-month intervals. During my time on board, we performed numerous exercises and drills, primarily in the waters along the West Coast. This allowed us to visit a number of very interesting ports from Southern California to Vancouver, Canada.

It was quite common for coastal cities and towns to invite a U.S. warship to visit during special events. To the best of my knowledge, there was never a charge to the public for such visits. The crew always looked forward to ports that were rarely visited. When entering infrequently visited ports, the ship was prepared for public tours. During each and every port visit, and to our complete enjoyment, we were overwhelmed with the kindness and generosity shown by our hosts.

Naturally, before the ship could be opened to the public, a great deal of preparation was in order. It probably goes without saying, all stations containing classified documents or information, sleeping quarters, engine room, ammunition magazines, etc., were off limits to the public. Following preparation, the public was free to explore the entire exterior of the ship and walk through the Bridge, with the mess deck being the only open space available below deck. I must have been asked hundreds and hundreds of times to take pictures of adults standing in front of our 5-inch cannons. On the other hand, most kids showed a preference for the gunner's mate's seat, associated with the antiaircraft guns (AA). Another popular photo hot spot was in front of or leaning up against the rack of depth charges. While the public was never in any danger, I wondered if they would have reacted differently knowing these were live weapons.

While San Diego was our home port, the ship made frequent stops to San Francisco. Entering and departing San Francisco Bay was both interesting and challenging. The temperature of the bay is surprisingly cold, and its currents and tides are extremely strong. As the ship approached the Golden Gate Bridge, the ship began feeling the impact of these strong currents. While San Francisco Bay is a large bay, the span

Photo taken on the *Stoddard* showing antisubmarine depth-charge weapons, circa 1965. Though it was not recorded, the author believes the land shown in the photo is the South Vietnam coast. (Author's collection)

beneath the Golden Gate Bridge is narrow by comparison. During incoming or outgoing tides, this area acted more or less as a venturi, causing a substantial increase in the water's velocity. After navigating into the bay for the first time, I struggled to understand how a convict may have escaped from Alcatraz Island. The water temperature and currents provided what seemed to be a perfect natural security system. Much like San Diego, San Francisco was also considered a naval town.

Though it was common for a city or town to request a naval ship as part of a major celebration, the waterways were unable to accommodate ships much larger than destroyers. This turned out to be a windfall for the destroyer sailor. The physical size of an aircraft carrier or cruiser limited the number of ports they visited. While on board the *McDermut*, and later the *Stoddard*, I was fortunate to have visited San Francisco numerous times. On the other hand, I wish we could have visited other ports of call more frequently, e.g., Portland, Seattle, Long Beach, and Vancouver, Canada. While each had its own unique offering, far and away I enjoyed the Portland, Seattle, and Vancouver visits the most.

My overall stay on board the *McDermut* was brought to an abrupt end on September 10, 1963, while conducting ASW off the coast of San Diego. On this date, a collision occurred between the *McDermut* and the USS *Gregory* (DD-802). The collision resulted in several injuries, generally of a minor nature. I recall one sailor on the *McDermut* did suffer a broken leg, but thankfully there were no casualties on either ship. As they say, bad news travels fast. By the time we limped back to the entrance of San Diego Bay, word of the incident had spread. As we entered the harbor, and during the entire route back to the 32nd Street Naval Station, people were lined up on both sides of the bay. Along the starboard side were naval personnel, on the aircraft carriers and cruisers, lining their main decks. On the port side were thousands of civilians, all gathered to observe the damage incurred by the "Mighty Mac."

Photo showing the bow of the USS *McDermut* following a collision with the USS *Gregory*, while conducting Antisubmarine Warfare (ASW) exercises off the coast of Southern California in September 1963. (Author's collection)

We also had an abundance of news crews acting like piranhas as they rallied their watercraft around the injured warrior. I'm sure you realize it was an embarrassing experience, but an experience just the same. This was proof conducting ASW exercises was extremely dangerous, with ships operating at close quarters and at high rates of speed.

After a complete and thorough investigation, the Review Board concluded poor communications between the ships was the ultimate cause. Both captains were determined to be at fault and disciplined accordingly.

Following a minor repair involving a flat plate being welded onto the bow, the ship sailed to the Long Beach Naval Shipyard. Upon arrival, it was put into dry dock and the decommissioning process commenced. All of the major devices, equipment, and systems were removed before being officially decommissioned on December 16, 1963. On January 4, 1966, the ship was sold to the National Metal & Steel Corp. and towed away as scrap in February 1966.

While the decommissioning work was on going, the radar team continued conducting frequent drills. Although we were in port, we conducted simulated exercises; these exercises occasionally included ships at sea. With the more senior radarmen working hard at avoiding the drills, it became a potential treasure trove experience for the radar strikers.

Throughout the time spent in dry dock my interest, knowledge, and understanding of radar systems, as well as fleet operations, increased exponentially. Much of our day was devoted to training exercises. One question that continued to haunt me was, "Why the delay in transferring or reassigning us to another command?" We had absolutely nothing to do with the removal of equipment and components; that task was being handled by civilian workers attached to the base.

During our stay in dry dock, to "keep busy" the senior radarmen were required to prepare a constant flow of simulated exercises. To say they appeared bored with this assignment would be an understatement. Therefore, they assigned much of the grunt research work to junior radarmen. Personally, I welcomed and accepted it as an opportunity. Being able to participate in the simulated drills sharpened my familiarity and knowledge of CIC functions on every level. While I was just a seaman at the time, given the opportunity, I could have easily passed the test for 2nd class petty officer. My professional skills and knowledge as a radarman increased that dramatically.

On November 21, 1963, I was asked to report to the executive officer's (XO's) office. I was confident I was about to learn of my next assignment. Instead, I was informed my younger sister was involved in a horrific car accident. She was in critical condition, with her injuries being life threatening. I was immediately granted emergency leave and departed the ship within the hour.

I took a shuttle from the Naval Air Base San Pedro to North Island Naval Air Station. Shortly after arriving, I boarded a MATS (Military Air Transportation Service) flight to the Naval Air Station, Lakehurst, NJ. When I arrived, my parents were at the hospital, so one of my sister's friends picked me up and drove me home.

On November 22, 1963, as my Uncle Harry and I were on the way to St. Elizabeth's Hospital, in Elizabeth, NJ, the radio station was interrupted with breaking news. The news anchor reported President Kennedy had been shot in Dallas, TX. As we entered the hospital, I couldn't help but wonder if the news would impact me. The news report stated the military was placed on a heightened state of readiness.

We stayed with my sister, who was heavily sedated, until evening. Sometime in the afternoon, one of the nurses informed us that the president had passed. When my parents returned, my uncle and I headed back home. Upon arrival, I called the ship to check my status. I was authorized to remain on emergency leave until my sister was removed from the ICU.

Miraculously, in less than a week my sister's condition improved, and she was moved to a private room. Several days after she was moved from the ICU, I made travel plans to return to the ship. But this tragedy did have a happy ending; a few years later she married her boyfriend, the driver of the vehicle involved in the accident, and had two wonderful girls.

After about 10 days of emergency leave, I boarded a flight back to California. Though I didn't realize it then, it would be the last time I would see my family until I was discharged in May 1966.

Days prior to the decommissioning ceremony, I received orders to report to the *Stoddard*. The day before the ceremony, I learned the *Stoddard* had recently departed San Diego and was in the early stages of a WestPac cruise. Therefore, I would be boarding it in Yokosuka, Japan. Transportation arrangements were in the works and would be available the following day.

Early the next day, I learned I was booked on a series of MATS flights. Immediately following the decommissioning ceremony, I boarded a Navy bus heading from Long Beach to the North Island Naval Station, Coronado, CA.

CHAPTER 8

From Gatekeeper to Buckboard

I arrived at North Island and boarded a flight headed north to the Travis Air Force Base. Travis is located in Fairfield, CA, about 50 miles northeast of San Francisco. Upon arriving at Travis, I was informed the next leg of my journey would be departing the following morning. This flight would be heading for the Tachikawa Air Force Base in Japan. When I asked for the expected arrival time in Japan, the answer was "in a few days." Really? That's the best you could offer? In a few days?

Shortly after arrival, I was assigned to a base barracks. Unquestionably, the sleeping quarters were much more luxurious than on board a destroyer. The food at the mess hall was well prepared, plentiful, and delicious. While I never considered enlisting in the Air Force, this evening I began to envy my hometown friend, Willard.

The following morning a group of military personnel, from every branch of service, reported to flight operations. Within minutes, we boarded a bus and were transported to an aircraft. Bear in mind, in the 1960s, passenger jet aircraft were just gaining popularity. The bus pulled up next to a four-engine propeller-driven plane. So, this is the reason we'll arrive "in a few days." Unlike commercial flights, on MATS flights the seats face the rear of the aircraft. I'll bet you're thinking that sure sounds safer, and you'd be right. Before I could register my objection, we were airborne and heading west. A few minutes into the flight, the pilot announces we are headed for the Hickam Air Force Base, near Honolulu, Hawaii. Hickam is located close to the naval base at Pearl Harbor. Thankfully, the flight was uneventful, although it seemed as if we were in the air for days, rather than hours. During the flight I fell asleep, woke up, fell asleep again, woke up, and we were still in the air. Upon arrival at Hickam, an Air Force bus transported us to a barracks, and later to the mess hall. Again, the accommodation and food was outstanding. Unfortunately, we weren't given a liberty pass to explore downtown Honolulu.

Early the following morning, we boarded the aircraft and took off for our 4,000-mile flight to Tachikawa, Japan. A few hours into the flight the pilot announced that "the headwinds are strong, causing the engines to consume more fuel than anticipated." If these headwinds continued, they would calculate the remaining distance versus the amount of fuel available to determine if an unscheduled refueling stop was necessary.

Several hours later, the pilot confirmed the strong headwinds created fuel concerns, necessitating an unscheduled refueling stop. He continued, "We'll be landing on

Midway Island to refuel, have a meal." This unscheduled event became more than just an adventure; it turned into an eye-opening experience.

Midway Island, circa 1964. This photo shows just how small the island is, with a significant amount of its land consumed by the airfield. (U.S. Navy, public domain, via Wikimedia Commons)

I'm sure everyone is familiar with the battle of Midway, which involved 3 American aircraft carriers, along with 25 cruisers and destroyers, for a total of 28 U.S. warships. The Japanese forces included 4 aircraft carriers, 2 battleships, and 15 destroyers, for a total of 21 warships. I incorrectly assumed the battle probably included a considerable amount of real estate on the island. But this was not the case at all; the Midway real estate was important because of its physical location. In reality, Midway isn't an island at all but more of an atoll.

Midway is located nearly "midway" between the U.S mainland and Asia. It's about 1,500 miles from Hawaii and 2,500 miles from Japan. For this reason, it was an important military asset for both the United States and Japan during World War II. Its overall size is 2.4 square miles, and it consists primarily of a runway and several support buildings. The island was solely populated by military personnel. Its actual residential or civilian population is zero. The island is absolutely beautiful, but I for one could not imagine being stationed there for more than a few days.

We landed, deplaned, and were transported to the mess hall. A little more than an hour later, we took off for the final leg of our journey.

We arrived at the Tachikawa Air Force Base and once again were transported to a barracks on the base. Shortly following our arrival, I was informed the *Stoddard* was expected to arrive at the naval base in Yokosuka within a few days. I was also informed I would remain at the Tachikawa base until the morning of the ship's arrival. Struggling to sleep on the plane left me exhausted. I simply wanted a bite to eat and to hit the rack, and that was exactly what I did.

Over the course of the next few days, I was free of any duty or assignments, so I had liberty until the ship reached port. During the flight I met another radarman who was also waiting for his ship to return to port. Every day, following morning muster, we were given liberty. But this liberty included the stipulation we return to the base before midnight. Each morning, we would board an Air Force bus for the short trip into Tokyo. There were buses leaving to or from Tokyo several times an hour, so transportation was never an issue.

Unlike the present day, it was quite inexpensive to visit Japan; the exchange rate was around 250 yen to the dollar. During our trips we spent much of our time enjoying the local attractions, the delicious cuisine, while hitting any number of bars. In Japan, we could get legally served in any business selling alcohol. On our final day, we found ourselves around the University of Tokyo. Being of college age made it easy to enter into a conversation with the students. With World War II almost 20 years behind us, the students were pleased to meet and talk to us.

USS *Stoddard* (DD-566)—A Fletcher-Class Greyhound

After getting to know much of what Tokyo had to offer, the experience sadly came to an end. We boarded a Navy bus headed for the Yokosuka Naval Base, which is less than 50 miles to the south. Late in the morning, we arrived at the base and I boarded the *Stoddard.* The following is a little background on this greyhound of the sea.

The *Stoddard* was a Fletcher-class destroyer of the United States Navy. It was named for Master's Mate James Stoddard, who was decorated for heroism during the Civil War. The *Stoddard* was laid down in Seattle, Washington, by the Seattle-Tacoma Shipbuilding Corp. on March 10, 1943; launched on November 19, 1943, sponsored by Mrs. Mildred Gould Holcomb; and commissioned on April 15, 1944, with Commander Horace Meyers in command.

The USS *Stoddard.* (*STODDARD '65*/the USS *Stoddard* 1965 cruise book)

The USS *Stoddard*'s Specifications (DD-566)

Category or Number	*Specification*
Displacement	2,050 tn
Length	376'6"
Beam	39'8"
Draft	17'9"
Propulsion	60,000 shp, geared turbines, 2 propellers
Published speed	35 kn (40 mph) published speed
Range	6,500 nm at 15 kn
Complement	329 (officers and enlisted)
Armament	• Four 5", 38-caliber dual-purpose guns • Four 40 mm antiaircraft guns • Four 20 mm antiaircraft guns • Two depth-charge tracks • Two torpedo tubes (removed when recommissioned during the Korean War)

The ship's final claim to fame was being the last Fletcher-class destroyer to be stricken from the U.S. Navy, in 1975 (there were 175 Fletcher-class destroyers built and commissioned). The *Stoddard* was towed to a predetermined position, near the island of Kauai, Hawaii. Seal Team One installed and set off charges, which sank her 64 nautical miles (119 kilometers; 74 miles) NNW off the island of Kauai, in the Barking Sands Missile Range, on July 22, 1997. The ship lies at a depth of 2,550 fathoms (15,300 feet). Such an appropriate resting place for such a valiant warrior.

***

With both the *McDermut* and *Stoddard* being Fletcher-class destroyers, getting around was quite easy. I was fully aware of every nook and cranny on the ship from the second I reported on board. Within a few hours, I had become a crew member and was beginning to feel at home. By the end of the day, about a half dozen of us were heading into Yokosuka to hit a couple clubs, have a few beers, and celebrate our arrival in Japan. And if there's one thing you should know about sailors, we know how to celebrate. We celebrated each and every time we entered a domestic or foreign port. As a matter of interest, when deployed on a WestPac cruise, Yokosuka was commonly referred to as our "home port."

After spending less than a week in Yokosuka, we set sail south and headed toward the port of Sasebo, Japan. Sasebo is located on the southwestern coast of Japan, where it meets or joins with the East China Sea. It's approximately 800 miles from Yokosuka and is located on the island of Kyushu. Many people are unaware that Japan is an archipelago or chain of islands. Japan consists of 14,125 islands of various sizes; only about 430 are inhabited. The four largest islands are Honshu, Hokkaido, Kyushu, and Shikoku. Mount Fujiyama (Mount Fuji), Tokyo (Japan's capital), and Yokosuka are all located on Honshu.

Sailing south, we passed the 12,000-foot Mount Fuji, an absolutely breathtaking sight. There were a number of places I wanted to visit while in Japan, with Mount Fuji being high on the list. While it was just over 50 miles from Yokosuka, unfortunately I never found time to schedule a trip.

After a few hours of being underway, we began conducting exercises. We were cruising on our own, so the training focused on shipboard drills. Unlike the training off San Clemente, when in foreign waters all drills were simulated; we never fired live ammunition. All exercises involving guns were conducted using shells designed for simulated training.

It was around this time that I realized ASW drills seemed to have ceased. I wondered if the collision between the *McDermut* and *Gregory* accelerated the Navy's decision to discontinue these close-quarter exercises. Stemming from this accident, along with the development and deployment of the ASROC, the Navy changed its approach to ASW. The use of helicopters and ASROC made ASW much safer, while providing better overall results.

When operating in the Far East, and strictly for political reasons, warships made frequent visits to many Asian ports. They acted as a reminder of America's presence and continued support. During the Korean War, the base at Sasebo played a major role as the main staging and launching point for the United States and our allies. The base was scaled down following the Korean War, which included less frequent visits by naval vessels.

While in a foreign port, liberty call was much more liberal. Following lunch, if a sailor was off duty, he was given liberty. After arriving in Sasebo and following lunch, five of us decided to pool our money and rent a driver and vehicle for a trip to Nagasaki (remember, the exchange rate between the dollar and yen was very favorable). The town of Nagasaki is the site where the second nuclear bomb was dropped during World War II. Believing the United States had a stockpile of similar weapons, the Japanese surrendered six days after the Nagasaki bombing.

Before departing Yokosuka, we learned ground zero in Nagasaki was less than 50 miles from Sasebo. Our research also revealed the bombing mission's code name was "Fat Man." Most people think the hypocenter crater was created as the bomb impacted the ground and exploded; however, this is completely false. To achieve the maximum impact of the nuclear weapon, the bomb was actually detonated at an altitude of 1,650 feet above the surface. This low yield nuclear blast produced a crater 20 feet deep and more than 1,000 feet wide. The area within a three-mile radius of the hypocenter or ground zero was demolished, with the city flattened and reduced to rubble. In the years following the bombing, thousands upon thousands of people also lost their lives from injuries or illnesses attributed to radiation exposure.

The "Fat Man" atomic bomb that was dropped on Nagasaki on August 9, 1945. (National Museum of the United States Air Force)

The transit time from Sasebo was a little more than an hour. We arrived at ground zero and, while the driver waited, we departed the vehicle. As we were observing the crater, we couldn't help but notice a number of people staring at us. As we looked around, we realized their numbers were increasing, with many beginning to point in our direction. Suddenly they began casting anti-American rhetoric or expressions in our direction. While we were visiting the site for historical purposes, as we were dressed in uniform, they must have thought otherwise. They may have believed we were there in support of or endorsed the destruction and massive loss of life caused by the explosion. After several more minutes, the people began to sound angry. Concerned they may become aggressive and concerned about our safety, we thought it prudent to return to the rented vehicle and head back to the base.

Years later, while waiting for a Navy craft to take my family out to visit the USS *Arizona* (BB-39) memorial, we were watching a movie about the attack on Pearl Harbor. The video was quite explicative; it didn't mince any words in describing the actions of the Japanese Navy. A few rows ahead of us were several families of Japanese tourists, and it was obvious some of the language disturbed them. At the conclusion of the movie, I introduced myself and mentioned I thought they appeared uncomfortable. After a brief conversation, I shared my experience in Nagasaki. After a few minutes they appeared more comfortable, we shook hands, bowed, and parted saying "the past is the past."

Just a side note, our visit to the Nagasaki site struck me on so many levels, leaving a lasting impression. For many years I thought it had scarred me, but later in life realized it affected me in a very positive way. Both the Nagasaki and Vietnam experiences changed my outlook on life itself. I had a completely different view or tolerance when it came to deploying our troops into harm's way, as well as the use of nuclear weapons. Since 1945, we have manufactured more than 75,000 nuclear weapons, with each being an order of magnitude more powerful than those dropped on Japan. Does this really increase our security or safety? I almost feel an *amen* is in order!

***

During a typical WestPac cruise, many foreign ports of call are visited by naval vessels. But the one most frequently visited was Subic Bay in the Philippines. The naval base at Subic Bay was a major ship repair, supply, and R&R (rest and recreation) facility of the U.S. Navy. The base is located on the western side of the island of Luzon, in the province of Zambales. The base was one of the largest in the world, covering more than 262 square miles (about the size of Singapore). It was located about 100 miles north of Manila.

When a sailor on liberty departed the base, he crossed a small bridge and entered the town of Olongapo. In the 1960s, the town was exclusively made up of rundown hotels, bars, and restaurants (applying the term "restaurant" here is really a stretch of its definition). Much like the rundown buildings within the town, the streets were half unpaved and crammed with "jitneys."

The main source of transportation was the jitney. Jitneys were open World War II jeeps with wild color schemes, much like the hippie peace movement vehicles of the 1960s. For less than $0.10, a rider could travel anywhere within the city (the Filipino currency was pesos and centavos, and at the time the exchange rate was 45 pesos to the U.S. dollar and there were 100 centavos to a peso). Without the naval base, the town of Olongapo would not have existed.

The town had but one industry, serving the "wants and needs" of sailors and Marines visiting Subic Bay. As a result, Olongapo was heavily populated with "barmaids" (aka, "ladies of the evening") who made their living drinking with and "servicing" Marines and sailors.

I always enjoyed visiting the Philippines. Overall, the people were very welcoming and they had the best beer I've ever tasted. The name of this world class beer is San Miguel. At the time we could buy a case for less than $2. Several of us would "invest" in a few cases when we entered port. Part of the deal was that the bar we purchased them from would store the cases and keep them cold. Any beer that remained after we set sail would be returned to the bar's stock. It was a great deal for all involved; it was less expensive for us, the bar was assured we'd frequent their establishment, and their profits increased when we left port. We visited Subic Bay quite often and usually negotiated with a different bar during each visit.

When visiting the Philippines, the only port of call was Subic Bay; however, the country is so much larger. The country is made up of over 7,000 islands, of which approximately 2,000 are inhabited. In the 1960s, with the exception of the largest cities, many even lacked electricity. While the country had its own currency, much of the economy operated more as a barter system. The country was more or less divided into three island groups: Luzon (which contains the country's capital of Manila and the Subic Bay Naval Base), Visayas, and Mindanao.

As I mentioned, I always looked forward to visits to Subic Bay. Besides making many friends, I always felt welcomed, respected their culture, and their food was delicious. While Japan was my favorite country to visit in the Far East, the Philippines was a close second.

During one of my visits, I volunteered to participate in a program called "Project Concern." By volunteering, I was relieved of any duty or watches and given daily liberty. Part of the program involved a medical element; it was devoted to inoculating the residents, especially children, in the town of Olongapo. During the onset of the program, people lined up far as the eye could see. A few days into the program, one of the nurses and I became friends. My assignment was to ensure she had an ample amount of the vaccine available, while hers was to administer the shots.

Entrance to the Manila American Cemetery, taken in 1965. (Author's collection)

A typical example of many of the village homes on the island of Mindoro. This photo was taken in 1965 and is believed to have been taken on Mindoro Island. (Author's collection)

Knowing I was fascinated by their way of life, at the end of the project she invited me to tag along as she scheduled a visit with her family. We took an open-top bus for two hours along a surprisingly decent highway to Manila, the nation's capital. We spent a few hours in Manila, as I wanted to visit the Manila American Cemetery Memorial. It consists of 152 beautifully manicured acres on a large plateau. The cemetery contains more than 16,000 graves of American service members. The cemetery has the largest number of graves, honoring U.S. military personnel, killed during World War II. Every Christian serviceman, who made the ultimate sacrifice, is represented with a white concrete cross headstone. For the servicemen of the Jewish faith, the headstone was made of white concrete in the shape of the Star of David.

After visiting the cemetery, we boarded a second bus and continued south for almost three hours. After leaving the bus and boat ride, we arrived on the Island of Mindoro where her family lived. It immediately became apparent there was a limited use of currency; the barter system definitely ruled. During our boat trip, I learned her father traded freshly caught fish for most of his family's needs. Occasionally, he provided physical labor for more expensive items.

After a short ride, we arrived at her parents' poorly constructed home. After being introduced, we were invited to join them for dinner. For the next two days, the nurse was the only person who spoke English and was kind enough to act as my interpreter.

The next two days were quite educational, although eye-opening may be more appropriate. It wasn't long before I realized just how basic a life they lived. I recall being more than thankful and happy to be returning to the ship; however, as I look back, it truly was a once in a lifetime experience. To be fully transparent, more than once while I was living it, I questioned my sanity. I wondered how I ever concluded that such a trip was a good idea. I'll say this, even to this day, I can't help but think there's nothing like the good old U.S. of A. So many of us fail to appreciate just how fortunate and privileged we are to be an American.

Taiwan

Following the outbreak of the Korean War, President Truman "neutralized" Taiwan, over concern it could trigger another world war. He wanted to avoid the country falling back into the hands of China and vowed to stop the spread of communism in Taiwan. To back up this vow, Truman directed the 7th Fleet to the Strait of Formosa. Their sole assignment was to prevent the PRC (People's Republic of China) from attacking the country. It also prevented the ROC (Republic of China, Taiwan) from attacking China.

Even today, China considers Taiwan a renegade province, a province that must be returned and controlled by China. Our relationship with Taiwan was greatly enhanced when President Eisenhower signed the "Formosa Resolution" in 1955. This resolution protected Taiwan against an armed attack by another country. Taiwan is only 100 miles off China's mainland coast. It's smaller than Maryland and Delaware combined, and it is an extremely hilly country. Most of the country's farms are located on relatively steep slopes. Taiwan is an industrial country, resulting in very little tourism.

To show our continued support, in the 1960s, U.S. naval vessels of all sizes visited the coastal city of Kaohsiung. Beside industrial factories, the city maintained a large concentration of bars and clubs. I always enjoyed sailing in Taiwan; it was relaxing, safe, the people were friendly, the food was great, and it was just a cool place to spend a little time.

Hong Kong

Another frequently visited place, and one of every sailor's favorite ports of call, was Hong Kong. Our visits to Hong Kong were during the period when the United Kingdom had a long-term lease with China. The span of the lease was for 100 years, expiring in 1997. Hong Kong is one of many islands along the Pearl River, and is separated from Kowloon (the Chinese mainland) by Victoria Harbor.

Being one of the deepest natural maritime ports, the port of Hong Kong experiences some of the heaviest ship traffic in the world. With mainland China on the port side when entering the harbor, navigating in and out of Hong Kong was sometimes an ordeal. Navy ships were frequently confronted with unusual challenges,

Photograph of Hong Kong harbor at night from Victoria Peak, taken in early July 1965 just before the author left Hong Kong and headed south for Da Nang harbor. Center right, you can see the *Stoddard* in a dressed-ship condition. (Author's collection)

originating on the China mainland. During my many visits to Hong Kong, I'm unable to recall a single time we paid heed to such challenges. It was common for one or two Navy ships to be in port at any given time. When in port, we served as "Station Ship Hong Kong." This assignment required us to frequently communicate directly with, and act on behalf of, the U.S. Embassy.

When visiting Hong Kong, we anchored in the harbor and used a motor launch to travel ashore. It was one of the few ports where we anchored in a formal setting. This setting was referred to as "dressed ship." Under the condition of dressed ship, a massive string of lights was run from the ship's bow up to the top of the main mast and down to the fantail. The lights associated with dressed ship were illuminated from dusk to dawn. It was quite a sight to see from Hong Kong's Peak Tram.

For me personally, Hong Kong was one of two cities where I was assigned shore patrol (SP) duty, aka the Navy's military police. San Francisco was the other. In Hong Kong, my assignment was in the area around the U.S. Embassy.

While serving as shore patrol, we randomly roamed the assigned area which afforded us the opportunity to meet many local merchants and residents. It was from one of these encounters that I learned of a well-known tailor. This tailor crafted handmade, custom-fit clothing at reasonable prices. I mentioned it to several shipmates, and we took a bus to his shop.

I ordered two custom-made suits, a uniform made of gabardine, and a few monogrammed shirts. After completion, I took the uniform on board the ship and wore it whenever dress blues were required. I arranged to have the suits and shirts shipped home directly from the tailor. I loved all their clothes but especially the monogrammed shirts. I stayed in contact with the tailor and, for several years following my discharge, he made additional shirts and shipped them to me.

I also have to mention the food in Hong Kong; I absolutely loved it! Rather than being what I'd call "typical" Chinese food found in every U.S. city, Hong Kong's food was strongly influenced by the Cantonese culture. Across from the Hong Kong pier was a small but delicious Cantonese restaurant. I enjoyed—no, craved—their Cantonese chow mein. My first and last liberty stops frequently involved having a serving of chicken chow mein, Cantonese style. My mouth is watering just thinking about it. My visits were so frequent, and my orders so predictable, the chef would begin preparing the meal as I crossed the road from the pier. In the last 55 or more years, I have been unable to find a restaurant that could even come close to duplicating this Cantonese chow mein. Over the years, I have attempted to make chow mein Cantonese style. So far, I have failed; in fact, the most positive thing I can say is that I believe I'm making progress.

Beside U.S. Navy ships, Hong Kong is visited by warships from other countries as well. During one of our visits, an Australian destroyer also tied up in the harbor. While having a few drinks at a local bar, we ran into a group of Aussie sailors, struck up a conversation, and began drinking together.

I recall that after consuming a tremendous amount of alcohol during a drinking marathon, one of the American sailors said something along the lines of, "Look, I'm shitfaced and can't drink another drop without pissing my pants or passing out. It's one thing to get drunk but this is getting ridiculous." In response one of the Aussies said, "I felt that way an hour ago but wasn't about to let any fucking Yank drink me under the table." We all laughed, exchanged goodbyes, and staggered back to our respective ships. To this day, I have yet to meet an Aussie I haven't liked.

Midway Island

How many people can say they made two trips, in less than five months, to Midway Island? During our return to the States, we entered Midway's port to refuel before heading east to Pearl Harbor. As mentioned, Midway is more of an atoll than an island and beautiful in every aspect. Regardless of its beauty, it's a place you look forward to leaving within minutes of your arrival. It's a paradise hidden from civilization. The island (or atoll) has only two claims to fame; first, of course, is the famous World War II, battle of Midway Island and the other, gooney birds.

During our brief stopover, it was breeding season for the gooneys (aka albatrosses). We quickly learned they were a constant source of entertainment, amusement, and unquestionably the highlight of our visit. After spending years at sea, the gooneys' attempts to land or take off were an absolute scream! It was like watching the Keystone Cops of the bird world. Let me try to explain.

Their birthing season was well underway when we sailed into port. Less than 100 yards from the ship, we roamed among hundreds of nests. Each nest contained two birds and their fledglings. And let me mention, they were anything but frightened by our visit. In fact, their behavior could be described as indifferent or uninterested. These are very large birds, standing almost 36 inches high, with a wingspan in excess of 80 inches. The young fledglings reminded me of brown bowling pins. The adult birds' clumsiness or awkwardness comes from being at sea continually for six to seven years. Albatrosses were known to fly close to 50,000 miles without touching land. The ship could be hundreds and hundreds of miles from the closest land when an albatross would appear. During my time at sea, I'm unable to recall a single day when we failed to see at least one, regardless of our location. Ancient mariners firmly believed that albatrosses were the souls of dead sailors.

A gooney bird (albatross) and her fledging on Midway Island. Photo taken in early 1964. (Author's collection)

Midway Island is home to both the ka'upu (black-footed and black in color albatross) and the moli (Laysan albatross; white in color). We laughed, as we accused them of being prejudiced; neither type of albatross would tolerate or allow the other colored bird from even approaching their nest. Regardless of color, they nested in the same area with minimal room between nests. It was obvious by their movements and attitude that they were always prepared to fight. One interesting feature about the chicks was their color. The fledglings of both the black and white albatross were identical, yet their parents had absolutely no difficulty telling them apart.

As mentioned, their gawkiness became apparent whenever they attempted to land or take off. Once in flight, they are indescribably graceful. They could glide almost endlessly as they rode the air currents without flapping their wings a single time. At sea, sailors would watch these beautifully elegant legendary airships of the sea for as long as they remained within view. Effortlessly, they would glide in and out of sight, as if hiding below the waves; just an unforgettable sight and treasure of nature. However, when landing, they were the exact opposite. As they closed in on their "runway" and just before touching down, they would begin to run. They did this without realizing the speed of their feet differed from their air speed. This confusion caused them to tumble and cartwheel down their "landing strip." And it was equally funny when they finally stopped. As they stood up, they shook their heads while appearing to look around, wondering if anyone witnessed their dreadful arrival.

Taking off was equally challenging. They would begin by running and flapping their wings in an effort to get enough ground speed to take off. Being experts in air current management, even with just a mild breeze they would successfully become airborne. But, when the wind was dead calm, it was a completely different outcome. After running and flapping their wings for a relatively long distance and being unable to take off, they seemed to lose sight of what they were doing. Rather than becoming airborne, they appeared to give up and returned to their tumbling routine. After finally stopping, they got up, shook away their shame, and looked around to see if anyone witnessed their latest crash and burn sequence. Obviously, their difficulty in landing or taking off is the reason they were referred to as gooney birds.

While in port, I spoke to a civilian who was studying the gooney birds. During our conversation, he mentioned that about 90 percent of the world's population of gooneys call Midway Island their home. After spending a stint at sea, they return to Midway for the sole purpose of mating.

Guam, the Jewel of the Mariana Islands

While less frequently visited by naval ships, on two occasions we pulled into Guam to refuel. Guam is located a bit over 1,300 miles east of the Philippines and about 2,600 miles from Midway Island. Guam is known as "Where America's Day Begins."

Guam is a U.S. territory and one of the Northern Mariana Islands. Within hours after Pearl Harbor was attacked, the Japanese attacked Guam and occupied it for about two and a half years; the United States liberated Guam on July 21, 1944. Most people are unaware that in the 1960s, Guam was very instrumental throughout the Vietnam War. Our B-52 bombers, America's largest bomber, flew numerous missions out of the Anderson Air Force Base on Guam.

Superstitions are almost a way of life for many sailors, and this one is a prime example. Approximately 70 miles off the coast of Guam lies the Mariana Trench. It is the deepest part of any ocean or body of water on earth.

With that background, whenever we crossed the Mariana Trench, there were a few shipmates who intentionally limited their time outdoors to an absolute minimum. These men had a fear of falling overboard and were so easy to recognize. As they made their way from bow to stern or vice versa, they held onto the lifeline with both hands, as if we were in a Category 5 hurricane (or typhoon, in the Pacific Ocean). Take just a moment to consider this: normally when underway there are thousands of feet of water below the ship's keel. So, falling overboard in over 1,000 feet of water is far less dangerous than 36,000 feet.

Okinawa

In the spring of 1964, as we were returning stateside, we made a brief stop in Okinawa, known as "Churashima" or "beautiful island" in Japanese. It stretches along 160 islands, 49 of which are inhabited, and is referred to as a "rope in the open sea."

Okinawa is where one of the bloodiest World War II battles took place. Over an 82-day period the Japanese Imperial Army lost 95,000 soldiers, and the Americans 12,510. But the general population fared even worse, with 149,193 either killed or committing suicide.

My most memorable island experience had little to do with the country. We arrived in Okinawa in late March 1964, for a one- or two-day port visit. While many of the ship's crew was on liberty, we learned of the Great Alaskan earthquake. This 9.2-magnitude earthquake was devastating and also spawned a number of huge tsunamis. The highest wave was recorded in Shoup Bay, Alaska, at a height of 220 feet. Most people are unaware how the power of an earthquake is measured. A 6.0-magnitude earthquake is 10 times more powerful than a 5.0.

When the report of the earthquake was received, the ship was tied up on the eastern side of the island. This meant we were in the direct line of the tsunami, a wave that would later be felt along the coasts of Japan, New Zealand, Papua New Guinea, and even on the continent of Antarctica.

Our primary unknown and fear was the tsunami's strength when it approached Okinawa. The question was the effect or impact it may have on the ship. Would the tsunami be of sufficient strength to "lift" up the ship and carry it over land before receding and leaving us grounded on the island? Not knowing the answer to this question, the decision was made to ride it out at sea. The word spread quickly, the ship would be departing port within the hour and for all sailors to report back ASAP.

With transportation limited on the island, coupled with many sailors never receiving the news or order, only half the crew made it back on board in time. I made it back just minutes before getting underway. Our intent was to proceed at full speed to the leeward side of the island. If we were able to make it to Okinawa's western side, the land mass would block or greatly reduce the impact of the tsunami. If there was any strength remaining in the tsunami, it would carry the ship away from land. While communications were limited, updated reports suggested we may not reach the end of the island in time. The captain made the decision to change course and head out to sea. His intent was to "confront" the wave dead on.

The captain broadcast his decision over the 1MC, ending with instructions to "batten down the hatches and any loose material." His concern was, at impact, any loose items (i.e., cups, pencils, compasses, stools, glasses, coffee pots, etc.), could become dangerous missiles and compromise safety. To avoid injury, some of the nonessential or uninvolved shipmates tethered themselves in their bunks. The crew members on duty were instructed to identify a permanent structure close by and firmly hold onto it as the tsunami approached.

While "batten down the hatches," in nautical terms, meant "to prepare for trouble," it also meant to close and secure every horizontal and vertical opening on the ship. This would prevent water from flooding the compartments at impact. By battening down the hatches, if the ship's superstructure was compromised, the only compartment affected would be where an opening was present. This is the same condition used during GQ, with the intent of limiting the amount of damage. The primary objective was simple; allow the ship to remain afloat and continue normal operations.

While waiting for the tsunami, word was passed around that a Fletcher-class destroyer is one of the most seaworthy vessels to ever set sail. It would not capsize until water began running into its stacks. In short order, the ship was prepared and everyone in CIC surrounded the surface search radar. We were all wondering if the tsunami would be powerful enough to appear on the radar scope.

Suddenly, after a relatively long wait, the winds picked up and the waters began getting rougher and rougher by the minute. All signs we were getting closer to the main wave. With the ship prepared for the worst, about five miles out, a "line" appeared on the radar scope and the Bridge was notified. While we could see a line, it was less than clearly defined; it appeared somewhat erratic and static like; more typically like "noise" on the scope, which made it difficult to project an accurate distance.

Being well after sunset, we would be unable to take advantage of any visual observations. Moments later, we reported the line appeared to be closing and recommended a course for striking it dead on. The captain would decide the ship's speed; remember, any increase in engine speed increases the relative speed at impact. If two cars are heading in opposite directions at 50 miles per hour and hit head on, the relative speed at impact is 100 miles per hour. With that said, both the Bridge and CIC knew we had to travel at sufficient speed to prevent the force from stopping or controlling our forward progress.

We continuously fed our distance from the line, and the estimated time of impact, to the Bridge. When we were under than a mile away, the 1MC blared out, "Standby for heavy rolls!" Shortly thereafter the ship took what was later reported as a combined 100-degree roll; 50 degrees to port, followed by 50 degrees to starboard. Was that accurate? Who knows? But I'll say this, the instruction to "standby for heavy rolls" was a common phrase used as the sea changed moods and the ocean became rougher. But for my remaining years at sea, I never experienced another roll (side to side) or pitch (bow to stern) that even came close to matching what occurred that March night. Days later we learned the strength of the tsunami continued to weaken, causing a "minimal impact" on Japan and other countries.

While taking a bit of a beating, the ol' tin can survived; it kept its crew safe and sound. It did suffer a bit of minor damage; the most major being that the force at impact damaged our port running light, located near the top on the main mast. But, most importantly, no one was severely injured; nothing more than a few bumps, scrapes, and bruises. In the end, we all had a renewed respect for this greyhound of the sea.

Early the following morning, we arrived back in port and picked up a bunch of drunken and broke sailors. For the coming days, the bantering between those who "abandoned" the ship versus those who "rode it out" continued back and forth. But the best part was the embellishment contributed by both sides. At its peak, the crew that was "abandoned" reported they were "kidnapped" by the locals, forced to drink heavily, with their beer glasses replaced with funnels. They were also taken advantage of, stripped of their uniforms, and forced to pleasure the local women, while facing the constant threat of castration. Whereas those who rode the tsunami out at sea told of a rogue wave, at least twice the height of an aircraft carrier's flight deck, which caused the ship to take a 360-degree roll. Passing through the wave resulted in a great white shark being stranded temporarily on the main deck. God, there's nothing like the imagination of a sailor!

During my time in the Far East, again for political or diplomatic reasons, we did make other ports of call. Some of these included Kobe, Osaka, and Beppu, in Japan. While points of interest may have differed from port to port, from a sailor's perspective they were similar in the most important of ways: booze, women, and great food; not necessarily in that order.

I'll again mention my favorite country to visit was Japan, with the one exception being the foolish trip to Nagasaki. Personally, the Japanese people and their traditions were the warmest and most welcoming. To this day I envy the way the Japanese youth respect and honor their elders. Besides having some of the most hard-working people, Japan had, and continues to have, one of the lowest crime rates, making it one of the safest countries in the world. With only a third of the U.S. population, annually the total number of citizens killed by gunfire is less than 10.

During the spring of 1964, following a final port of call in Hawaii, we returned to San Diego. Most West Coast-based ships made a WestPac cruise once every 18 months. This being the case, and with my enlistment ending in January 1966, it was likely this would be my one and only cruise to the Far East. Well, as they say, "The best laid plans of mice and men" frequently go wrong. Well, I'm here to confirm the accuracy of this statement; let the games begin!

CHAPTER 9

Train, Train, Train, and When You're Finished—No, Wait, You're Never Finished!

> The more you sweat in training, the less you bleed in combat.
>
> UNKNOWN

Up to this point, all of the training had involved a minimum amount of live ammunition. We had also spent a significant amount of time training as part of a task force, training which had always involved simulated exercises. But let me assure you, this represents only part of the picture.

The crew of the *Stoddard* was already a well-oiled machine. However, in the fall of 1964, following the Gulf of Tonkin incident, the training of the crew was taken up to even higher levels. It became more focused, with the frequency and intensity of each exercise ramped up to new heights.

While in port, training continued at an "almost as usual" pace. The crew spent most of their day cleaning and keeping up their assigned spaces, as well as performing routine and preventative maintenance on the equipment. CIC was "cleaned up" and prepared for the next time the ship got underway.

However, when at sea, it became what seemed to be an endless day. Standing watches and being at general quarters consumed most of our day. For an unknown reason, GQ was ramped up to a higher level. This included the number of times we were called to GQ, the time spent more than doubled, and visits to ports along the West Coast became less frequent. This impacted the amount of time we had for writing home or just relaxing. We participated in an exhaustive number of informal drills; unbeknown to the crew, with the sole purpose of honing our wartime skills. That may sound harsh until one realizes wartime missions lack second chances or do-overs, so off time or casual time wasn't part of the equation. A combatant and his enemy are engaged in what can only be described as "it's us or them," "live or die" situations, with only one of them likely to enjoy tomorrow's sunrise. It's the reason every serviceman's proficiency must be sharpened and honed to their highest levels. Being prepared means he or she is able to enter their "combat readiness mindset" at a moment's notice. Once in that mindset, they must be able to execute their duties "professionally"; defined as instantaneous, crisp, flawless, and enduringly!

I mentioned this phrase a time or two before, but it's worth repeating. It describes the Navy's focus and intensity when it came to training and training exercises: "War is hell, but peacetime is worse." While most civilians probably find this adage amusing, I can assure you every combatant serviceman or servicewoman knows and has lived its exact meaning. And for this, I would like to thank the Navy.

Please allow me to retrace my steps and momentarily return to the decommissioning phase on board the *McDermut*. Although we were in dry dock, we participated in simulated exercises for hours and hours throughout the day. At first, I thought it was a form of punishment; why are we conducting so many exercises both in terms of type and volume? At the time, we were in port and decommissioning a ship. For some time, it failed to make any sense at all. After more than a month into our decommissioning "sentence," in what could only be described as an "aha" moment, it all became clear. In fact, it hit me like a sack of potatoes. At the conclusion of an exercise, I suddenly realized the importance of these simulated drills. Radarmen were confined to CIC; a space that never saw the light of day. It was dimly lit and basically isolated from the outside world. From a naval protocol perspective, whether it was a simulated exercise or an actual wartime mission, the activities, language, and interaction within CIC would be precisely the same. So staged or actual combat missions were basically the same way. I'll attempt to clarify or explain:

Let me begin by mentioning that all exercises were prepared well in advance. The development or preparation may include the bearing and range of the enemy's vessels, including countermeasures to avoid enemy shells. Most drills addressed specific topics so, rather than using the 1MC to call general quarters, the exercise commenced at a predesignated time. Any and all disciplines involved in the exercise would be at their battle stations, many times in full battle gear. With CIC being the ship's war room and accountable for managing the movement and responses during battle, we participated in the majority of exercises, simulated or live. The majority of our exercises also included the Bridge and the gun mounts. If a drill dealt with tending to injured shipmates, damage control issues, or engine room concerns, it was unlikely we'd be included in the exercise.

An exercise would be conducted or managed by an exercise coordinator. This individual wrote and acted as the drill's narrator. Many began with the report of a blip showing up on the surface search radar (the same type of event during a war time condition). After reporting it to the Bridge, calculating its course, speed, and CPA (closest point of approach), we would identify it as being friendly or hostile. When determined to be an enemy vessel, the Bridge would request a course and speed to intercept the skunk at a specific range, which always included the time of the intercept. During such a drill, the exercise coordinator may make adjustments reflecting movements an enemy may take. Or he may make adjustments impacted by sea or weather conditions. It would be the responsibility of those involved in the drill to respond accordingly. This always included recommending the best course, speed, position, and profile for an attack or the action necessary to manage a situation.

Any questions would lead to discussion, but in the end, it was imperative for all attendees to find themselves on the same page. This type of exercise usually concluded once the mounts were provided with the bearing, range, selection of weapon or weapons, type of ammunition, fuse, and a release to "fire for effect." Of course, a good exercise coordinator would keep the participants on their toes by frequently including numerous obstacles; obstacles requiring immediate reactions, decisions, or recommendations.

After participating in numerous drills, I began to realize the undeniable value of these simulated exercises. It was a resource that was essential in the training of new sailors. Plus, repeating similar training kept our most seasoned shipmates razor-sharp and operating at peak levels. And for this, I must once again thank the Navy!

The vast majority of exercises, both actual and simulated, were conducted at sea. The drills involving the firing of live ammunition, or interacting with other ships, were usually run between 0800 and 1600. In contrast, simulated exercises were conducted between 2000 and 0400. Of course, wars aren't only fought during daylight hours. For safety reasons, exercises involving live ammunition were infrequently conducted after sunset. However, in CIC (the cavern or grotto of a warship) there was very little difference between actual and simulated exercises. In reality, the only difference between these two types of exercises was the actual movement of the ship and the sound of guns firing. This became even more apparent when entering a combat zone and engaged in actual wartime missions and conditions.

Being the focal point of ship operations, whether it was navigating between two ports or participating in a combat mission, CIC was continually being challenged with every type of drill or exercise imaginable. These drills ran the gamut from navigating, air attacks, sea battles, shore bombardment, and even responding to a nuclear attack. Such drills were frequently run and repeated often. While many exercises were similar in nature, I'm unable to recall when any two were identical. Each contained unique and challenging features or characteristics. Many would run for about an hour, while others for the better part of an entire watch. Some drills were limited to the crew on our ship, while others included all the ships within a task force. When a drill involved the entire task force, it was usually limited to the CICs on every ship within the formation. When conducting this type of exercise, the task force commander assigned a specific frequency that connected the CIC on all ships. This avoided any interference with actual task force operations. All simulated exercises were closely monitored by senior level personnel on board the flagship.

For ship-only CIC exercises, the quality and results of the exercise would be evaluated by the most senior officer or petty officer. Beside evaluating the staff's ability and effectiveness in executing the drill, they also evaluated the exercises complexity and difficulty levels. If the exercise was poorly designed or its execution was less than stellar, a similar type of exercise would be scheduled focused on the weaknesses exhibited during the initial drill.

For exercises involving ships within a task force, the flagship representative evaluated the quality of the exercise and reported his observations to each ship's captain. The captain shared the critique with his senior staff, who would discuss the results with their respective division. Having the report mention a weakness or deficiency demonstrated by all ships is one thing, however having criticism directed specifically toward "your" ship's performance was another matter entirely.

The importance of gun crews can't be overstated. Their performance was always in the captain's crosshairs. I mentioned one drill where a gun crew's poor performance was addressed by the captain. In all fairness, the following involved a gun mount on a different ship. In this case, a major weakness or concern was mentioned in the exercise coordinator's summary. Following this unfavorable report, I witnessed what could only be described as being how God would react if you pissed Him off. The captain's rage and ferocity was intense and absolute; it made my boot camp DI's demeanor seem trivial by comparison. For the next few days when not on watch, eating, or sleeping, the deficient gun crew were in their mount practicing and sharpening their craft. In short order, they became a top-performing gun mount. The Navy always found a way of turning lemons into lemonade; negatives into strong positives. This is why the U.S. Navy is so often recognized as the strongest and most respected in the world.

It may sound unfair but during actual battle situations every sailor was expected to perform at 100 percent; however, the gun mounts were expected to operate at even higher levels. But then again, even one slipup could be catastrophic.

After being discharged, I never witnessed anything even close to this demand for excellence or perfection in civilian life. If pushed, I'd say the closest in pursuit of such excellence was exhibited by the management of our nuclear power plants. However, this may have been the case because our nuclear power plants are primarily managed by trained and seasoned former Navy personnel. The Navy simply asks every man or woman to perform at their highest level. The term "productivity" is defined differently in civilian life versus the military. In civilian life, productivity is measured by product output or yield. Whereas in the Navy, it measured by a person's work ethic, standard, and commitment to striving for the highest degree of performance excellence achievable.

Getting back to the topic; realizing the complexity of the exercises, one begins to understand and appreciate the time and effort invested in their preparation. The CIC exercises were generally prepared by the senior radarman, primarily 1st class and chief petty officers.

If I recall correctly, we infrequently had more than one 1st class petty officer and 1st class chief petty officer on board; the rest of the department was made up of radarmen with less than four years of experience. During my first six months on board the *McDermut*, I was totally unaware of how the senior staff spent their day in port. I would see them at morning and evening musters, but they seem to disappear for the remainder of the day. It wasn't until I came on board the *Stoddard* that I learned a significant part of their day was spent planning and preparing simulated training exercises.

As I mentioned earlier, when we were hundreds of miles from land, an entire four-hour watch could pass without even a single surface or air contact showing up on our radar screens. This provided an excellent opportunity for conducting simple training exercises for radar strikers. It would not only be a learning experience but helped pass the time during what could be a very boring four hours. If, during an exercise, an air or surface contact showed up on our radars, the drill would be paused until the contact was identified and was safely exiting the area.

Many of the exercises focused on training junior sailors, whereas those involving more complex issues, especially GQ events, were generally prepared and focused on 3rd and 2nd class petty officers. I understood that much of the training of the 1st class and chief petty officers, who were generally career sailors, was conducted off ship in base classrooms.

As you can imagine, it was somewhat of an honor to be asked to prepare and execute a training exercise. The pressure is really ramped up when asked to prepare such an exercise involving an entire task force. And the pressure usually included the selection of the topic, the thoroughness in its research and execution. Conducting an exercise for the task force was a direct reflection on the ship. Unquestionably, when the flagship critiqued the overall exercise, every ship was hoping for positive feedback. You can be assured, the sailor responsible for the exercise and its execution was relieved when the exercise was over. He was equally pleased to receive affirmative or constructive comments about his work and effort.

As I'm sure you've concluded, in order to create a successful exercise, the author must possess a substantial amount of knowledge of the topic. This was especially true when creating an exercise for a task force. For a task force exercise, the coordinator had to have more than basic knowledge and operational awareness for every type of ship involved in the drill. This awareness had to come from both an offensive and defensive perspective. This knowledge resulted from prior training, experiences, and extensive research into the subject matter.

***

I'm confident my passion for the duties of a radarman has become apparent. Being a noncommissioned officer, I accepted the responsibility and accountability of this very important activity; I respected and treasured being a member of this critical classification. And may I add, this feeling was generally felt by most sailors for their specific classification. For me personally, this passion grew and peaked around the time I was tested and promoted to petty officer 3rd class in March 1964.

Shortly after being promoted, I found myself longing to learn more and more about my trade. By doing so, I would become a more valuable asset to the operation and readiness of the ship. It was also around this time that I realized every knowledgeable, successful, and respected crew member had one major factor in common; they were afforded the opportunity to visualize/create, write/prepare, and execute complex training exercises.

Following the promotion and after participating in a countless number of drills, I began to get the urge to create a challenging exercise. Unbeknown to anyone, I began sketching out a rather complicated exercise. Early on, I realized it was more difficult than I expected. To do so, I had to expand my overall knowledge of the topic. Within a week or two, I noticed my understanding of everything radar wasn't just expanding, it was exploding. The more I learned, the more I wanted to learn. I found my overall interest in the field extending into all aspects of the profession. This expansion included offensive and defensive actions, onboard weapons, and their selection for use in air, surface, and NGFS missions. In short order, I also became fascinated with a ship's tactical movements and capabilities in different situations. In order to continue my growth, I realized I had to confide and rely upon people with extensive knowledge in radar, CIC, ship movements, weapon selection, and 7th Fleet operations. The three people who best fit this description were the captain, the OI Division officer, and our radar chief petty officer.

Let's start with the captain. Simply put there was absolutely no way the captain would ever consider meeting or interacting with a 3rd class petty officer. The OI Division officer was an ensign; while he may have superior management skills, he lacked knowledge and experience in CIC activities. So, my confidant would hopefully be a man with unparalleled knowledge of radar: our chief.

The next morning, following muster, I made my move. I did so by requesting a one-on-one with my targeted mentor. He immediately responded by suggesting we get together in the chief's mess, about an hour before the noon meal. This caught me completely off guard; even before I mentioned the topic, he showed his willingness to meet. I was pleased with the schedule, as it gave me a few hours to review the draft I'd prepared and get my act together.

I arrived a few minutes early with a draft of the exercise, notes, and presentation in hand. As anxiety began to peak, I was pleased when he asked if I'd like to grab a cup of coffee. Coffee with the chief! This simple gesture settled me down and relieved some of the anxiety. He began our conversation with some small talk involving a few general issues, before asking why I requested the get together. OK, I had to present the idea in a brief and concise way; I wanted to avoid sounding like I had verbal diarrhea. Suddenly, I began wondering if I had all my ducks in a row. In reality my goal was quite simple, I simply wanted to convince him to at least give the idea a chance.

In less than half an hour, he approved my idea and couldn't have been more supportive. He liked the outline of the exercise and offered several suggestions to improve its overall concept. He also volunteered his help whenever I ran into an obstacle, while authorizing use of the ship's "library." For the record, the term library may be an overreach. The library generally contained publications pertaining to the operation of the ship. These reference documents would be essential to the success of my work. Before using any of the publication, classified or unclassified, I would have to request and receive permission from the chief. As a point of interest, there were several publications I could only use in his presence; remember the Navy operated on a "need to know" basis. Loose lips sink ships! As I was leaving, he loaned me the exam study guides for 2nd class, 1st class, and chief radarmen.

About a month later our newly promoted 2nd class radarman, responsible for keeping the ship's navigational charts updated, received reassignment orders. Just days before his departure, the chief notified me I would be assuming the duties of this position. The ship's charts were stored in a small, securely locked space below the main deck in the stern of the ship. This new assignment involved receiving a monthly publication called *Notice to Mariners* which described changes that impacted our navigational charts. Generally, it involved changes in water depths and the addition, deletion, or the relocation of buoys. The *Notice to Mariners* recorded each change by referencing the name/identifying number of a specific chart, a description of the modification, along with its longitude and latitude. When a chart became worn due to frequent or numerous changes or usage, I would simply write a requisition and order a replacement.

The new assignment provided the time and space I needed to read the study guides and any other relevant publications. I must admit, the chief's overwhelming support did have an impact as well; I felt I had to succeed or I would have let him down. The chart room was locked with only the chief, the supply officer, and I having keys. This security afforded me the opportunity of storing classified publications for as long as required during the development of an exercise. Several days after beginning my new assignment, the chief stopped by the chart room for an update. During our conversation, he suggested I go through each of the study guides before going any further in the development phase. This approach allowed me to read a topic that may impact the exercise, make a note, and return to it later. I thought it was an excellent suggestion and proceeded accordingly.

While in port, my assignment allowed me to spend numerous hours reading and preparing the exercise. It was a different story when the ship was underway. While at sea, I could only devote a minimal amount of time to the exercise. Besides standing the two 4-hour watches and GQ each day, I also spent a considerable amount of time participating in a variety of training exercises. Also, when the ship was underway, the fantail of the ship was constantly pitching and rolling. And to top that off, the sound of the screws in the chart room was almost deafening. These conditions made reading and concentrating practically impossible. But on many evenings, rather than playing cribbage, hearts, or watching the same movie over and over again, I found myself relaxing in the radar equipment room. There, as I listened to recorded music,

I was able to devote time to reading, planning, and making notes for my exercise. In less than a month, I reached the point where I had the knowledge and confidence to prepare a solid exercise. Also worth mentioning, my increased knowledge in the field of radar became apparent to my peers. During exercises I was able to answer most questions or provide the most acceptable approach to almost any challenge.

My sudden knowledge turned into somewhat of a game with several of our more senior staff. During the execution of an exercise, they added "unique" challenges to their exercises. Later on, they revealed these challenges were intended to bamboozle me. For the record, I'm unable to recall a single case when they succeeded. Before going any further, let me point out, these "challenges" didn't create even the slightest bit of animosity; instead, they became more of a competition. My interest and commitment to learning was completely unrelated to future promotions or increases in pay. Remember, to even be tested for a promotion a sailor had to serve time in grade; so, my commitment to or hunger for learning was never a threat to anyone. It was so different than civilian life, where my actions could have been misconstrued or misinterpreted. With that said, I quietly accepted the "stump" challenge game.

Announcements for upcoming exercises always included the timing and topic of the drill. So, to be fully honest, I stacked the deck just a bit. The chart room contained publications that addressed every topic related to radar, the duties for every position within CIC, and then some; thank you, chief. And I took full advantage, by using these publications to review the subject matter before attending the drill. At first, it was simply to get a brief understanding of the topic; with just basic knowledge, I could get the most out of the exercise. However, it did turn into a means of preparing for the numerous questions that would be coming my way. This challenge game went on for months and while everyone benefited, in my opinion, the Navy was far and away the greatest benefactor. Before long, several of my peers suspected something was fishy but failed to understand my source for such broad knowledge.

Finally, one day after all the participants arrived for a prescheduled exercise, the exercise coordinator announced he was unable to complete the scheduled exercise in time. Therefore, he would be presenting an entirely different drill. I remember it clearly to this day. The topic turned out to be naval protocol following a nuclear attack on a carrier strike force. It included course adjustments, the individual ship's tactical movements, and who assumed the position of OTC (officer of tactical command), concluding with how and when the OTC was transferred post-explosion. Now this was the best part; his "unannounced" exercise was the topic I had been working on for about a month. I had completed all of the research but hadn't begun laying it out on paper.

When the outline of the exercise was presented, I recall taking the grease pencil from the exercise coordinator's hand and sketching out the entire set of maneuvers on a plastic display board. This was followed by explaining the procedures set forth by Navy paradigms. As a silence fell over the group, coupled with a few of the most senior staff smiling, the exercise coordinator asked, "How did you know I was going to run this drill"? I assured him I had absolutely no advance notice. After letting it sink in for a few more minutes, I confessed he selected a topic I was developing; one to be presented sometime in the future. We all had a good laugh and wished the Navy had similar competitions between ships; what a great learning tool and experience. But then you have to remember, competition in the Navy is generally frowned upon. Our training was focused on working as a team, and this team could be a group of sailors on a destroyer or a group of ships assigned to a Carrier Strike Force. The only "competition" was between "us" and our enemies.

Man Your Pen, Compass, Maneuvering Board, and Reference Guides

Over the coming months I was given the opportunity to prepare and execute numerous exercises. At the time, we had two 1st class radarmen assigned to our ship. The chief decided prior to beginning a new exercise, I was required to discuss its concept and obtain the approval of one of the 1st class radarmen. This approach worked out very well for all parties. So, following a discussion and approval by a 1st class, along with a second nod from the chief, I would begin the research and development phase. Throughout the process, the 1st class and I would informally meet a few times a week. These interactions were to discuss the project's progress and direction. In turn, the 1st class radarman would not only act as a resource but also update the project's progress to the chief. This way, while the 1st class may not have been doing the grunt work, they remained within the loop. It's important to mention that throughout an exercise's development they provided significant input. This was especially the case during the writing and assembling phases. Their involvement was essential to my development, while acting to advance their skills as well. It also supported the internal chain of command, a major element within the military.

After being assigned to keep the ship's charts up-to-date, when in port I stood the normal watches but was relieved of other duties. As you would expect, as time passed my proficiency in developing exercises grew exponentially. Please don't get the wrong idea, I never became overly gung-ho to the point where it affected me personally or interfered with my personal life. While I enjoyed what I was doing, I was extremely careful in "managing" the assignment. As I gained experience, especially as it related to the research activity, I began to pace myself. I did so by ensuring most projects took about the same amount of time, conception through execution.

It's worth mentioning, in all my years, I believe it may have been the only time I woke up looking forward to and excited about my "job." As I became a more seasoned author, the complexity of the exercises increased. My approach and the goal for all my exercises was simple: the program had to advance the knowledge and wisdom of both the targeted audience and me. Of course, there were many times the exercises were similar in nature, but not unlike a good James Patterson novel, each contained unusual twists and developments. It didn't take long before I was combining two exercises into one.

All my exercises encouraged questions; I quickly learned a "hard" question is only hard if you don't know the answer. It was during this time when my peers began to realize my knowledge of radar and CIC had well surpassed that of most other 3rd class petty officers. In fact, many began to actually show a different degree of respect to me versus others of the same rank. It was more or less their way of reflecting their appreciation and recognition of my hard work. As with any sailor, they began busting my stones by referring to me as a "lifer." A lifer was a sailor who was serving a self-imposed life sentence in the military. However, I was also aware the term lifer was also a Navy acronym for "Lazy, Inefficient Fucker Expecting Retirement." It was used to describe someone who does as little as humanly possible and was simply waiting to begin collecting his pension. Either way, I knew it was all in jest.

You may find it of interest that as an enlisted man I had somewhat of an unusual relationship with many of the officers. When on shore, my relationship with officers was the same as with any other enlisted sailor. However, when on watch there were numerous times when conversations with officers went beyond the Navy. During these conversations, we shared personal experiences about family and background. I feel they benefited both of us, making future conversations easier and more comfortable. From the Navy's perspective, I may have expanded their knowledge of CIC functions; in turn, they expanded my knowledge of 7th Fleet operations and naval protocol. Many times, I felt I was being groomed to make the Navy a career and study to become a commissioned officer. The topic of "shipping over" (aka, extending my enlistment) and making an eight-year commitment was a constant theme among all the officers I interfaced with. If I agreed, the Navy would absorb the cost for any college or university, but it also meant I would have to serve a minimum of four years following graduation. By then, I would have served a total of 12 years and would become eligible for retirement after 20 years. But I had other plans; as it turned out, through the GI Bill, the Navy footed the entire bill for me to attend college.

After a few months of preparing training exercises, I received a request to meet the chief following the 1600 muster. He mentioned our ship had been selected to prepare an exercise, lasting an hour or so, to be executed with an entire task force. The exercise would be conducted in six weeks while at sea. I was being "asked," under the supervision and direction of our 1st class radarman, to lead the assignment, including being responsible for its creation and execution. He concluded by mentioning that with the approval of the OI Division officer, the chief, and the 1st class radarman, I could select the topic.

Are you kidding me? He hadn't even finished and my head was reeling. Shortly thereafter, my joy and happiness turned to apprehension and possibly even fear. Dear

Lord, what have I gotten myself into? Can I really pull this off? Oh yeah, I can see the letter to my family: "After failing to provide a challenging exercise, and just prior to diving from the air search radar antenna platform onto the main deck, your son shit his pants and lost his hat." As we were discussing the exercise, the XO passed by. I was floored when he joined the conversation and congratulated me on the assignment. Well, at least I think he did, my nerves still had the best of me. But I do recall that, seeing I was a bit frazzled, he offered up a thought that was comforting: "You may feel stressed or overwhelmed by the assignment but remember, you've earned this assignment and we're confident you'll make our ship proud." Holy shit! But then what followed made me realize—and it has lasted for a lifetime—I was being asked by others who believed in me and I should not doubt them.

I walked away thinking, what have I gotten myself involved in? To pull this off, the first objective was to be fully knowledgeable and aware of your audience. It's extremely important to respect the attendees or participants receiving your presentation; such respect must never be taken lightly. But it's equally important to recognize that the reason you've been invited to make a presentation is because of your knowledge of the topic. As the speaker, or coordinator in this case, it's likely you'll have a greater knowledge of the subject matter than most attendees. This came to mind every time I was asked to develop a naval exercise. And remained with me whenever I was called upon to make a presentation throughout my civilian career.

After a few days of mulling over ideas, which included numerous discussions with my peers, I approached the chief and 1st class radarman with my suggestion. I proposed an exercise involving a nuclear attack on the fleet. It would include the detonation of a low-yield nuclear bomb, its impact, and the post-explosion responsibility of every vessel within the task force. If you recall, it was a topic a peer used earlier during the game of stump. As I thought about it, I recalled that the complexity of the exercise contained all the elements needed to be successful. These elements included guidelines to minimize damage and injury to ship and crew, the maneuvering technique all ships were required to follow, and the evolving fleet chain of command, which required an extensive knowledge and understanding of naval protocol.

Following the discussion with those above me, the concept was approved by the end of the day. But there was a caveat, that being concern over "airing" classified information during its execution. After further discussions between the OI Division officer, our chief, and 1st class radarman, I was given the go-ahead. I was informed, once completed, all data involved in the exercise had to be reviewed. This was necessary to ensure it was free of any classified information. To this day, I'm unsure who was on the review panel, except that it was off the ship and totally independent of the exercise. As mentioned, the military takes the handling of classified information very seriously. From the onset, I was committed to limiting my research to unclassified documents. But it's worth noting, when one or more unclassified documents are combined from different sources, the result could end up in the creation of a classified document.

I found it extremely challenging to write an exercise of this complexity. The degree of complexity grew not only from the topic but intensified with the sheer type and number ships participating. I remember the OI Division officer used the analogy of a "composer writing a musical piece; one that included a large variety of instruments." My initial plan was to keep all the ships engaged but somewhat isolated from one another. I provided an "exercise-only exit speed" from which to maneuver from the impact zone; this way the actual flank speed of each class ship would remain classified. However, the turning radius for each class of vessel remained unchanged. To make the exercise as realistic as possible, at the time the nuclear device was detonated, a number of ships would be lost. I concocted the names of the ships severely damaged or sunk, along with their call signs. This way the actual ships within the task force, while possibly sustaining some damage, would remain operational.

To ensure everyone understood how the OTC functioned and changed, I intentionally slowed down several of the "damaged" ships, so the full impact could be realized. I'm less than certain what may have been declassified or changed in the last 50-plus years. But for the record, my ultimate goal was simply to involve every destroyer, cruiser, and carrier to the max. The plan ensured every ship had events and conditions where snap decisions were essential. Close to the conclusion of the exercise, I scheduled one of the actual ships to simulate the order to abandon ship. This was necessary to see how the crew on the damaged ship responded. It also addressed how the recovery or rescue of the sailors would be handled by the current OTC and the remaining ships. Oh yeah, I was creating what could only be described as a true shitstorm. God, I loved it!

OK, typically running an exercise for your ship and shipmates was one thing, but I quickly learned running it for an entire task force was a far different challenge. With that said, I was so fortunate to have so much experience and knowledge available from our 1st class and chief radarmen. There were times I felt the assignment might be over my head, but the help from our senior staff completely relieved this concern. My interaction with these two professionals substantially increased my respect for each of them.

Shortly after review and approval, we learned the exercise would be conducted on our third day at sea, during the 2000 to 2400 hours watch. Just a few areas of clarification: when operating in a task force each ship (CIC and the Bridge) is tuned into a common frequency. As you may expect, radarmen on watch were not involved with the exercise; they remained focused on normal operations.

With the guidance of the 1st class radarman, about 30 minutes into the watch and after we laid out the conditions and parameters of the exercise, we "detonated" the nuclear weapon. Almost immediately, based upon the quality of responses and questions, it became apparent people of higher rank had taken notice and joined the exercise. Both the 1st class and I became aware our audience had expanded; unexpectedly, several ships began debating naval protocol, especially when addressing to whom and when OTC passed from one ship to another. While the debates were brief, they included the station location where the ships would regroup based upon wind and sea conditions.

I'm unable to recall a time when I was more nervous. However, in the end, the exercise turned out to be more than any of us ever imagined (thank you chief and thank you 1st class radar petty officer) and could only be described as a complete success. You're probably wondering how we knew it was successful. Well, first of all if it was a flop, it wouldn't have appeared in this book, and the book would have been more than 10 pages shorter. Or possibly even worse, if the exercise had failed, the consequences could have impacted the remainder of my enlistment and my involvement during actual combat conditions. But its most defining moment came the following day.

While on watch, as the captain was leaving the wardroom, he stuck his head in CIC and said something along the line of "Calder, great job on the exercise, keep up the good work. Now we've been assigned plane guard duties, get me the course and speed to get us on station by the time I return to the Bridge." It was one of the very few times I remember the captain stopping in CIC. Whether it was at sea or in port, it was unusual for the captain to interact with or compliment any sailors under his command. After all, we were expected to perform our duties at the highest level at all times. I think the visit could best be summed up by the officer on watch. After the captain left, I looked at him and he simply said "holy shit!" as I began calculating the requested course and speed. The striker on the surface search radar, who first noticed the captain and called "attention on deck," asked if the captain came into CIC often and he got a brief, firm, and unanimous "no!"

A few months later, our 1st class received an assignment to teach at a Radar Class "B" or "C" school, and the chief mentioned he used the exercise as a course outline; that in itself was a great compliment.

Before long, all this work was about to pay off in spades, and I believe it resulted in a unique opportunity and the privilege to further serve my country, the U.S. Navy, my ship, and possibly as being an honor to my family. I would do so by assuming one of the more key roles for any enlisted man stationed aboard a destroyer, during wartime conditions. However, before going down that avenue, let's first discuss what led up to the United States' involvement in Vietnam.

CHAPTER 10

The Gulf of Tonkin Incident

During the 1940s and 1950s, conflict existed and continued to mount between the countries of North and South Vietnam. The North was inspired by Chinese and Soviet communism; whereas, in an attempt to retain its fragile position as a democracy, the effort in the South was led by the French with support from the United States. In years prior to our involvement, the Viet Cong's popularity and growth steadily increased in the South. The United States sided with and supported the leaders of South Vietnam, with most of this support coming in the form of military aid. It was our attempt to prevent the North from returning it to a socialist-style country.

With that brief overview, the question becomes: what circumstances or events propelled us from providing aid to becoming an armed conflict participant? Even to the present day, the answer is very controversial; well, at least for some. Of course, I'm referring to the "alleged" attack by North Vietnamese PT boats (short for Patrol Torpedo) on U.S. destroyers in the Gulf of Tonkin. But did it ever occur? After 60 years, the answer still remains contentious. As a warning, research into the "incident" can only leave you more confused than when you began. It is difficult to find any two articles that are in agreement. The "facts" vary because they are so misleading and outlandish; they were manipulated and altered as needed to support the attack. I wonder if this is where the phrase "alternative facts" originated.

On August 2, 1964, while conducting intelligence operations in the Gulf of Tonkin, the U.S. destroyer USS *Maddox* (DD-731) allegedly came under attack by three North Vietnamese PT boats, in international waters. Now, let's put this "attack" into perspective.

A North Vietnamese PT boat was a small (63 feet long with a 12-foot beam), fast, but short-range craft, used for coastal scouting and attacking enemy transport, tankers, barges, or other supply ships; but never warships. With a crew of four, they posed no threat whatsoever to a warship.

China delivered 12 P-4 torpedo boats to North Vietnam between 1961 and 1964. These aluminum-hulled vessels were fast and maneuverable but lacked radar. They contained two torpedo tubes and twin 14.5-millimeter guns. These guns had a firing range between 1,600 and 2,200 yards. In the late 1960s, China provided radar-equipped PT boats, but these boats were used sparingly and never as a weapon against a U.S. Navy warship. Regardless of where they were built, PT boats were greatly hampered by their ineffective torpedoes, limited armament, and fragile construction. Because of these weaknesses, every nation limited the use of their PT boats to coastal waters. Their torpedoes were highly ineffective, as they lacked any form of homing, controlling, or steering capability.

Simply explained, firing a torpedo from a PT boat, at a moving target, was basically an attempt to create a collision between the target and weapon. Any variance, such as changes in the target's speed or course, would result in a miss. Also, weather and sea conditions impacted the effectiveness of the weapon. The most successful launching platform for a torpedo was the submarine. A submarine could fire at close range, which increased the likelihood of a torpedo striking its intended target. These weaknesses were the primary reason most torpedo tubes were removed from all Vietnam-era destroyers and eliminated from the future design of all U.S. destroyers. Torpedoes were most effective when fired against fixed targets or supply-type ships. These ships moved slowly and lacked any defensive weapons. If fired at a destroyer, the sonar system would pick up the sound of a torpedo motor immediately after launch, regardless of distance, allowing the ship to take evasive action.

The *Maddox* was a Sumner-class destroyer: 2,200 tons, 376 feet long with a 40-foot beam, and a crew of 336. It was armed with six 5-inch cannons, twelve 40-millimeter AA guns, and eleven 20-millimeter AA (antiaircraft) guns. Their fire-control system was capable of engaging high-speed subsonic aircraft. Their 40-millimeter antiaircraft guns could fire 160 rounds per minute and their 20-millimeter guns over 300 rounds per minute. This highly decorated vessel saw extensive action in both World War II and the Korean War.

The USS *Maddox*, DD-731. Based upon the radar antennae shown, this photo was most likely taken in the 1960s. (The Naval History and Heritage Command, NH97804)

As you can see, a completely unsophisticated PT boat attacking a Sumner-class destroyer is like a Peterbilt tractor truck being driven off the road by a Schwinn bicycle. It makes no military, political, or common sense whatsoever. If the North Vietnamese wanted to start a war by attacking or sinking a U.S. warship, they could have employed their Russian-built MiG-15 jet aircraft. Also, let's remember, the relationship between the United States and North Vietnam may have been strained, but it had lacked any exchange of gunfire since July 8, 1959. On that date, two American soldiers were killed in a guerrilla raid just outside Saigon. So, if the North Vietnamese objective was to sink a U.S. warship, it could have accomplished this goal by means of a surprise aerial attack. Using this scenario, much like Pearl Harbor, it would have been unlikely the *Maddox* could have responded in time to react to such an air attack.

From the above, you can only begin to realize why I refused to accept the notion that an attack ever took place. And to complicate matters even further, just the thought of a Sumner-class destroyer firing in excess of 250 rounds of 5-inch high-explosive (HE) shells—with each round weighing 55 pounds and blanketing the area with 4,000-plus pieces of shrapnel per shell—yet missing the target every time, is just plain stupid, insane, or both. It's unfathomable for me to comprehend how anyone could believe such moronic gobbledygook.

At the time, I was very familiar with the awesome firepower and capability of a U.S. destroyer; so, this nonsense just made my head hurt. A U.S. destroyer is basically a downsized battleship. If you look closely, a destroyer is armed with a variety of weapons from bow to stern. On the other hand, a PT boat is nothing more than a glorified Chris-Craft, with a twin machine gun and a pair of torpedo tubes. The sailors on board the *Maddox* were well trained, like every other sailor who donned the Navy uniform. However, media reports painted a completely different picture. Based upon these reports, if an attack took place as described, the sailors on board should have been court-martialed for incompetence, disgracing their uniform, and falsely posing as members of the U.S. Navy. While subjected to criticism, few were ever asked to provide their observations.

Consider this: during World War II our destroyers hunted down and sank Japanese aircraft carriers, battleships, cruisers, and destroyers, plus numerous other naval vessels. In addition, there were thousands of enemy aircraft downed by U.S. destroyers. The destroyer was, and continued to be during the Vietnam War, the Marines' primary artillery when landing on beaches and defending coastal regions. Yet, the public was led to believe they were completely ineffective against North Vietnamese PT boats. And for the record, during any previous war, the total number of U.S. warships sunk by enemy PT boats totals 0, zero, nada, zippo, zilch! The total number of U.S. destroyers sunk during World War II from enemy weapons was 71. Of these, 47 were sunk by enemy aircraft, 19 by enemy submarines, and the remaining 5 by other means (i.e., shore batteries, other surface ships, etc., but not once by a PT boat).

PT boats were only effective against commercial and unarmed military freighters, barges, etc. Our PT boats were able to sink 38 of these types of ships during World

War II. So, this false claim was, and remains, an absolute embarrassment and slap in the face to every destroyer sailor who donned a naval uniform. If a PT boat or group of PT boats ever attacked a Sumner-class destroyer, their service life expectancy would be measured in seconds. The threat would have ended long before every sailor arrived at his assigned battle station.

So many other "facts" of the incident were equally mindboggling and completely erroneous. They had to have been fabricated by politicians or spin doctors in Washington. The objective of these individuals was to pull the wool over the eyes of the American public, and it was completely void of reality. There were numerous, inaccurate and misleading claims and reports, generated by individuals who possessed the basic naval knowledge of a doorknob. While completely erroneous, they were written with such detail the reader wouldn't question the qualifications or experience of the author. This false and misleading narrative even carried over in a declassified report released by the Center for Cryptologic History, NSA.

Let me offer up a list of the major issues that came immediately to mind after hearing the media report coming from Washington. And these facts were altered, manipulated, and changed numerous times over the weeks, months, and years, in an attempt to stay ahead of a constantly changing story. The story was so outrageous. Seeking to add some degree of credence to their political fodder, days later there was a report of a second PT boat attack. However, this time they added a second destroyer and several naval jet fighters. It's important to mention this rendition, which remains questionable, resulted in Washington authorizing the military to commence retaliatory strikes against the North.

Here are some of the claims reported in the news:

- Claims regarding the distance from which the *Maddox*, and later the *Maddox*/USS *Turner Joy* (DD-951), were sailing from the North Vietnamese coast. While most reported the ship to be in excess of 35 miles off the coast, one report stated the *Maddox* had violated international law by sailing under 10 miles from the coast. Later, reports indicated they were closer to Hainan Island, which was under Chinese rule and over 125 miles from the North Vietnamese coast.
- The time of day at which the attack took place. The original attack supposedly took place during daylight, but even that is debatable. If this were the case, it would make the "tale" an order of magnitude worse. During the first attack, it was reported the weather conditions were "ideal." The second attack allegedly took place at night, in stormy weather.
- The type and number of enemy PT boats involved in the attacks varied, along with the number of torpedoes fired. Some reports stated more than 30 torpedoes were fired. This number exceeded North Vietnam's total inventory; so, this lie went under numerous and frequent modification. In addition, with each torpedo weighing over a ton, a North Vietnamese PT boat could

only carry a maximum of two torpedoes and they had to be loaded in the tubes before leaving port.

- The duration of the attacks; some stating the *Maddox* versus PT boats, as well the *Maddox* and *Turner Joy* versus the PT boats, were engaged in battle for more than an hour.
- The number and type of U.S. military hardware involved in the attack. We're talking about two decorated destroyers and jet fighters scrambled from a carrier. Yet, all failed in their attempt to neutralize the enemy's poorly armed, poorly constructed watercraft.
- How close the attacking PT boats were able to get to the destroyers. Some reports would lead you to believe the closest point of approach was 10,000 yards or 5 nautical miles, while others reported the PT boats maneuvered so close that the bullets from their pop guns struck the superstructure of the *Maddox*. The maximum range, not the effective range, for the North Vietnamese mounted machine gun was just over 2,000 yards.
- I read several media reports claiming the PT boats were able to fire on and either damage or down one of the "attacking" naval jet fighters.
- Prior to the Vietnam War, the proximity shell was perfected for many different-sized weapons and applications. This included all the 5-inch guns mounted on all U.S. destroyers. The proximity shell contained a fuse that detonated the shell at a preset distance, before impacting the actual target. This detonation spreads a field of shrapnel in excess of 100 yards in diameter. Created during World War II, proximity fuses used in Vietnam increased the lethality projectile by 10 times and were effectively used against ground forces. These fuses incorporated updated technology referred to as "Doppler radar fuses." This automatic proximity fuse was revolutionary because it allowed artillery shells to explode just before hitting the ground or an aircraft, making them more effective against targets. However, their advanced design also allowed them to be used against enemy ships, aircraft, and missiles. The blast field created by the high-explosive rounds of 5-inch shells, each containing 4,000-plus pieces of shrapnel, would have neutralized the crew and demolished the watercraft.

OK, let's explore this alleged attack in even greater detail. Let's begin by understanding more about the Gulf of Tonkin and the likelihood the PT boats could have even located the *Maddox*. Please take note of the two destroyers' locations in relation to the closest land or islands when the attacks took place on the chart below.

The Gulf of Tonkin is 48,750 square miles of open water, and it's 150 miles wide. To put that in a more understandable perspective, it's about 2,000 square miles larger than the state of Pennsylvania. And before going any further, as a reminder, the North Vietnamese PT boats lacked any radar or similar technology. In order to locate the *Maddox*, they had to strictly rely upon locating the ship visually.

Chart of the Gulf of Tonkin, reflecting the location of the USS *Maddox* on August 2, 1964 and the location of the USS *Maddox* and USS *Turner Joy* on August 4, 1964.

Using these figures, we'll assume Pennsylvania is a body of water and you're in a Chris-Craft crossing somewhere along the Maryland border. Your assignment is to locate an object about the size of a football field within these 48,750 square miles, using only your vision. Approximately 2,300 destroyers could fit into one square mile; your odds of finding an object of this size are astronomical.

Part of the equation is the distance the PT boat crew could "see" after entering the Gulf of Tonkin. At a height less than 10 feet, visually, the horizon appears less than four miles away. As a further point of reference, the State of New Jersey has approved windmills to be installed 13 to 20 miles off its coast. When completed, the turbines will soar more than 900 feet above the waterline and the blades will be between 170 and 360 feet in diameter. Yet, these huge machines will appear as small white crosses along the ocean's horizon, about ⅛ inch in size, as viewed along New Jersey's beaches and shore communities. The top of the radar mast on the *Stoddard* was approximately 65 feet. And, for the record, the maximum effective range for the surface search radar, on a 1960-era destroyer, was 10 to 12 miles or 20,000 to 30,000 yards. And this radar was an order of magnitude more advance than those used by the North Vietnamese.

Let's continue, if you're searching at night, you and your crew are blindfolded and are attempting to locate a football field-size object, which is constantly moving. It would be easier to locate a toothpick dropped on the ground somewhere in the Grand Canyon (and that's under 2,000 square miles). Think about that for a moment, because that's the scenario presented to the American public by politicians and the media in order to justify the aerial attack.

Let me explain why a blindfold was necessary in the above example. I can only hope the reader has been at sea at night and beyond the horizon. If so, you realize how ridiculously preposterous locating the *Maddox* and *Turner Joy* visually would have been. When a ship is beyond the horizon, even if the sky is clear, the only light would come from the ship's exterior lighting and the moon. Even a clear night, in the direct path of a full moon, lacks the illumination to see a surface contact as far as the horizon. I'll try to describe what night or darkness is like at sea.

I'll use a simple example to make my point. Before going to bed, shut off all the lights, go into a closet, and close the door. Now try to see your hand in front of your face. A better illustration tracks directly with a combat mission discussed later in the book. I'll start with a little up-front information. When operating in a combat zone or involved in a combat, sensitive, or special operations mission in the 1960s, a warship operated in a condition known as "darkened ship." The *Maddox*, and later the *Turner Joy*, were operating in darkened-ship mode while conducting operations in the Gulf. This condition requires that all external lights be extinguished, including the ship's running lights. It prevents any light whatsoever from leaking from the exterior of the ship. The only active lights are a few interior lights which are dim and red in color. These dim red lights can only be seen for a very short distance. Their rays aren't reflective, nor can they bend around corners or up ladders, etc.

With that background, we were operating in the condition of darkened ship, under a mile off the coast of South Vietnam. As we were preparing to take up station and begin an NGFS mission, I was communicating with three Marine helicopters. I informed the pilots we were under a mile from their location and would be on station within a minute or two. They immediately took exception to my broadcast and began questioning our actual location. They did so because they were unable to get a visual on the ship. I assured them of our location, confirmed we were tracking them on radar, and they were under a mile to our north. From the ongoing conversation, it was apparent they continued struggling with or disbelieved we were in the area. This remained the case until we fired the first salvo.

Another example involved a spotter, who thought he was directing the fire of a large cruiser or battleship. He did so because of the number of guns being fired and the size of the firing field. Instead, he was witnessing two destroyers firing on the target in a mass firing operation. Even with range-finding binoculars, he was unable to see the profile of the two ships.

With these examples in mind, how close would a PT boat have to get before they could make visual contact with the *Maddox*? I suggest it would be under the length of a football field.

About 10 years ago, I was talking with a veteran who suggested the PT boats may have been supported by land-based radars. These land-based radars may have directed the boats to the location of the *Maddox*. An interesting concept until you realize several key factors. First, the North Vietnamese radar systems could be defined as primitive at best. In addition, a surface radar system simply records a blip on a screen. The technology only identified a contact by means of a blip; it lacked the ability to identify the blip as a military ship, a commercial vessel, or a junk. Finally, neither radar nor radio signals bend to conform to the curvature of the earth. The maximum distance a PT boat could have communicated with the land was approximately 14 miles, provided the land-based transmitter tower was at least 100 feet high. As a reminder, in the 1960s, satellite and Bluetooth technology was only available in the world of Flash Gordon.

Next, let's discuss the enemy's torpedo. We'll start with the report of the enemy's torpedoes being picked up on the ship's radar. Let's be clear, torpedoes travel below the surface at about 35 to 40 knots; regardless of the sea conditions they would never be picked up by radar. An incoming torpedo would be picked up on the ship's sonar. But once again we're dealing with reporters who haven't the foggiest knowledge or experience of the topic on which they are reporting.

Staying with the torpedoes, there was a great deal of confusion over the range from which the alleged torpedoes were fired, with most stating the weapons were fired at 10,000 yards (which is completely out of the torpedo's range) to as little as

5,000 yards or 2.5 miles. I'll sum it up this way: because they lacked any type of homing or controlling components, even at 400 yards (around the range used by submarines), and assuming the *Maddox* failed to take any evasive action whatsoever, based upon the reported sea and wind conditions, the chances of the weapon finding its target were very low. It lacked the means of locking in on a target. At 5,000 yards, with the top speed of 40 knots, at launch it would take 3 minutes and 42 seconds for the torpedo to reach its target. The odds of a torpedo striking a ship from this range were as likely as the PT boats finding the *Maddox* in the first place.

I read reports stating the North Vietnamese PT boats were able to get less than 2,000 yards from the *Maddox* and fire their .50-caliber pop guns. At this range, and with them just firing their 40- and 20-millimeter AA guns at the PT boats, it would be like a marksman firing a shotgun at a target under 3 feet away. Each 40-millimeter gun fired 160 rounds and each 20-millimeter gun fired 450 rounds per minute, with each mount having a very effective fire-control radar system. If the Maddox had made either visual or fire-control radar contact, once they confirmed they were under attack, the PT boats would have been obliterated in seconds.

And if the August 2, 1964 insanity wasn't enough, it was reported a second attack took place two days later. But this second attack involved the *Maddox* and a second destroyer, the Sherman-class *Turner Joy*. In "defense" of the two destroyers from this horrific PT boat attack, several jets were scrambled from the aircraft carrier USS *Ticonderoga* (CV-14), operating in the South China Sea. Although a fair distance away, the carrier was able to scramble several jets "to join the battle," with the reported attack lasting in "excess" of an hour. Other reports suggested the jet aircraft were flying overhead to defend the destroyers from coming under attack by North Vietnamese PT boats.

To clarify, you may feel my reference to "defense" is being sarcastic, but it isn't. A declassified report stated that Captain John J. Herrick, Commander Destroyer Division 192 and on board the *Maddox*, had "added a concern that the DRV's (Democratic Republic of Vietnam) torpedo boats, especially at night, could hide and then approach the destroyers with little warning." He stated that the *Maddox* and the *Turner Joy*, with their 5-inch guns and top speed of 33 knots, were inadequately armed for defense against such boats. He suggested that the Desoto patrol would be safe only with a cruiser and continuous air cover. Try digesting that one for a few minutes. This same individual also reported that the *Maddox* had originally picked up the PT boats on its surface search radar when they were over 40 miles away. As a reminder, at sea the range of a destroyer's surface search radar was in the 10- to 15-mile range.

At a later date, a report was released stating that following the "alleged encounter, the aircraft thoroughly searched the area and were unable to find any signs of damage, wreckage, bodies, oil slick, or any evidence an enemy PT boat even existed." With the jet pilots unable to support the "attack," the story began falling apart. In fact, the report was later "revised" to state there may not have been a second attack.

The report stated 250-plus shots were fired in the direction of an unusual "weather event." With the bombing campaign already underway, it supports or may explain any reluctance in reversing the "fiction" surrounding the first attack.

As the politicians and the media were dumping all this nonsense on the American public, it made me suspect they had been exposed to too many heroic stories about PT boats. Approximately a year earlier a movie titled *PT-109* had been released. It overly exaggerated and embellished the power and operations of a PT boat. In the *PT-109* movie, the skipper was named JFK. In this case, JFK's PT boat was dramatically rammed and sunk by a Japanese destroyer. This event took place on August 2, 1943. And if that wasn't enough, the American public had to also navigate its way through a television show around the same time called *McHale's Navy*. It was a comedy involving a PT boat with a dysfunctional crew that portrayed a PT boat having what could best be described as supernatural powers.

I have a vast amount of experience and knowledge of the Gulf of Tonkin. We spent a considerable amount of time cruising and conducting numerous assignments in the Gulf. Occasionally, when operating in the Gulf, skunks or unidentified surface contacts appeared on the surface search radar. It was not uncommon for these contacts to appear as if they were traveling at high rates of speed and suddenly jump erratically on the radar scope. There were times when they appeared to instantaneously reverse course. But never once did I, or any of the other radarmen, ever consider it to be a vessel or an act of aggression by a hostile nation. These events occurred occasionally in the Gulf and were identified or classified as nothing more than weather phenomena. These unusual weather events were commonly referred to as the "Ghosts of Tonkin Gulf." And let it be known, similar events were known for many, many years prior to the Gulf of Tonkin incident.

Phantom images known as "radar angels" had been recorded since radar was first introduced in the 1940s. These radar angels occurred when hot and cold air in the atmosphere was present. The turbulent mixing of layers of different temperatures gave rise to phantom images, in the forms of both ships and aircraft. The "Tonkin Gulf Ghost" or "Tonkin Spook" is a phenomenon that became familiar to U.S. Navy radar operators. Even on clear days, it can produce blips that appeared to be a ship or plane on the radar scopes, even though nothing can be seen visibly. When first reported, the word of an attack on a destroyer spread quickly, with almost every crew member thinking "this is insane; it must be some kind of a prank or joke?"

This Gulf of Tonkin reported "attack" was a reflection on every sailor who donned a naval uniform. The crews on U.S. Navy destroyers were highly trained professionals; the readiness of a destroyer sailor is legendary. Personally, there was absolutely no way I was buying into this nonsense; the media had gone batshit crazy, with reports that were irrational, misleading, and completely false. They even reported that although the *Maddox* was operating in international waters, it tried to flee when coming under attack, causing the PT boats to chase after them. I can assure you, the U.S. Navy never conducted exercises involving the physiological reaction of fight or flight! I must confess, I became obsessed with these reports; I had to learn more about what had actually occurred on August 2, 1964. But unfortunately, the *Maddox*'s home port was Long Beach, CA, which is about 100 miles north of San Diego.

During the fall of 1964, I learned of a navigational course being offered by the Navy in Long Beach. Being responsible for updating the ships navigational charts, I felt I should attend. For days, I tried to persuade the chief and OI Division officer to approve my request to register and attend. And you can be assured, I pulled out all the stops, but in the end my request was denied. Regardless, I wasn't giving up. I had to get to the bottom of this insanity!

In late 1964, a few of us were enjoying a beer at Patrick's Tavern, in downtown San Diego, when I noticed a 2nd or 3rd class radarman at the bar. Most importantly, he was wearing a ship's patch that read "USS *Maddox*"; I almost lost my cookies. Could this be real? I went up to him, introduced myself, and told him, "We have to talk."

Initially, I may have come on a bit too strong; he resisted and told me they were sworn not to discuss the incident with anyone. I apologized for being too forward, explaining I wasn't any part of the media organization but just a radarman who would likely be deployed to the region in the near future. I reminded him that as sailors, and especially with both of us being radarmen, we were like family. I stretched the truth just a bit by mentioning I had just received a new shipment of charts. These charts suggested we were slated to spend considerable time in the Gulf of Tonkin. This claim may have been less than true at the time, but I had so many questions that needed to be answered. After more prodding, and throwing in a beer to seal the deal, he agreed to share what he felt was "pertinent" information about the incident.

To be honest, the conversation started off a bit on the vanilla side. He mentioned they were assigned to a Desoto patrol (DeHaven Special Operations off Tsingtao). This assignment involved collecting electronic intelligence in what may be considered unfriendly waters. Similar missions were conducted for years in the South China Sea. He talked, and I mostly listened, for the better part of an hour. Finally, he began talking more openly in the direction I was interested in. During our conversation, I mentioned a major part of my job was writing training exercises. It turned out he was doing the same on board the *Maddox*, and we agreed to exchange a few in the near future. But in all honesty, that never happened. But in the end, this is a summary of what I learned during our conversation:

- Their 5-inch guns were fired in the direction of the blips appearing on the surface radar scope. No PT boats were ever visually observed. The PT boats never got close enough to engage their 40- or 20-millimeter guns.
- After an extensive search, no signs of personnel or wreckage were ever found. As a side note, the daytime pictures that surfaced years later were not taken on board the *Maddox*. If they had been, I can assure you they would have

taken pictures of the debris field after "successfully sinking" one or more of the boats (as reported).

- He mentioned the blips on the radarscope, which were first observed less than seven miles from the ship, were thought to be anything from noise on the scope due to sea conditions to being a high-speed skunk. He was adamant that the majority of the senior sailors in CIC did not think they were under any sort of an attack. Several were aware of the unusual weather phenomena occasionally present in the Gulf of Tonkin. This was especially true when the contact suddenly appeared on the radar scope, acted erratically, and then just as suddenly disappeared. Being unable to fully explain the nature of the blip meant it had to be reported. Per Navy protocol, as soon as the contact was observed on the surface search radar, it was reported to the Bridge.
- When the speed and the unusual movements of the contact or contacts couldn't be explained, the Bridge assumed it may be hostile. The contact's movements and tracks were so irrational, CIC was unable to calculate a course and speed. Resulting from the contact's unusual behavior, per naval protocol it was immediately reported to the captain, who in turn reported it to command. Such action was necessary because, if the skunk was hostile, the ship needed guidance and permission on when and how to engage it. Remember, up to this point, no shots were fired by either the North Vietnamese or the Americans. Also in August 1964, no American combat troops had mobilized in Vietnam. The only American troops in-country were involved in training the South Vietnamese.
- The *Maddox* received orders that if an attack was imminent, they were authorized to fire warning shots over the contact's bow. Although the contact was never visually observed, the ship fired two rounds in the direction of what was believed to be the skunk's bow.
- When the command received word a destroyer "may have come under attack," they notified every ship in the region of a "possible hostile act" against a U.S. destroyer. They also reported the incident up the chain of command, eventually reaching Washington. Again, this would also follow normal naval protocol. However, I'm confident the report underwent a significant change between the *Maddox*'s captain's lips and the president's ears. In communication with the local command, the *Maddox*'s captain requested "rules of the engagement" be followed if they determined the ship was under attack.

Let's assume for a moment that there was a chain leading from the *Maddox*'s captain to the president. This chain would have contained a series of many, many links; let's say the links on the military side were blue in color, whereas the links on Washington's political side were red.

Knowing military protocol and how they handle and report sensitive information, the embellishment of the facts surrounding the incident, likely occurred after it left the blue links, and occurred along the series of red links, before reaching the president's desk. At the time, there were reports that many politicians were looking for a reason to become more militarily involved in the South Vietnamese effort to remain a democracy,

- While many *Maddox* crew members may never have heard of or been exposed to such unusual weather conditions, the captain certainly had. While his action could be described as an abundance of caution, he precisely followed naval protocol; putting the safety of his men and ship over the possibility of a false alarm. However, within a few hours following the alleged attack, the captain of the *Maddox* notified command that an attack may not have occurred. He stated, "Freak weather effects on radar and an overeager junior sonarman may have accounted for the erroneous reports. There had been no actual visual sightings by *Maddox*."
- It was later learned the captain was simply looking for direction on how to react if the contact was deemed to be an attack by a hostile nation (rules of engagement). Had he suspected the command was going to do any more than simply provide direction, he would have presented the situation much differently. Apparently his what-if was received and interpreted in Washington as "an enemy attack is underway," thus raising all sorts of red flags. The following day, the captain was overheard saying he thought he'd be allowed to conduct an investigation before determining if an attack actually occurred.
- The following morning, and after a careful, thorough review and investigation, the captain's report concluded the chance of it being an attack was "highly unlikely." The report also mentioned there were no visual observations or concrete signs that any hostile boats were even in the area. In his opinion, the blips on the radar screen were caused by freak weather events known to exist in the region. As mentioned earlier, the report of a torpedo being fired resulted from an "overly eager" junior sonarman.
- Sonar and radar operate in a similar fashion; they transmit and receive signals. With sonar, when an incoming torpedo or contact is picked up, the sound and quality of the ping increases as the torpedo or contact nears. Whereas, during the investigation, it was reported neither the sound nor the quality of the ping improved. Instead, the sound frequently faded and at times completely vanished. I remain confused as to how a weather event could have been picked up on sonar and continue to suspect that the operator "imagined" he heard a ping. Some suggest this junior sonarman actually misinterpreted the sound of his ship's screws for a ping, as the speed was abruptly increased to "all ahead full," and they commenced maneuvering in a zigzag pattern.

- Following the alleged attack and exchange of gunfire, the Navy had several aircraft search the area. These aircraft were dispatched and were unable to find any wreckage or signs an incident or exchange took place.

The radarman from the *Maddox* and I ended our conversation with a laugh, while agreeing that the legend of PT-109 and *McHale's Navy* had strongly influenced or, at a minimum, tainted the public's perception of PT boats. This false narrative about PT boats was exploited by politicians and the media to their advantage. Of course, the ill-informed public wholeheartedly accepted the misinformation as fact; how indescribably sad.

In the strictest of confidence, prior to our deployment, I shared this discussion with the other radarmen on board the *Stoddard.* This knowledge advanced our ability to properly observe and better interpret conditions when entering the Gulf of Tonkin.

As a further follow-up, many Americans are unaware this would not be the last reported "attack" by North Vietnamese PT boats. On September 18, 1964, a little more than a month following the Gulf of Tonkin incident, another Desoto patrol reported they came under attack by North Vietnamese PT boats. The USS *Morton* (DD-948) and the USS *Richard S. Edwards* (DD-950), both Forrest Sherman-class destroyers, were assigned a Desoto mission. At 1730, the two destroyers picked up radar contacts on their surface search radars. The destroyers reported five ships showing up on their scopes.

After about an hour, the *Morton* fired a warning shot; a shot that had no impact, as the PT boats continued to trail them. This resulted in both ships opening fire on the attacking boats. The firing continued for the next hour, as blips on the screens remained constant with every sweep of their radar antennas. It was later reported that at no time did the attacking ships return fire. In fact, it appeared the attacking ships remained about the same distance from the destroyers. During the alleged encounter, the *Morton* and *Edwards* reported that the number of attacking PT boats increased. At the conclusion of the confrontation, they stated they'd fired over 250 rounds and were successful in sinking five enemy boats. A search was ordered, as a retaliatory strike was being planned. The area was thoroughly searched and re-searched several times, but nothing was found; no debris field or oil slick was observed. Regardless of whether such an attack ever occurred, on September 20, 1964, the destroyers were ordered to return to the task force and all future Desoto missions were permanently suspended.

CHAPTER 11

What Genius First Uttered Those Words: "War Is Hell, but Peacetime Is Worse?"

In early January 1965, as I was leaving CIC the chief asked me to take a few steps toward the wardroom, an area where it was unlikely our conversation would be overheard. I was informed I'd be attending a naval course off the ship. Following a successful completion, I would be designated as the *Stoddard*'s naval gunfire support communicator or coordinator. This is a position responsible for all communications between the ship and Marine spotters during shore bombardment missions. Transportation to the naval station at Point Loma would be leaving within the hour. This allowed a relatively limited amount of time to pack and prepare for a somewhat extended stay. I would remain at the installation throughout my training, which I believe was the better part of a week in duration. To say I was shocked would be an understatement.

After it sank in, the first question that came to mind was why was such a course—one devoted strictly to naval gunfire support—necessary? In the past, the position was passed between coordinators as an activity better defined as on-the-job training. Being unable to answer the question, I began focusing on: why was I selected? Could it be a "reward"? Regardless of the reasoning, I felt honored and truly appreciated the ship's senior staff's trust in me. I was confident my family would feel likewise.

An hour or so later I boarded a Navy bus, along with radarmen from other ships, and headed for Point Loma. Upon arrival, we were taken to semi-private rooms to drop off our belongings. I recall being very impressed with sharing a room with just one other sailor or student. It would be much easier to focus on my studies without the barracks noise. The barracks setting usually involved a group of loud, rowdy, and fun-loving shipmates; but as they say, there's a time and place for everything. While the room may not have been spacious or luxurious, it was more than adequate, especially when compared to shipboard accommodation. The room contained a stocked bathroom (soap, towels and wash cloth), two single beds (not bunks), with mattresses thicker than an inch or two, and two desks. It was still the Navy, so it contained only the very basics; forget about any extravagances such as a TV or radio. If I recall correctly, it even lacked pictures on the wall or any daily domestic service.

But it was clean and well kept, so I may have been hoping for too much. Regardless, even after more than 50 years, it remains a very memorable experience.

An introduction to the course was presented within an hour following our arrival. Near the end of our first session, one of my classmates raised a very pertinent question: "Why did the Navy feel it was necessary to develop and present a course focused on or devoted specifically to naval gunfire support?" If I recall correctly, the simple answer was "to further increase our wartime readiness and capabilities." Now that's a canned phrase or response that would apply to any and every training exercise past and present. Regardless of his reply, it just didn't sit well with me. In an earlier conversation, we all agreed this was a first. None of the students were able to recall any former NGFS communicator receiving any sort of "formal" shore bombardment training. Rather than challenging his answer with another question, we simply accepted his response as presented. We were confident it was highly unlikely the instructor would, or could, provide any further information. He was there to teach a segment of the course and nothing more.

The course was extremely condensed and intense, with each segment taught by seasoned senior petty officers and Marines. Our class size was less than 10 (if I recall correctly, five or six may be a better estimate). The course included a sizable amount of one-on-one training. It was a no-nonsense course, with the instructors demanding our constant and unabated attention. I mention this because, after several days of reminding one student to pay closer attention, the instructor paused his presentation and asked to speak to the student outside the classroom. A few minutes later he returned, mentioned it was better for all involved if the student returned to his ship, turned around, and continued the course.

The course focused primarily on our main armament, the four 5"/38 guns. As a point of reference, the designation "5 inch/38" means the barrel diameter was 5 inches and the barrel length was 38 times the diameter. The course also addressed the fire-control computer, a component of the gun fire-control system. Remember this was 1964, so keep in mind the definition of a computer system differs considerably from today's technology. Before going any further, and to avoid any confusion, I would like to clarify the definition of the word "computer." First, let's go back to 1965, when the word computer had a completely different meaning than today. Even in a press release to the wire services involving a mass firing mission, our captain used the phrase "computer solution."

To be clear, in 1965, we did not have the benefit of electronic computers, GPS, satellite imagery, nor anything even closely resembling Bluetooth technology. For the most part, our systems hadn't even been upgraded to include transistors. But even back then our fire-control system, coupled with gyroscope technology, resulted in extremely accurate gunfire. After inputting data into the fire-control system, the analogue system "computed" the angles to impact the target by considering corrections involving gravity, relative wind, and the effects of a spinning shell. It even took into account the different location of the guns along the length of the ship, as well as calculating the shell fuse time. It sent this data to the gun mounts via synchronized motors. Bottom line, the calculations and hydraulic machinery data were used to aim the guns. Once the system was "locked" on target, it produced a continuous firing control solution. The original fire-control system, developed and utilized during World War II, was later modified and upgraded when the ships were recommissioned during the Korean War. This upgrade significantly increased the long-range accuracy during shore bombardment or NGFS missions. These modifications allowed illumination and airburst rounds to explode above the targeted area, rather than detonating upon impact with the ground or other objects.

I touched on this earlier; during heavy sea conditions it was fascinating to watch the movement of the gun mounts when locked on a target. The rolling and pitching of the ship made it appear the gun's movements were utterly out of control. They moved completely independently, as they swung wildly up and down at different speeds. In reality, the guns remained stationary, locked on target, as it was the ship that was actually moving.

The course included extensive information regarding the different types of ammunition, fuses, and their usage. The types of ammunition primarily addressed were illumination and high-explosive rounds, whereas fuse discussions addressed the different conditions for their use. For instance, under normal circumstances when firing on enemy forces, a "fuse quick" (a proximity fuse) would be utilized for both illumination and high-explosive rounds. Both of these shells exploded at different elevations over the target and were commonly referred to by the Marines as "airbursts."

As the course continued, we began to fully understand and realize the importance of the position. As NGFS coordinators/communicators, we were taught and charged with focusing 100 percent of our attention on the mission, along with the precise execution of our duties. It was essential for us to remain focused on our duties, while ignoring all surrounding activities or dialog. The importance and impact of blocking out of our environment was expressed within examples. These examples reflected how the lives of friendly forces may have been impacted if we failed to devote 100 percent of our attention to the mission.

Let me try explaining it this way; in today's world an NGFS coordinator is similar to a 911 emergency operator. When in dire need and requiring help (police, firemen, EMTs, etc.), a victim calls 911. It was much the same way for a destroyer's crew when operating off the coast of Vietnam. The minute command assigned the ship to a mission, the NGFS coordinator established communications with the designated Marine spotter. The spotter was properly authenticated and an immediate bond was formed. It began feeling as if you were communicating and working with a close dear friend on a common objective. And not unlike 911 operators, each call was unique and special. When the event concluded, you remained concerned over the whereabouts and safety of your "friend." As time passed, these encounters frequently crossed your mind, as you hoped all remained well with your "special friends." While you never met the Marine spotters, through this extensive training, you were aware of a spotter's needs and the spotter was equally aware of your capabilities. By their needs and your capabilities, I'm referring to the training and relationship between the Navy and the Marines in general; it was exceptionally professional on every level.

We spent countless hours and days practicing mocked-up missions. The language structure had to be followed precisely, no variations whatsoever. Using and understanding the exact same terminology allowed the NGFS coordinator and Marine spotter to communicate on the exact same level. From the time communications were established, the NGFS coordinator and Marine spotter were so well trained, they knew the type and format of information upcoming in the next sentence. There was never a time when either party questioned what had been conveyed or how to respond. It's important to repeat, when it comes to training the military is far and away the hallmark by which to measure all other institutions. Following my tour of duty, I attended college as well as numerous industrial seminars; none came even close to the standards set forth or required by the Navy. When a student graduated from a Navy school or course, he was fully trained in the topic and prepared to perform at his highest level.

The course remained intense throughout its duration. There wasn't any time allotted for socializing or liberty. While there may not have been a final written examination, there were frequent and numerous quizzes throughout the week. But most importantly, to qualify or be certified as an NGFS coordinator, each student had to have the blessing of the Navy and Marine instructors. This was accomplished by conducting mock drills, with the instructors posing as Marine spotters. And I can assure you, the trainers truly put us through our paces. They covered every scenario conceivable and then some. Many of these oral-style evaluations ran continuously for hours with the same evaluator. Other simulations involved multiple missions conducted with a variety of trainers. These evaluations tested the student's knowledge of NGFS, as well as his stamina or endurance. It measured the coordinator's ability to remain focused on the mission during long and drawn-out hours of simulated combat conditions. While the exercises lacked any physical demands, this was more than compensated for by how remarkably exhausting and challenging they were mentally.

As more exercises were conducted, the exhaustion was replaced with a degree of calmness and confidence. This calmness developed as we effectively addressed each and every challenge thrown our way. In the end, in addition to learning the skills and demands of being an NGFS coordinator, I also discovered so much about myself. Most importantly, I learned how to accept and respond to challenges, regardless of how hopeless or bleak they may appear. Being just shy of 22 years of age, I realized everyone has and deals with stress differently. What differentiates us is

Another successful NGFS mission, circa July 1965. This photo was taken within eight miles of Da Nang harbor. Notice the smoke in the left-hand side of the photo, a result of the NGFS. (Author's collection)

how successfully we are able to react, manage, and process stress. Let me offer up a few examples to explain.

I recall watching an interview with Lee Trevino following a PGA win. The interviewer asked Mr. Trevino if he felt pressure knowing sinking the putt would win the tournament, a two putt would cause a playoff, and a three putt would result in a loss. Mr. Trevino replied, "That's not pressure; pressure is when you're preparing for a 15-foot putt and someone says, 'I'll bet you 10 bucks you don't make it.' You step back and say, 'You're on'; all the while knowing you have only a dollar in your wallet; now that's pressure!"

Maybe a better example is comparing the stress of a professional baseball player to one in high school. Let's assume both athletes are preparing to bat in the team's final championship game; one the World Series and the other a state championship. The opposing team is up by one run, bases are loaded, and there are two outs in the bottom of the 9th. A hit wins the game, a walk ties the game, and an out loses the game. People are people, and in this scenario both athletes are feeling the same degree of stress. When you think about it, the only real difference is the financial reward. The outcome is largely influenced by how a person is able to react to and manage stress.

As the course was ending, we were given an unusual opportunity; one to observe a live NGFS exercise. Several of the Marine trainers were being taken, by helicopter, out to the practice range located on San Clemente Island. At the conclusion of the course, rather than returning to the ship, we were invited to accompany the Marines to witness an actual exercise. In a few hours, we would return to the naval air base and catch a Navy bus back to the 32nd Street Naval Base.

When we arrived on the Island, we were taken to a location where the Marines had a structure set up for conducting NGFS exercises. It became obvious that the training of both Marine and naval personnel was occurring simultaneously. Although we may have been classified as "spectators," in reality we were also engaged as students or trainees. Each sailor was assigned to a Marine involved with the exercise. While the atmosphere could be described as casual, there frequently was a certain degree of uneasiness whenever different services interacted. This was even apparent when servicemen, from different military organizations, met on liberty.

I was assigned to a Marine trainer whose nickname was "Gunny." After a few questions and some random discussion, we both began to feel more comfortable. The exercise was absolutely remarkable, especially seeing the effect or impact of a 5-inch high-explosive shell. I was also struck by how the exercise tracked precisely with our training. As the training mission evolved, I mentally found myself responding to the Marine spotter, as he completed his transmission. While I was at awe with the entire exercise, I was even more impressed with Gunny. He knew his craft and was more than ready to share every component of his knowledge. But the most memorable event happened as the exercise was winding down. It was when I was thanking him for his guidance and for answering all my questions. As we shook hands, he made a statement that basically changed everything.

As if talking to his best friend, he looked directly at me and put one hand on my shoulder as he raised his index finger just in front of his nose. He began speaking words that will remain with me forever. "John, there's something I want you to remember, from this point on we are both teammates and friends. Keep this in mind as you work with different Marine spotters. As a teammate, I'll keep count of enemy casualties; as a friend you keep count of the Marine lives you may have helped save!" I can assure you, I returned to the *Stoddard* a much different sailor. From this conversation, especially when it came to actual combat situations, even with a limited amount of sleep, it was easy to get the adrenaline flowing when called to general quarters. And this message resonated with me every time I participated in an NGFS mission, whether on board the *Stoddard* or the *Samuel N. Moore*.

Before going any further, I'm sure many readers have mixed reactions and may not fully understand what Gunny was attempting to convey. For some, Gunny's statement may appear to be insensitive to human life, and nothing could be further from the truth. I'll attempt to explain the meaning of his message.

Civilian and military life could not be more different. Remember, the military isn't manufacturing pencil erasers or car fenders; it has no product output. Many people relate or connect military personnel to police officers, believing they are very similar in nature, but they are far from it. Police officers are responsible for enforcing and maintaining law and order, while respecting and keeping community members safe and out of harm's way. Frequently, they are called upon to restore peace when there's quarreling or disagreements within families, between neighbors, within neighborhoods, with large groups of emotionally charged people, or with individuals who are dealing with mental issues. There may even be times the National Guard may be called upon, when large groups or mobs become unruly, and hopefully find a means of deescalating a tense situation. However, the primary mission of one serving in the military is very different; it is condensed to defend the United States and its interests.

It's summarized in the oath taken on the day they are sworn in. As the recruit raises his or her right hand, they repeat the words:

> I will support and defend the Constitution of the United States against all enemies, foreign and domestic; that I will bear true faith and allegiance to the same; and that I will obey the orders of the President of the United States and the orders of the officers appointed over me, according to regulations and the Uniform Code of Military Justice.

Being in the military comes with the understanding that "defending" includes the likelihood there may be the loss of life. When a conflict between the United States and an adversary reaches a boiling point, military action may become necessary. When this occurs casualties (wounded and fatalities) will likely result. For this reason, military training by all countries focuses on "neutralizing" the enemy or opposing forces. I'm unable to recall a single training exercise focused on employing deescalating tactics or measures. Our training was focused on eliminating a threat. When a member of the military goes into battle, they go in with the training and sole understanding enemy forces must be dealt with and neutralized as efficiently and expeditiously as possible. Achieving this objective would likely result in the loss of life; coming in second was not an option; there is no room for mistakes, apologies or do-overs.

So, when we were conducting air, surface, or ASW exercises, we were preparing for a battle against enemy forces. NGFS (shore bombardment) is part of this training. As the Marines' primary coastal artillery, our mission was to defend, protect, and support the Marines, as they executed their assignments and duty. A major objective in every mission was preventing harm or death to our Marine "brothers." A successful mission meant they survived, were available to fight another fight, and someday return safely home to their loved ones and friends.

When confronted with this life-or-death environment, you learn the true meaning and value of life. In battle, it isn't anger that drives you, it's the immeasurable concern and the unknown of the outcome; especially for your fellow combatants. Let me give you an example, which I'll explain in more detail in a later chapter. One evening as Da Nang harbor defense ship, we received emergency orders to change course to a location north of the harbor. While en route, we learned a squadron of 20 Marines were up against a fighting force of more than 700 Viet Cong. Throughout this night battle, our ship's only concern was keeping those 20 Marines safe and alive. The thought of losing even one Marine was overwhelmingly unacceptable; we're talking about the lives of our American warriors.

Gunny was not in any way making light of or disrespecting human life, including that of our enemies. "Giving" our Marine counterparts the ability of "counting enemy casualties" meant we had succeeded in the most important ways—we'd neutralized the enemy's attack, the Marines were safe, survived the battle, and were available to continue to carry out their duty.

CHAPTER 12

How Great Thou Art!

O Lord my God, When I in awesome wonder
Consider all the worlds Thy hands have made
I see the stars, I hear the rolling thunder
Thy power throughout the universe displayed!

Several weeks after returning to the ship, we began to hear more and more rumbling and sword rattling from the media. It was focused on the buildup of North Vietnamese troops in the South. However, it was an attack on Camp Holloway that tipped the scale, necessitating a heavy retaliatory response by the United States. Camp Holloway was located just over 200 miles southwest of Da Nang and about 50 miles inland from the South China Sea. The camp was originally constructed by the U.S. Army in 1962, in the Central Highlands of South Vietnam, as a helicopter facility. Its intent was to support the operations of the Free World Military Forces.

Early in the morning on February 7, 1965, approximately 300 Viet Cong guerillas attacked Camp Holloway. This attack left 8 American servicemen dead and 126 wounded, while destroying 10 aircraft and damaging another 15. Within hours, President Johnson authorized a bombing campaign on selected targets in North Vietnam. Following a second attack on an U.S. installation, and killing 23 more servicemen, on March 4, 1965, the United States began Operation *Rolling Thunder*.

As with every naval vessel in the 7th Fleet, the impact on the *Stoddard* was immediate. The *Stoddard*, along with numerous other destroyers based in San Diego and Long Beach, began frequent and extensive training in the waters off San Clemente Island. Rather than ship-to-ship or ship-to-air exercises, more than 90 percent of our training focused on NGFS. As in the past, during the NGFS exercises we were on target after firing two or three rounds. The remainder of our training was focused on operations with a carrier task force.

I recall the first time we conducted an NGFS exercise, after completing NGFS school. As we approached the San Clemente firing range, general quarters was called. As the crew mobilized at their battle stations, I initiated radio contact with the Marine spotter. Once contact was established, the spotter asked if we were prepared for the exercise and my reply was "ready, over." The Marine spotter (call sign "Ceremony 26 Charlie") and the *Stoddard* (call sign Buckboard) were operating with the exact same detailed grid map of the target area. These classified maps contained "X" and

"Y" numbered coordinates across the top and down the side of the map. As a point of reference, during the communications, the letters in the coordinates would have been expressed phonetically: the "X" as "X-ray" and the "Y" as "Yankee." Using these coordinates as markers, the Marine spotter—officially known as a supporting arms observer—was able to clearly convey the location or position of the target. Once communications were established, the dialog would begin and continue as follows:

Marine spotter: "Buckboard this is Ceremony 26 Charlie, coordinates X-2356, Y-9673, one-gun, main armament, high explosive, fuse quick, at my command, will adjust."

As we received and plotted the data on our map, we began the process of converting and entering the information into our fire-control computer, as I repeated and verified the target data back to Marine spotter.

Stoddard: "Roger Ceremony 26 Charlie, coordinates X-2356, Y-9673, one gun, main armament, high explosive, fuse quick at my command, will adjust."

As the remaining information was being entered into the fire-control system, one 5-inch gun mount was loaded with a single round of high-explosive, fuse-quick ammunition. When the fire-control system reached a computer solution, CIC would be notified, and I'd relay our readiness to the spotter.

Stoddard: "Ceremony 26 Charlie, this is Buckboard, Ready, over."

Marine spotter: "Ready break, Fire, over," to which I responded, "Fire, out"

In under a second, following the release to fire, the gun mount was notified and the round fired. Even before the round struck the target, the powder casing was removed and another round was loaded. Upon hearing the gun mount fire, I notified the spotter of the incoming round.

Stoddard: "Shot, over."

Marine spotter: "Shot, out."

The length of time from when the Marine spotter began to provide the target coordinates to when the first round was fired was under a minute.

The initial coordinates were manually calculated by the spotter using a pair of range-finding binoculars. These were used to estimate the target's position and magnetic bearing on the map. After observing and evaluating the effectiveness of the initial salvo, the spotter recalculated and provided an adjustment. But this adjustment was in yards rather than with new coordinates. It went something like this.

Marine spotter: "This is Ceremony 26 Charlie, left 75 up 50, over."

As we calculated and entered this yardage adjustment into the fire-control system, I acknowledged receipt of the adjustment by saying:

Stoddard: "This is Buckboard, Roger, left 75 up 50, out."

Once I was notified the revised computer solution had been reached, I informed the spotter by saying:

Stoddard: "This is Buckboard, ready, over."

Marine spotter: "This is Ceremony 26 Charlie, ready break, fire over."

Stoddard: "This is Buckboard, fire, out!"

This cycle continued until the adjustments caused the rounds to strike the target. For the *Stoddard*, our system and crew were so in tune or focused, we usually were on target following a single adjustment (two rounds). Once the adjusted rounds were striking within an acceptable range of the target, the spotter would confirm we were on target.

Marine spotter: "This is Ceremony 26 Charlie, fire for effect, over."

Stoddard: "This is Buckboard, fire for effect, out."

At more than $1,200 per round, no additional rounds were fired and the exercise ended.

***

Between February and when we departed San Diego for the Far East on June 4, 1965, we conducted similar exercises a countless number of times. All the exercises were while the ship was underway and varied in both course and speed. Some of the exercises lasted less than an hour, while others lasted much longer. During all exercises the crew remained at GQ, in full battle gear, until ordered to stand down. Most unusual was when daytime NGFS exercises were supplemented with nighttime exercises; many running well after midnight.

Mission accomplished! This photo taken from the *Stoddard* shows the result of an evening mission (evening defined as any time between sunset and dawn) and was taken mid-1965. (Author's collection)

Then late one night in mid-April, as we were returning to San Diego following a rather long day, the unthinkable happened. While the crew was sleeping, the sound of the bosun's whistle blared out of the 1MC. This was followed by, "*Now hear this, general quarters, general quarters, all hands man your battle stations;* this is a drill, only a drill, general quarters!"

You have to be friggin' kidding me, the United States sure as hell better be under attack. What kind of deranged person would do this to an exhausted crew? Well, not only did it occur over the coming weeks, but it recurred several times. The practice continued periodically until we departed for the Far East. But it was comforting knowing the captain had a soft spot in his heart; he never called for GQ during chow time or while in port.

It wasn't until we were called into actual battle when we realized the reasoning behind such strange behavioral training. It also acted to confirm serving on a destroyer certainly is not for everyone. It takes a special kind of person to be able to keep going, knowing you're exhausted, and your ship is being used (or abused) as a workhorse. But this is the way it was, and in all honesty, I wouldn't have wanted it any other way. This was why I enlisted in the U.S Navy. Enough complaining; let's get on with it!

CHAPTER 13

Let's Go on a WestPac Cruise

Stand Navy out to sea,
Fight our battle cry
We'll never change our course,
So vicious foe steer shy
Roll out the TNT,
Anchors Aweigh.
Sail on to victory
And sink their bones to Davy Jones, hooray!

Anchors Aweigh, my boys,
Anchors Aweigh.
Farewell to foreign shores,
We sail at break of day
Through our last night ashore,
Drink to the foam,
Until we meet once more.
Here's wishing you a happy voyage home.

Blue of the mighty deep
Gold of God's great sun.
Let these our colors be
Till all of time is done.
On seven seas we learn
Navy's stern call
Faith, courage, service true,
With honor, over honor, over all

—"ANCHORS AWEIGH," THEME SONG OF THE U.S. NAVY

On June 4, 1965, the *Stoddard* set sail from San Diego, headed in a northwesterly direction. Resulting from our extensive and rather unusual training, the crew sensed this cruise was going to be unlike any other. The families living locally gave us a heartfelt send-off. It may have been the first time I really missed having someone to wave or say goodbye to. As we departed the harbor the thought crossed my mind that I should have called home to say goodbye. Telephone rates for even a relatively short call could cost a day's wages; a collect call was even more expensive. It was a thought or regret that would frequently haunt me over the course of the next year, especially during the holiday season.

Shortly after exiting San Diego harbor, we joined up with a number of other destroyers attached with DESRON 21 (Destroyer Squadron 21). We took the Great Circle Route coming within 300 miles of the Aleutian Islands. A quick review of our charts revealed we were en route to Subic Bay, the Philippines, rather than Yokosuka, Japan. The first port of call for most naval vessels heading to the Far East (WestPac cruise) was normally Yokosuka. This uncharacteristic route added more than 1,800 miles to this first leg of the cruise.

The U.S. Navy patch. (Wikimedia Commons, U.S. Navy)

Just days out of San Diego, the weather took a major turn for the worse. The wind began howling and gale force gusts continued for much of the trip. Contributing to the poor conditions were air temperatures that dropped dramatically, becoming unusually cold, rainy and at times icy. These conditions caused the waters off the coast of Alaskan to be extremely rough, resulting in the ship pitching and rolling endlessly for days on end. Lacking indoor passageways made commuting fore and aft extremely challenging, if not dangerous. With the seas so angry, and the ship moving in every direction, we had to hold on tightly to the lifeline or life rail to avoid falling overboard. Night watches became more challenging or even treacherous. First, we had to find our way to the lifeline or life rail before making our way forward. Maintaining one's balance required the almost constant flexing of different muscles. By the end of a watch, we were physically spent. In order to maintain our balance, we constantly held on to an immovable object and it was downright exhausting.

I'll try explaining how it felt serving on a destroyer in rough seas. Picture yourself walking up a continuous flight of stairs for hours on end, with every step a different height. This continued as the staircase pitched and rolled simultaneously side to side and fore to aft (right to left, up and down). This constant movement not only beats you up, but it also wears you out. It was one of the few times I wished I was stationed at a Navy base near Great Bend, Kansas.

As the waters began to calm, we realized we were just days away from tying up in Subic Bay, the Philippines. We arrived and docked on June 22. As we were pulling alongside the dock, the 1MC came alive to inform the crew we'd remain in port until July 6, 1965. After the long, hard, and cold days since departing San Diego, the crew began to thoroughly enjoy the warm subtropical climate; it was just what the doctor ordered. While in port, the crew spent much of their off time on liberty in Olongapo, as well as attending a relaxing ship party on Grande Island. Following our recent voyage, it was unusually thoughtful of the Navy to give us such a wonderful and relaxing party.

Grande Island's most famous asset was Fort Wint. The fort was built by the Philippine government and the Department of the United States Army between 1907 and 1920. Although abandoned and in disrepair, the Fort contained two 10-inch cannons to protect the island. But for us, it was the beaches and swimming that were most memorable. While on this private island we also enjoyed a few, well maybe more than a few, San Miguel brews. As a reminder, San Miguel is one of the best brewed beers in the world, and for less than $2 you could buy a cold case of God's nectar. Best of all, this time the Navy picked up the tab.

During our stay in the Philippines, there were several additions made to the ship; additions that raised more than a few eyebrows. First, we welcomed on board a division medical officer and a chaplain. Both were absolute firsts, confirmed by the most seasoned sailors. Why were a medical officer and chaplain being stationed on board a destroyer? What was going on that made this cruise so different from any other? If that wasn't unusual enough, days before setting sail a series of .50-caliber machine guns were installed along both the port and starboard sides of the ship. I began thinking, well, this certainly can't be good. Could this be related to the Gulf of Tonkin incident? Please, for the love of God, and the sanity of every man serving on this destroyer, don't tell me the Navy is buying into this political and media gibberish?

Days passed as we began preparations for getting underway, with many shipmates growing ever more suspicious of these unusual events. It quickly became the topic of all scuttlebutt. Knowing I handled the navigational charts, I wasn't surprised when more than a few shipmates asked if I knew what was going on. I told them everything I knew; a day earlier I was asked to confirm that the charts, necessary for leaving Subic Bay and setting sail for Hong Kong, were up to date. Just knowing our next port of call wasn't in any way comforting. OK, there was the possibility we were nothing more than a means of transportation for the medical officer and the chaplain, but that theory failed to explain the increased armament. As with all naval ships, its itinerary was classified and only known by a few beyond the captain. Remember, "Loose lips sink ships." Because of CIC's navigational duties, we were always one of the first groups to learn of our next destination. Once the chief was notified, he normally requested I pull the appropriate charts for sailing from point A to point B.

It may be important to point out that the crew's curiosity in no way involved fear. The people back home have much more time on their hands, so we'll let them do the majority of worrying and praying. Every man on board had been well trained and prepared to handle whatever came our way. The *Stoddard* had become a well-oiled war machine. The entire crew was aware of its awesome firepower and confident we had no weak links. This may be best explained through an old military adage involving a warrior preparing to enter battle. The adage goes, as the warrior is making final preparations before battle, Fate leans in and whispers in the warrior's ear, "You cannot withstand the Storm!" Hearing Fate's warning, the warrior turns to Fate and whispers back, "But I am the Storm!"

Following our well-deserved rest and "additions," we departed Subic Bay on July 6, and two days later arrived in the BCC (British Crown Colony) of Hong Kong. OK, this was absolutely great, but once more the crew was left scratching their heads.

Normally, when getting underway for a WestPac cruise, the first stop is Yokosuka, Japan. Yokosuka was generally regarded as the fleet's "home port" when in the Far East. Not to mention, it also shortens the first leg of the trip by 1,800 nautical miles or about five or six days. Then for a month or longer, we visited a number of Japanese coastal ports. Once our assignment in Japan was complete, we set sail for Taiwan, followed by Hong Kong, and finally the Philippines. Laying out the ports of call by distance is much more cost effective and efficient. This approach also makes it easier to schedule and conduct exercises while in transit between ports.

With my curiosity peaking, I felt the navigational charts may offer up a clue to the mystery. I pulled all the charts reflecting the vast amount of water and land masses in the Far East. In less than an hour, it all came into focus. I had to almost laugh, remembering how I embellished a story to draw information from the *Maddox* sailor. It was at this time I realized our next destination was likely to be Vietnam. When viewing the charts from a macro perspective, the Philippine Islands and South

A photograph of the *Stoddard*'s main deck after a .50-caliber machine gun was installed near the bow of the ship. (Author's collection)

Vietnam were almost on the same parallel, separated by approximately 850 miles. Whereas Hong Kong was to the north and less than 500 miles from the border with South Vietnam, geographically, it was even closer to the Gulf of Tonkin and North Vietnam. So how did all this correlate? By evaluating the events surrounding the last month, I reached this conclusion based upon:

- For months leading up to our departure from San Diego, we spent an unusual amount of time and effort conducting NGFS exercises off San Clemente Island. However, it may be important to point out, as of this July date, the Whitehouse had not approved the Navy to conduct NGFS or shore bombardment operations in Vietnam.
- The recent raids conducted by North Vietnam initiated the onset of Operation *Rolling Thunder* on March 4, 1965. This led me to suspect a much more aggressive posture may be about to unfold in Vietnam (but at this juncture, I was unsure if that involved the North, South, or both).
- Our participation was likely to be very soon, which was the reason we bypassed Japan and headed directly for the Philippines. Calculations showed Japan was more than 2,000 miles from South Vietnam, whereas the Philippines were less than half that distance.
- We spent an unusual amount of time in the Philippines and added .50-caliber gun mounts to the ship. If they were added in San Diego, it would have raised many questions from the crew and family members. There was also the possibility such a modification would leak out to the general public. Even other destroyers tied up at the naval station would have begun asking questions. Having them installed in Subic Bay was less risky or controversial. The guns were installed well after normal working hours, when most sailors were not on duty and more than likely in town raising hell. This meant the only people aware of the modification would be the ship's crew and those who performed the installation. While it didn't matter, I wondered if the installation was conducted by crew members, as they certainly had the qualifications to weld a gun mount to the main deck.
- But this additional armament did raise an important question, one that wasn't answered until we arrived in Da Nang. A .50-caliber gun is considered a very short-range weapon, so why were they being installed on our ship? The effective range of our 5-inch guns was measured in miles, whereas the effective range of a .50-caliber gun is measured in yards.
- The next clue was the addition of a medical officer and a chaplain to the crew. This was probably the one that raised the red flag the highest. When you think about war and war-type conditions, how do a doctor and chaplain fit in? Need I say more?

- Finally, we were navigating into Hong Kong, and just before entering the harbor our .50-caliber machine guns were covered with a canvas-like material. However, the general shape of the cover mount would suggest it was a weapon. At first, this threw me a bit of a curveball. Whenever a U.S. naval vessel entered Hong Kong harbor, it was assumed it would act as a Hong Kong Station ship. Hong Kong was a BCC and shared a common harbor with mainland China. With that said, every U.S. vessel, naval or otherwise, was heavily scrutinized by the Chinese government as it entered port. For this reason, when entering the harbor, we only employed our surface search radar for navigational purposes. All other radars and electronic devices were silenced. So, it's likely the Chinese recognized the unusual nature of a U.S. destroyer anchored in the harbor; one outfitted with a series of unusual objects installed along its main deck. Inasmuch as this was so early in the Vietnam conflict, the unknown armament would likely have been seen as a form of "saber rattling." We knew differently. In addition to the machine guns, our ammunition magazines were filled to the max; and this was certainly outside the norm. Of course, the Chinese would have had no way of knowing any of this.
- Finally, if it wasn't Vietnam, why was the Navy being so generous? It failed to follow any normal pattern. First, we'd spent several weeks in a beautiful tropical environment, with weather patterns similar to those found in Naples, Florida. This was followed by two days at sea, before spending almost a week in one of the most dynamic cities in the world. Telling me this was normal for the Navy was much like telling me it's raining, all the while you're peeing on my boots. It just didn't add up, but if it did, standby for heavy rolls!

Just before noon on July 13, 1965, I was requested to meet with the chief in CIC. When I arrived, I was told to keep this conversation "under my hat" until we left port. There was no need for me to respond to this; he was not asking a question. He was giving an order. I was told to pull all of the navigational charts associated with the fastest and most direct route to Da Nang harbor, South Vietnam. As I was listening, I was mulling over the definition of the word "harbor." Did he just say harbor? Was it actually a poor choice of words? Did he really mean "off the coast of?" There's a huge difference between "harbor" and "off the coast of." As I was replying with "Aye, aye, chief," I mentioned the chart room contained numerous charts of the Vietnam coastline but lacked any detailed charts necessary for navigating into Da Nang harbor. As I mentioned this was the case, he handed me a roll of charts laying out, in extraordinary detail, Da Nang harbor. The roll included charts of the surrounding coastline, including rivers and land masses to the north and south of Da Nang.

Leaving the chief for the chart room, with my heart pounding and having forgotten all about lunch, I realized, "Holy shit, this is it. We're about to go where no naval vessel has gone before!" Then it hit me: I had to get off the ship ASAP. I wanted to avoid any questions about charts or if I've spoken to the chief about our next destination. After pulling the charts and sealing them in a round tube, I changed into my dress whites, jumped on a launch, and headed ashore.

Arriving at the pier and per my normal routine, I walked across the street to my favorite restaurant. As I walked in, I noticed the chef had begun preparing my usual order. Yeah, they knew me. As I wondered if they realized just how much I've enjoyed every one of their meals, I began calculating if I had enough time to make a second stop before catching a motor launch back to the ship. After scoffing down the food, I headed downtown to meet up with my shipmates and hopefully enjoy the rest of the evening.

We met at our favorite bar and I was actually struggling a bit to get a few lines of "Anchors Aweigh" out of my mind: "We sail at break of day; Through our last night ashore; Drink to the foam; Until we meet once more." With that, we began downing a few beers. A few hours into the evening, one of my shipmates noticed I was drinking much less than normal. When asked, I responded by telling him I was giving my liver a rest and wanted to avoid a hangover as we left port. I also added, "Shit you just reminded me, the chief is going to be pissed. I came ashore before pulling charts for getting underway." This simple statement avoided any questions about our next destination; they knew that when the chief asked me to pull charts, I was heading to the chart room before taking my next breath. Fortunately, it was assumed I would learn of our next destination by speaking with the chief and pulling the charts after returning later in the evening.

By the way, knowing our world was about to change had little to no impact on my last night in Hong Kong. Actually, in retrospect, I may have even enjoyed myself a bit more. And yes, I did make a final stop, for a "nightcap," at the dockside Chinese restaurant. It seemed like a fitting way to end our stay in Hong Kong. As I boarded the ship, I felt both physically and mentally prepared for "tomorrow!"

CHAPTER 14

Chào Buổi Sáng Việt Nam[1]

On July 14, by the time we completed breakfast and prepared to leave port, the word spread we were heading for the coastal waters off Vietnam. As the crew learned Vietnam was our next destination, an unusual quietness seemed to fill the air. The news didn't strike fear in any of my shipmates, but it did promote a feeling of uneasiness. I recalled what Mark Twain wrote about courage in relation to fear: "Courage is resistance to fear, mastery of fear—not absence of fear." Most of the uneasiness centered on what the future may bring. We were confident in our degree of training and readiness, but at the same time we were sailing into "uncharted waters"; waters last experienced during the Korean War, some 12 years earlier.

Once we left port and were 15 or 20 miles south of Hong Kong, the 1MC came alive with the captain confirming we had set course for the waters off South Vietnam. He continued by advising that more details would follow as we approached our ultimate destination. Most memorable was a phrase the captain used when referring to our assignment. He suggested "we earned our place as the first destroyer to be deployed to the Vietnam coast." Those in CIC looked at each other and wondered about the definition of the word "earned." But, in reality, it actually made sense.

During the previous year, the crew operated at such a high level or standard, the *Stoddard* was awarded the Battle Effectiveness Award. This award authorized the ship to exhibit an "E" on her stack, signifying this accomplishment. The benchmark for the Battle Effectiveness Award is the overall readiness of the command to carry out its assigned wartime tasks. It was based upon a year-long evaluation of the ship's performance during fleet exercises. The competition for this award always has been extremely intense. To earn this honor, a ship must demonstrate the highest state of battle readiness. It is an annual award presented to only a small number of naval vessels. So, when the captain used the phrase "earned our place," most were confident it was in reference to the Battle Effectiveness Award.

Not trying to be cocky, but it was an award we all accepted, maybe even expected, without giving it much thought. We knew we operated at a high level, higher than most comparable ships, and felt we had earned it. Whenever a new radarmen boarded our ship, especially from a similar command, they quickly learned, whether it was training or enjoying liberty, our crew was "all business." Usually following

1 Translates to, "Good Morning Vietnam."

their arrival, new sailors frequently complained about our "no nonsense" (I believe the actual reference was "chickenshit") approach to training. But in short order, they came around to the *Stoddard* way of conducting themselves. And I'm willing to wager, they were pleased with the transformation from being just another crew member to being a team member on this well-organized greyhound of the sea.

The following morning, the 1MC came to life with the captain announcing, "Today we became eligible for federal income tax exclusion." In other words, we had officially entered the combat zone. By definition, a combat zone is a general term used by the IRS and includes all hostile areas where the military may serve. Actual combat areas, as well as combat support areas, qualified for hazardous duty. This may have been the most sobering announcement of my entire enlistment: *good morning, Vietnam!* Besides tax relief, being in a combat zone had other perks including:

- Combat Pay (also called Imminent Danger Pay) was an extra $65 per month.
- Sending letters to family and friends was free. After sealing the envelope, in the area normally reserved for a stamp, we simply wrote the word "Free." This may sound like it could cause anxiety at home. Although we were prohibited from offering up any detail, the division officers suggested we notify our family and friends we were participating in numerous "exercises" that prevented us from writing as often. In reality, this was true but contained a bit of a twist. Prior to arriving at our final destination, we were informed all letters would remain on board until we were safely outside the combat zone. For security reasons, during combat missions we were limited regarding taking photographs of specific items and areas. We later understood this directive, as many of the events we would witness should only be recorded in our memory; not on film. We were instructed to avoid mentioning anything about our missions; most would be classified and may be upsetting to the reader. There would be plenty of time, after returning stateside, to relive and describe our Vietnam experiences.
- While we're on the topic of mail, while outgoing mail was held on board the ship, incoming mail delivery was also quite rare. I'm confident this was intentional on the part of the Navy for a very valid reason. Operating within a combat zone is very challenging and requires each sailor to focus 100 percent of his attention on the mission. Receiving a distressing letter, such as a loved one being injured, the financial hardship associated with the loss of a job, or a "Dear John" letter from a wife or girlfriend, etc., could impact a combatant's performance. If there was a dire emergency, such as a life-threatening illness or a death, the Navy would try to accommodate the sailor in every way possible.
- During the cruise the crew was able to amass a considerable amount of money in the bank. When combining his regular and combat pay, the sailor returned

to the States with a sizable sum. This accumulation of funds covered the period from when we departed San Diego on June 4 until the ship returned on November 24, 1965. This period represents a total of 172 days, of which 135 days were spent at sea. This left only 37 days in port, including the 20 days in Subic Bay and Hong Kong, before heading to Vietnam.

- The development of a special bond among shipmates; one that could never be broken and would last a lifetime. I'm sure everyone is aware of the camaraderie shared among veterans from every branch of the military. One time or another I'm confident you've observed what I'm talking about. When in public places, such as stores or sporting events, you'll frequently see veterans wearing baseball caps signifying their branch of service. You'll notice as they pass, they may stop to chat or simply nod their heads acknowledging the others' service. Well, take that unique recognition of service and multiply it tenfold. And that only begins to explain the unconditional and special bond between servicemen and women serving during times of war.
- Of course, along with the positive perks comes at least a negative one. And it wasn't the length of time spent at sea but the awareness we would be dueling with enemy shore or field batteries; batteries attempting to remove our presence one way or another. And you can be assured, being fired upon quickly finds its way to the top of the "negative" list.

In mid-July 1965, with the coast of South Vietnam within sight, we changed course with the bow heading directly toward the land mass. Suddenly the land mass began to grow, with trees, a beach, and a fleet of small junks coming into view. With the ship at an elevated level of readiness, the boatswain's whistle breaks the silence followed by the captain's voice. "As you can see, we are three miles off the coast of South Vietnam, and are en route to Da Nang harbor. We will enter the harbor later today and commence our assignment as the first 'Da Nang harbor defense ship.' I'll provide additional information as appropriate."

Suddenly, the crew realized our assignment was much more than conducting surveillance along the coast of South Vietnam. Instead, we would actually be entering the port of Da Nang. The addition of a medical officer and chaplain to the crew, along with the additional armament, began to make sense. However, there were so many new questions, so many unknowns. For instance, with the .50-caliber machine guns having an effective firing range of 2,000 yards, it meant we were heading to a position less than a mile off the beach. Being so close to Da Nang, the crew began wondering about the details surrounding our assignment and how we would be executing them. I recall stepping back for a moment, realizing only a day or so ago, I was enjoying chicken chow mein in Hong Kong. Now we were in a combat zone and possibly about to make contact with the Viet Cong (aka VC or Charlie).

As we were nearing our destination, we received a classified message, a message that originated in Washington and had an immediate impact on the assignment. The message authorized the Navy to commence NGFS missions in South Vietnam. This authorization came with a caveat; NGFS could only be conducted in coordination with trained spotters. The purpose of this caveat was intended to prevent or limit collateral damage, especially as it involved the civilian population.

We entered the harbor midafternoon, unaware that Da Nang harbor would be our "home" for the next month. Being the first destroyer assigned as Da Nang harbor defense ship, and not knowing what to expect, we entered the harbor at a snail's pace. As we were reaching our destination, many of us questioned what Da Nang harbor may be like. I'm not sure what most of us expected, but I'm confident it was far from what we imagined. It was far from being a "combat zone" (whatever that may have been symbolized by)—it was the exact opposite. A panoramic view of the harbor revealed a peaceful, beautiful, quiet, restful, and serene atmosphere. However, that would all change in a day or so.

Da Nang could more accurately be described as a "seaport" rather than a "harbor." A harbor generally has land on three sides with an opening through which the ships navigate into a port, whereas a seaport is defined as a section along a shoreline or land directly connected with an ocean, sea, or gulf where ships may tie up to load and unload goods. Also, ports are usually equipped with warehouses, cranes, and docks for mooring ships.

The French Called It "Tourane"

Almost immediately following our arrival, we learned Da Nang was an absolute must-have tactical asset for the South Vietnamese–United States, as well as our enemy. Da Nang is located only 40 miles south of the border with North Vietnam, contained a deep-water seaport for large cargo ships to deliver troops, supplies, weapons, and equipment, while having the second-largest airport in South Vietnam; the largest airfield was located in Saigon.

In March 1965, the 3rd Marine Division landed in Da Nang, South Vietnam. These were the first combat troops arriving in South Vietnam, joining 23,000 military advisors, who had been stationed in the country since the 1950s. To avoid any confusion, the phrase "landed in Da Nang" meant they arrived and mobilized in Da Nang. This was not a Normandy invasion but rather the exact opposite. When I spoke to a young Marine, he mentioned they did not arrive with guns blazing and engaged in battle. Instead, they arrived under some very favorable conditions. A more detailed examination revealed they arrived following negotiations and agreements between Washington and the South Vietnamese government. Being part of the landing in Da Nang in March, the young Marine was told they would arrive as discreetly and inconspicuously as possible. They arrived on board the USS *Henrico*

(APA-45), an attack transport, in the early morning. Unaware of the conditions on the ground, they arrived in full battle gear.

As they hit the beach, they were greeted by the locals, a number of South Vietnamese officers, as well as Vietnamese women with flowers. He reported there were also a number of American servicemen among the group displaying a sign welcoming their arrival. It turns out, a negotiated agreement had been quietly discussed and approved by the U.S. and South Vietnamese governments. Apparently, the senior Marine staff were not expecting it and were less than pleased with the "welcoming" they received. The senior staff had hoped the Marines would be able to land without any fanfare. Shortly following their arrival, the Marines were allowed to enjoy shore leave or liberty in Da Nang; this remained the case until security concerns developed caused by increased military activity and tension in the area.

The Marines' orders were to establish a base and prevent Da Nang from falling into the hands of the enemy. With increased Viet Cong activity in the region, 2,000 additional Marines landed in May 1965, bringing the total of combat troops in South Vietnam to 5,000. These were the only combat troops in South Vietnam, until the United States committed to increase their numbers in July 1965. Following our arrival in Da Nang, during July 1965, President Johnson ordered another 50,000 combat troops to mobilize in South Vietnam.

At the time of the Marines' landing in March 1965, local conditions existed which allowed troops to visit Da Nang for R&R purposes. With the passage of time, the Viet Cong realized these were not advisers but combat troops. With this recognition, the VC began mobilizing additional forces to the region. In the past, the majority of the VC's personnel in Da Nang were in the form of agitators or sympathizers with the North. When they recognized the United States had mobilized combat forces, the VC began a major campaign to do this same. The buildup of combatants caused the tension between the Marines and Viet Cong forces to rapidly ramp up, as skirmishes began breaking out.

As the months passed, the fighting between the Marines and the Viet Cong saw a dramatic increase, both in frequency and intensity. With hostilities on the rise, this brought along an increase in the number of enemy attacks on the city, as well as an alarming increase in civilian casualties. Then on August 2, 1965, a Viet Cong suicide bomber attacked a Marine barracks in Da Nang, killing 8 Marines and wounding 50 others. This assault was followed by a surge of attacks on the city, including mortar rounds being fired on the airport and the bombing of a civilian market. On August 5, 1965, General William Westmoreland, the commander of U.S. forces in Vietnam, declared R&R in Da Nang off limits to the Marines. The declaration remained in effect for the rest of the war.

With this buildup and attacks by enemy forces on Da Nang, additional firepower was necessary to support the Marines protecting and defending this vital asset. With the city located on the coast of the South China Sea, a destroyer was the perfect choice for providing additional and immediate firepower. When it came to artillery, the effectiveness of our four 5-inch guns, along with an array of other weapons, provided the Marines with a game-changing weapon. It provided the Marines with the armament and flexibility for attacking targets to the north and south of the city, and as far inland as nine miles. In addition, we would also be called upon to manage supply ship and boat traffic attempting to enter the harbor. This would prevent the enemy from delivering equipment or supplies by sea.

When assigned as Da Nang harbor defense ship in July 1965, with the only combat Marines stationed in Da Nang, the *Stoddard* was the sole U.S. destroyer to conduct combat missions in South Vietnam. However, shortly after our arrival, recognizing the rapid buildup of enemy forces in the region, the Navy began reassigning more warships to South Vietnam's coastal waters. This redeployment of assets took time; it wasn't an activity that could happen overnight. This reassignment of assets was closely being coordinated with an increase in U.S. ground forces. Eventually, the U.S.–South Vietnamese militaries controlled most of the country's coast from the border with the North to south of the Mekong Delta.

The Transition

On the day of our arrival, a South Vietnamese officer was assigned as an interpreter on our ship. He confirmed what we had already known; specifically, we were the first destroyer assigned to this duty. He would board the ship each morning and depart around dusk. His assignment was limited to acting as an interpreter, as we patrolled and challenged vessels, small ships, boats, and junks attempting to enter the harbor. He was never on board during refueling, munitions and stores replenishment, or when conducting NGFS missions.

Early on, we realized being the first came with the understanding and realization that there were absolutely no precedents from which to follow. Virtually every activity, event, or mission was the first for a naval vessel stationed along the coast of South Vietnam. Being the earliest stages of the war, there was limited intelligence related to the enemy, their make-up, movements, intent, or capability. In contrast, neither the Viet Cong or our allies in the South were aware of the awesome firepower of a U.S. naval destroyer.

Within a day after arriving, part of our duties became clear. During daylight hours we would patrol the waters in and around Da Nang harbor. This duty included observing, boarding, and searching vessels and junks for contraband, weapons, and other VC and North Vietnamese paraphernalia. The purpose of this assignment was to prevent the VC from moving or delivering supplies via water. We also learned the VC had a half dozen or so small watercraft, not PT boats, outfitted with light armament. We were confident they could never get close enough to pose a threat; however, being a VC-controlled weapon, they had to be addressed.

On the morning following our arrival in Da Nang harbor, this South Vietnamese officer was assigned to the ship (lower center, right). His only duty was to act as a translator as we stopped and boarded seagoing traffic that was attempting to enter the harbor. The officer boarded the ship in the morning and departed each evening around dusk, before we conducted NGFS missions. He arrived on board circa mid-July 1965. (Author's collection)

Following our second day of coastal patrol, as we were returning to Da Nang, I was requested to meet the CIC officer on the quarterdeck at 1700. As Lieutenant "Bud" Bower and I met, I noticed a dinghy had pulled alongside. I also observed a sailor was dropping a rope ladder down to the boat. The boat had a coxswain and a gunner's mate; the gunner's mate was armed with a BAR (Browning automatic rifle).

Lieutenant Bower informed me we were going over to the Marine compound to "pick up some area maps." Had he said "maps," but did he mean charts of the harbor and surrounding waters? While he was talking, we were both handed a belt containing a loaded military .45-caliber pistol and two additional clips. I hadn't fired a small arms weapon since boot camp. Were we likely to be subject to an

Preparing for the trip to the Marine base in Da Nang. This photo shows the author after being given a .45 handgun. (Author's collection)

attack in the 1,000 yards between the ship and the beach? Well, it turned out to be nothing more than normal protocol when moving about in a combat zone. Actually, after a few trips it became routine. I must admit, however, the first trip between the ship and the dock was rather nerve-wracking. As we made our way toward the dock, it felt as if every small craft or junk contained an enemy preparing an attack. In reality, the armed gunner's mate standing on the bow was very noticeable. His presence led most boats and junks to steer clear of or move away from us. As we were approaching the dock, Lt. Bower mentioned we were actually picking up packets of NGFS maps.

I was somewhat relieved realizing the dock was within the limits of the Marine base. A Jeep, with two heavily armed Marines, was waiting at the dock and transported us to a building on the base. Its fabricated structure appeared to be temporary in nature. Upon entering the building, I noticed a number of men were working in different sections or stations. We were greeted by a junior Marine officer and an enlisted man, who escorted us to a small conference-like room. In the room was a stack of maps, very similar to the ones used during exercises off San Clemente. They were quite small, as both the Marine spotter and the ship worked from identical maps. If they were larger, the spotter might have difficulty carrying and using them. We opened one of the maps, which I'm sure was classified but lacked any classification stamp. From the strong smell of ink, I was confident they were recently printed. As I looked at the map, I was amazed at its detail. Studying it made me wonder who actually counted the number of slips in what seemed to be a marina; they contained that degree of detail.

With this being my first time on the ground in Vietnam, it left me a bit edgy. After packing up the maps, and thinking we had accomplished our goal, it was time to head back to the ship. But I was wrong. Instead, we were taken to a larger room. As we entered the room, we joined six or seven others who were already seated.

As instructed, we introduced ourselves by revealing our rank, position or classification, and affiliation (i.e., radarman 3rd class, NGFS communicator, *Stoddard*). We were instructed to refrain from using our actual names. The others did the same and, by the time the introductions were finished, I'm confident my mouth was wide open and my expression best defined as "what, in God's name, is going on?"

Did I hear this correctly? We're in a meeting made up of officers and enlisted men from the Marines, Navy, and now UDTs? Before the end of the Vietnam War the name of this group, originally known as Frogmen, would be changed from UDTs to SEALs (derived from Sea, Air, Land). From their creation as Frogmen, this unique fighting force was tasked with secretive aquatic operations in rivers, lakes and ocean; but why are they here? Maybe a much better question is "what the hell are we doing here?"

The meeting was weird from the start; it opened as if everyone knew and understood the nature of our get together. Yet in reality, with the exception of the most senior Marine and possibly the UDTs, all other attendees were completely in the dark. Being well before the era of electronics and sophisticated video screens, using a large paper map taped to a chalkboard, the Marine officer opened the meeting. He began by explaining the United States is an "occupying force" rather than an "invading force." As a defending force, the United States must prevent or repel the VC from advancing within the Da Nang region, as our military prepared for America's possible expansion. He continued to say that, in collaboration with the Marines and the UDT, they had identified roads and routes vital to meeting these goals. These roads must be protected and defended, while impeding those less traveled to prevent use by the VC. The primary way of limiting the use of these less vital routes would be accomplished by removing multiple bridges and trestles along their route.

The senior Marine continued and mentioned the Marines had watches posted on bridges along the Han River to the south, and the Cu De River to the north. They would protect all roadways falling within that area, including the mountainous region to the west. The UDTs would conduct missions to eliminate any unnecessary bridges, trestles, or structures outside the Marine-protected area. The UDTs had other missions as well; but these missions remained classified, unless support from others was necessary. It was further explained, the *Stoddard* would provide NGFS as deemed necessary, in support of both the Marines and UDTs. Holy shit, did I hear that correctly? Am I dreaming? Where the hell was any of this mentioned in the Vietnam visitors' travel brochure? As the meeting was drawing to a close, I noticed most of the UDTs were enlisted men, and decided I had to find a way of speaking to at least one of them. For the record, a UDT member may come from any classification within the Navy. Before becoming a UDT member, they had to prove their worthiness through extensive physical and mental testing. It was at this moment that the senior Marine informed us the UDTs would be using the *Stoddard* as a platform or base for staging their operations. The UDT team would mobilize on the ship after nightfall and commence their assignments immediately. Nothing more regarding their assignment or description of their duties was mentioned. Before departing the base, we were instructed to limit the topics discussed at the meeting to a need-to-know basis, and we returned uneventfully to the ship.

I was confident this arrangement would make it easier for me to talk to one of men assigned to the team and hopefully learn more about their covert operations. And how successful was I in my quest? Simply put, after all was said and done, I ended up wondering what white wine paired well with "eating crow." I was just about that successful.

As the sun began to set, I noticed the UDT craft was approaching. As it got closer, the captain's voice came over the 1MC, announcing a special operations team would be joining us. He continued by mentioning this group would be on the list of objects and people that we were banned from photographing. He completed his announcement by stating that the UDTs were not to be mentioned in any of our letters leaving the ship.

Within just a few hours after their arrival, we realized that with the exception of participating in joint missions, they would not be interacting with the crew. Wait, that is completely inaccurate and misleading. A much better description would be they intended to avoid interacting with the crew, in any and every way possible. At first the crew thought that by ignoring us they were just a snobby group. However, we quickly learned and understood they were basically on the clock 24/7. From the time they woke to the time they retired, they were working. They had their own routine; they even ate by themselves, and I have no idea where or when they slept.

I mentioned this before, early on one of the UDTs must have screwed up or taken an excessive amount of time during a drill. For the better part of the day, hour after hour, he sat blindfolded against a quarterdeck bulkhead assembling and disassembling his rifle, while mumbling something incoherently. If I had a dollar for the number of times he repeated this sequence, I could have easily covered the down payment on a new Corvette. It was just that insane. It's just the way they operated; they accepted nothing less than perfection.

The first time one of their team members and I met or interacted, I thought I'd open up the conversation by asking what ship he had previously served on. He looked at me coldly, and in a curt manner replied, "Just how does that involve the mission?" I mean come on, I wasn't asking if his sister was a virgin, it was a reasonable question. But his reply said it all; he wasn't interested in any small talk whatsoever. However, when discussing the parameters of a mission, he was all business. The entire team's focus on detail was extraordinary, especially as it pertained to our involvement. Discussions concentrated on the mission, targeted area, and always included confirmation we had sufficient munitions on board to carry out the assignment.

A few days later, a UDT member and I spent about an hour going through a mocked-up NGFS mission sequence. Unexpectedly, at least on my part, not a word was exchanged as we headed down to the mess deck. We sat at separate tables, about 10 feet apart, with our backs facing each other. Before starting the exercise, I asked his name, to which he replied, "That's unimportant" and mentioned he was thoroughly familiar with my NGFS training.

I'm unable to recall the exact call sign he used during the drill, so let's assume it was either "Rusty Nail" or "Shit-For-Brains." It didn't take long for me to realize this was more of an interview than a training session. He had to ensure or confirm I was adequately trained and could flawlessly execute my duties as an NGFS communicator, at least up to their standards. We covered several scenarios, with the last involving the possibility of multiple targets. At its conclusion, "Rusty Nail" ended it with "one-gun, main armament, high explosive, fuse quick at my command, will adjust, over." I repeated the information exactly as taught and after several seconds said "Ready, over." This meant a computer solution had been reached and we were prepared to fire the opening salvo. He replied with "OK, we're done," stood up, and began walking toward the exit. I countered with, "No we're not; your response should have been 'Ready break fire, over,' and I would have replied 'fire out,' and the mission would have continued until you gave the command to 'Fire for Effect.'" He turned and just looked at me as I said, "I just wanted to make sure you were properly trained in following NGFS protocol!" Amazingly, he kind of smiled and said "touché!" turned, and headed up the ladder. Well, well, well, his arrogance and attitude began to make sense; he must be French.

We reached the main deck and, as we went our separate ways, not another word was exchanged. Being well trained by the Navy, I wasn't at all surprised the exercise went off without a hitch. Do you know what really ran through my mind? "And screw you, too!" not realizing that thought would later return to haunt me in the form of concern, worry, and remorse.

As time passed the crew began to accept their brusque and terse behavior. Rather than a feeling of disdain, many of us felt somewhat sympathetic toward their demeanor. Unquestionably, they were a bunch of bad asses and determined to avoid the amazing camaraderie shared with being shipmates. From their behavior, no "outsiders" were allowed within their inner circle. But that was fine, and they were right, interacting with the crew was unnecessary in executing and succeeding in their assignment. Much more important was the relationship and respect they enjoyed with their peers. The "I've got your back" trust they had for one another was absolutely apparent and essential to their safety, mental well-being, and ultimately their survival. I was confident, in one way or another, their behavior was an integral part of their training and should be accepted accordingly.

CHAPTER 15

The Only Easy Day Was Yesterday

> A sailor is not defined as much by how many seas he has sailed than by how many storms he has overcome.
>
> MATSHONA DHLIWAYO

A few days later, we were directed to support the UDT team. They were assigned to remove a bridge and trestle in a territory approximately 25 miles north of Da Nang. The team would be removing these structures in a stealthy manner, in an area with a heavy VC presence. The afternoon prior to the mission, a meeting was held on the mess deck with the UDTs. The meeting began with their leader explaining the goal of the mission. One structure was a bridge along an infrequently used road and the other an underused, or possibly abandoned, railroad trestle. Both were connected to the Northern border and possibly used to smuggle weapons and supplies into the region. With both targets clearly in enemy-controlled territory, as a precaution, we were ordered to be stationed under a mile offshore. Our assignment was to support the team if or when they encountered the Viet Cong or any unexpected obstacles. Being early in the war, only basic or general details were available about the terrain or any other physical landscape characteristics. Such reference points or markers are frequently used by a spotter when calculating a target's coordinates. With limited knowledge of the terrain, it made the UDT mission's planning phase more challenging.

The UDT leader opened up his map and pointed to the two structures involved in the mission, and the order in which they would be removed. The strategy of his plan began when the UDTs departed the *Stoddard*. Operating in the darkened-ship protocol and following their departure, we would take up station under a mile off the coast. Upon arriving on station, the coordinates of the first bridge would be entered into our fire-control system. This way, as we cruised offshore our main armament would remain locked on the first targeted bridge. If the team encountered a problem, the targeted bridge would be the reference point from where the UDT spotter would adjust our gunfire. The purpose of this arrangement was to reduce response time.

The UDT spotter's call sign would be "Wolf Creek." If we were required to participate, it would likely be an emergency situation. Therefore, the UDTs decided to streamline the authentication process to avoid fumbling through pages, lines, and numbers. Making the process easier would allow the spotter to remain focused on the enemy, thus reducing the overall NGFS response time between identifying the enemy and firing. Once communications were established, the authentication process would begin.

Wolf Creek: "Buckboard, this is Wolf Creek, do you have the Tokens?"

Buckboard: "This is Buckboard, Roger Wolf Creek, they are in the jungle, the mighty jungle, ready, over."

Wolf Creek: "Roger, The Lion Sleeps Tonight."

This would be followed with the spotter providing adjusted or revised firing coordinates. Again, this adjustment would be calculated from the coordinates of the targeted bridge. This shorter process avoided the longer authentication sequence, However, if there was any discrepancy whatsoever during this exchange, we would revert back to the normal authentication process. (For anyone unaware of the connection associated with this identification sequence, early in the 1960s, a group known as the Tokens released a song titled "The Lion Sleeps Tonight.")

Assuming the frequency remained silent, hearing or seeing the explosion of the first bridge would act as confirmation that the UDTs were en route to the second bridge. For the team's safety, following the destruction of the first bridge, we would wait about five minutes before entering the coordinates of the second structure into our fire-control system. This way, if the Viet Cong were in the area and responded to the first explosion, we would be in the best position to offer up the most rapid response. Bottom line, the purpose was simple; be prepared for the unknown, be in the highest state of readiness, and prepared to react. Once the UDTs departed the ship, unless they required NGFS, there would not be any communications, with the frequency remaining silent.

Before ending the session, the UDT leader revealed he was uncomfortable with the initial plan and decided to make a major change. He was concerned that the initial explosion may draw unwanted attention or response from the Viet Cong forces in the region. As a result, he modified the mission to be a timed event. This meant the explosives would be secured to both bridges and detonated at approximately the same time. The only drawback is they would have exited the area before confirming the structures were rendered unusable. Without mentioning a word, I assumed the UDTs would increase the amount of explosive material to ensure the structures were completely destroyed.

This change would also necessitate a revision to the communications between the UDTs and the ship. If NGFS became necessary, the arrangement described above would apply and remain in effect. However, once the explosives were secured to the first bridge, and as the team was en route to the second bridge, the UDT spotter would notify us by saying:

Spotter: "Buckboard, this is Wolf Creek, I come to the garden alone, while the dew is still on the roses."

Buckboard: "This is Buckboard, He walks with me and He talks with me, and He tells me I am His own, over."

Spotter: "This is Wolf Creek, Roger, I'd stay in the garden with Him, though the night around me be falling, out!"

This reference is from the hymn "In the Garden." This communication confirmed and updated several key mission milestones: first, NGFS was not required during the first phase of the mission; second, the explosives to remove the first structure were in place, and the UDTs were en route to the second target. Five minutes after receiving this message, the coordinates of the second structure would be entered into our fire-control system.

Of course, at the end of the coordination meeting, once more I embarrassed myself by asking when and where the UDTs would be returning to the ship. In classic fashion, because the question was unrelated to the execution of the mission, I was given a snippy reply: "We'll be back on board in the morning, but thanks for asking; should I wake you when we arrive?" The UDT leader spoke up and said, "Is that something you should be saying to a guy who is in the chain that could impact our lives?" He replied with, "Well, maybe he should come along for the ride. I can see the news headline, 'Sailor is awarded the Purple Heart for getting shot in the back while charging.'" With a smile on my face I replied, "That's an interesting thing for a sailor to say, one who wasted an entire day trying to figure out how to disassemble and reassemble his rifle. I also understand, when they asked you to 'sign' for the NGFS maps, you wrote 'Sagittarius.'" As the meeting adjourned, we exchanged half smiles along with a cordial nod, as if to say "well done."

You're probably curious why I simply didn't reply with the old standard of "yeah, screw you and the white horse you rode in on!" But this interaction wasn't like that at all; in fact, it was the exact opposite. This exchange was only possible because we had developed a kind of relationship. To an extent, he acknowledged our small group from CIC were accepted within their close-knit circle. It reminded me so much of the bantering exchanged back home, as we were listening to the "Make It or Break It" radio show. And yet even to this day, I haven't even a clue as to any of their names. But let me add, it really didn't matter whether or not they were a bunch of mavericks. What really mattered is this UDT squad had the upmost respect of our entire crew; they earned and deserved it!

Showtime

Late July through August begins one of the wetter periods of the year in Da Nang. From a temperature perspective it meant a normal high of 94 degrees Fahrenheit, with an overnight low around 80 degrees Fahrenheit. With the monsoon season only weeks away, the humidity had already begun increasing to levels approaching the oppressive range. But the night of the mission could best be described as being perfect; the sky was overcast (ideal for operating in darkened ship), the rain had stopped, the temperature was in the mid-80s, with the humidity at a relatively high but tolerable level.

Shortly after sunset one day in late July, likely the 25th, we departed Da Nang harbor and conducted a brief NGFS mission. Just after 2300 hours we changed course, heading in a generally easterly direction. Once we were a few miles beyond the horizon, we came about to a more northerly course. Our speed was in the 5- to 6-knot range. At this stage, the entire crew knew we were about to participate in a UDT mission; however, only the UDTs and the captain knew the drop off point and when the mission would officially commence. Having a clear understanding of the UDTs' mission, I was fascinated watching them prepare. Naturally, this observation was done at arm's length. And for the record, never once did I ever entertain the thought of "riding along"; I wasn't overly fond of the prospect of getting shot in the back while charging!

I was confident their preparation involved more than the movement of equipment around the main deck. As I watched them assemble their gear, I was confident they were simultaneously rehearsing the mission over and over again in their heads. This thought came to mind because it's exactly what I was doing. Mentally I was completely consumed with the details of the mission, rather than the atmosphere around me. This was how I was taught; it was to be my norm. Whether it was in the classroom, an exercise off San Clemente Island, or in actual battle, the routine was the same. Being aware of the mission's complexity, along with the danger the UDTs may be facing, did cause a bit of an uptick in uneasiness. It was an uneasiness I knew I had to eliminate or control.

It wasn't a matter of getting over a fear but simply a matter of managing it. I would do so by being painstakingly prepared. As I was beginning the process, I remembered what one of the instructors said during my NGFS training. I later learned it could be attributed to James Carse: "To be prepared against surprise is to be trained; whereas to be prepared for surprise is to be educated." I was confident any uneasiness would fade when I was fully prepared to address the what-ifs; the expected and unexpected. To reach this level of readiness, I continually ran and reran the mission over and over in my mind. In doing so, I applied all I had learned in radar school and NGFS classes. Using these tools made it easier to identify and evaluate practically every variable, risk, and obstacle, along with preparing or devising potential solutions. I knew my preparation was complete when a kind of calmness and confidence came from within. Finally, I thought, "OK, let's go, bring it on!"

Around 2330 hours, the Bridge requested a course and speed to arrive at a specific chart location at 0130. At the time we were approximately eight miles from the location, so we had about two hours to cover eight miles. The CIC supervisor (petty officer of the watch or POOW) recommended remaining on the current heading and speed for another hour. At approximately 0100, the POOW recommended turning westward and coming about to course 270 degrees. This course allowed our bow to be heading directly in the direction of the desired rendezvous point, thus presenting the ship's most conservative profile.

When we were within 2,000 yards of the drop-off point, the UDTs were in their final stages prior to departing the ship. I wanted to leave my post and extend my wishes for a safe and successful mission. Fortunately, I was able to overcome this unprofessional gesture. I remained in CIC and silently said a Hail Mary, praying that She and Her Son watch over and protect our treasured shipmates. While it may sound unusual, most sailors and Marines I spoke to post war were quite religious on active duty, sometimes even more than their civilian counterparts. It may be interesting to learn that they remained that way even after leaving the service. It's never good to break a promise or vow made to God, especially during times of danger or while under duress. I can assure you, every combatant experienced times when a more intimate dialogue with God was necessary, and this was one of those times. But for the most part, we left the praying up to our family and friends back home.

The ship came to a full stop and within a minute got back underway. As the ship changed course and speed, CIC was notified the UDTs had departed and directed to load the coordinates for the first bridge into the fire-control system. I wondered if the captain would have been surprised to learn that request was completed as the UDT crew were departing the ship. He also requested a course and speed to cruise slowly in a zigzag pattern about 1,500 yards offshore, staying within an 8,000-yard north–south corridor. Each time we reached the end of the corridor, we made a sharp turn, with the bow facing the coastline. The sharp turn was necessary to keep a broadside profile, allowing our four main armament guns to be trained toward the coast. It took 15 to 20 seconds for the guns to rotate 180 degrees and face the coastline. Once the course change was completed, we resumed the zigzag pattern in the opposite direction. As a reminder, the zigzag pattern allowed the ship to become a much more difficult target for the enemy's shore batteries. For the record, throughout the duration of this assignment numerous changes in course, speed, and direction were employed, though always remaining within the designated corridor.

As we were waiting to hear from the UDT spotter, I continued to replay the coordination meeting over in my mind. I recalled, other than identifying it as a night mission, there weren't any other references to time. Looking at the maps, the two bridges were just over a mile apart, with the first bridge being well under a mile inland from the coast. Both of these distances were as the crow flies, so it didn't take into account the terrain or the route they may be taking. What I am leading up to is the unknowns in terms of time. The only given was that we would remain within striking distance of both structures throughout the night.

Although the crew was at general quarters, they were given permission to stand down in place. Three of our main armament crews were prepared to load high-explosive, fuse-quick shells at a moment's notice. The 4th gun had an illumination round already loaded. As I replayed the details of the coordination meeting, I was unable to recall any discussion involving illumination rounds. Illumination rounds are very effective in revealing the location and size of enemy forces. On the negative side they may be doing the same to our forces. After observing the UDTs for some time, I suspect their preference would be to operate within the shadows. In the end, their actions would be predicated upon conditions as presented. The firing of any illumination rounds would strictly be the call of the UDT leader.

An hour or so later, a radarman asked the Bridge if they could see or hear anything; the Bridge replied, "All is quiet." It was the same in CIC; the air search was clear, contacts on the surface radar were to our south and heading away from our location. Yet, the silence that filled this relatively crowded space seemed unusually loud and out of character. Even during training or exercises, when at GQ, CIC is normally bustling with activity, with each sailor focused on his area of responsibility. While I was communicating with the spotter and gunnery officer, there were radarmen on the surface and air search radars monitoring the ship's position, course, speed, depth of the water, calculating the next course and speed changes, radio frequencies, etc. As conditions changed, which was almost constantly, sailors updated information to the appropriate parties. The CIC officer, Lt. Bower, oversaw and was responsible for evaluating all data generated within CIC. If deemed necessary, at his direction, information is reported to the Bridge. If the captain wanted a recommendation to manage a specific condition or situation, he would call his CIC officer.

Let me offer an example that actually occurred after I was transferred to the *Samuel N. Moore*. One evening in February 1966, while communicating with a Marine spotter, it was determined a Viet Cong stronghold was just beyond the range of our main armament. Being determined to eliminate the threat, the captain asked the CIC officer for a course recommendation that would put the enemy's location within the firing range of our 5-inch guns. This meant taking the ship to a position under 1,000 yards from the coast. At the time, we were 4,000 yards off the coast. This may sound easy but the waters in the area were shallow. Without delay, the CIC officer carefully laid out a route on the navigational chart. The route was extremely challenging, requiring frequent and sharp changes in course, but accomplished the captain's goal. The CIC officer was fully aware and understood getting in was one challenge, but getting out was yet another. During the maneuver, CIC and Bridge were constantly fed the actual water depth below the hull by sonar. The CIC officer compared these readings to the depths reflected on the chart, as he also monitored the actual sea conditions, winds, and movement of the tide. It was one of the most brilliantly orchestrated operations I ever witnessed. At the conclusion of a successful mission, the captain called the CIC officer to the Bridge to congratulate him on a job well done!

In terms of the sailors within OI Division, the CIC officer's "stock" grew exponentially in value. He not only earned his stripes but also the upmost respect of every sailor who witnessed his performance. Rather than simply writing it off by saying, "The water is too shallow and dangerous," he understood the challenge, evaluated the risk, developed a solution, and executed it precisely, thus achieving the mission's objective, and he then returned us safely back to sea. The man was a true problem-solving leader! It was an absolutely amazing display of courage, confidence, and achievement; the true definition of what it's like serving in the United States Navy. He proved to truly be one of the best of the best!

Returning to the current mission, more than an hour had passed and the frequency remained quiet; the silence certainly added to the tension. Simply to stretch my legs, I requested to step outside for a moment to grab a smoke and get another strong cup of liquid energy. Moving only a short distance from CIC, I could feel the tension in the air. The sailors on the main deck may have been relaxing, and for the most part they were silent. About the only exchange I recall hearing was one of the crew asking, "What the hell is going on?" or "when is something going to happen?" However, even these brief exchanges ended with concern: "I hope those guys are OK!" Not unlike our training exercises, as were expecting to take station and shortly thereafter have all hell break loose, this slow cruising just felt out of character. After being absent for a few minutes, I returned to CIC and noticed the hour was a bit after 0300. This gut-wrenching pace continued for another 30 minutes or so, when suddenly the frequency came alive:

Wolf Creek: "Buckboard, this is Wolf Creek, I come to the garden alone, while the dew is still on the roses, over."

Buckboard: "This is Buckboard, He walks with me and He talks with me, and he tells me I am His own, over."

Wolf Creek: "Roger, I'd stay in the garden with Him, though the night around me be falling, out!"

I believe a smile appeared on every sailor's face in CIC, just knowing the UDTs were safe and not in immediate need of gunfire support. They had completed setting explosives on the first bridge and were advancing to the second structure. Although the NGFS authentication (the reference to "The Lion Sleeps Tonight") for the first bridge wasn't employed at this stage, it would play a major role in a future mission.

Whenever I was communicating with a Marine or UDT spotter, the communication was piped to a number of locations throughout the ship. This way the senior staff would have a general understanding of what was going on or an awareness that detailed instructions may be forthcoming. With only the personnel in CIC and a few on the Bridge understanding this unusual communication, it wasn't surprising when a sailor on the Bridge asked, "What's going on? Are the UDTs safe?" As a point of interest, sailors were known for their foul language, but such language was never acceptable during GQ. GQ was like a religious service, rite, or ceremony requiring a certain protocol and regiment.

More than likely the Navy would have classified this authentication sequence as "SECRET." The classification of "SECRET" is assigned to national security information or material which requires a substantial degree of protection. In all honesty, those who had knowledge of this arrangement handled it as if it carried this classification. However, once used it could be basically reclassified as "unclassified." It was standard for the Navy to assign any classified document a time or period before it was deemed unclassified.

Based upon the situation, and knowing the crew was concerned over their safety, well-being, and status, the captain allowed the word to spread that the UDTs were fine, had just completed the first leg of their mission, and were proceeding with the next phase.

So far so good, but it also meant it was our last communication unless they encountered a problem and required our involvement. So, we remained at our posts in a stand-down readiness condition. After about an hour, the unusual nature of the silence returned but this time felt less intense. Suddenly and without warning, the silence was shattered as the sky to the west brightened with several huge orange fireballs. Seconds later, the blast could be heard and felt throughout the ship. The mission was an explosive success.

Within the hour, the captain issued the order to stand down from general quarters, with one main gun mount remaining fully manned until dawn. Those on the 0800 to 2000 watch were released to catch some shuteye and would not be required to relieve the current watch until 1030. This allowed them a few hours of sleep and time to grab a bite to eat. Following his order, we remained a mile offshore until daybreak. We waited for the UDTs to reboard before changing course toward Da Nang harbor.

About 1030 I was relieved from my watch and headed down to the mess deck for something to eat. With the randomness associated with being on duty, I wasn't sure if I was having breakfast, lunch, or supper. If you go by what was being served, most would call it breakfast. After enjoying my powdered eggs and reconstituted milk, I was walking along the main deck when I noticed the UDTs had returned to the ship. As we approached amidships, a quick inventory confirmed all had safely returned. As you would expect, we passed without exchanging anything more than a glance and a head nod. It's amazing how much can be said or exchanged with this style of communication. It extended a greeting and acknowledged a very high degree of respect and thanks.

CHAPTER 16

A Quick Seasonal Change

A smooth sea never made a skillful sailor.

PRESIDENT FRANKLIN D. ROOSEVELT

On July 18, 1965, after completing our patrolling duties, we returned to Da Nang harbor. Just after sunset, we tied up about 800 yards offshore. As per the norm, when operating within combat zone all stations remained manned. From an armament perspective, this included manning one weapon of each type and at least two of the .50-caliber machine guns. The engines remained online and prepared to get underway at a moment's notice. Rather than the normal "running watches," a day or so prior to arriving in Da Nang harbor, the crew was put on a "Port & Starboard" or "Blue & Gold" watch rotation. This meant each crew member was on or off duty for 12 consecutive hours, plus additional time if or when called to general quarters. When GQ is called, regardless whether you were on or off duty, all hands manned their battle stations. It was essential to balance "on duty" and "down time" evenly across the crew. When tied up in the harbor, the various stations were manned by a minimum number of sailors; this approach never compromised crew safety. While underway, crews worked with each other to balance the hours on and off duty. This was accomplished by having either the port or starboard watch show up or remain on duty at the completion of a watch. This allowed the crew to manage the time spent at GQ. In the majority of cases, these adjustments could be measured in hours rather than minutes.

Almost immediately after tying up, we knew this evening would be different. As the engine room began to slow the engines to idle, and the crew began winding down from a very active day, we received an urgent message from command. We were ordered to get underway and proceed immediately to a position a few miles south of the harbor. Even before the ship got up to speed, the crew was asking, "What's going on?" As we approached our destination the 1MC came to life with the blaring sound of the bosun's whistle (boatswain's) with the announcement: "Now hear this! Now hear this! General quarters, general quarters, all hands man your battle stations; *this is not* a drill, I repeat *this is not* a drill; man, your battle stations, general quarters!"

As the men were hustling to their battle stations, I'm confident the thought, "Well, this is it" must have crossed each of our minds. We were thoroughly trained for whatever was coming our way. Yet we knew full well, we were about to cross the

Rubicon. The silence as sailors passed along the main deck was absolutely deafening. And this was the way it was every time we were called to GQ; no talking, bullshitting, bantering, just the dash of professional combatants preparing for battle and ready to demonstrate to Fate that we *were* the storm. Because we were about to participate in a combat mission, the ship was ordered to the condition of darkened ship. As mentioned earlier, this was when every exterior light, including the running lights, had been extinguished and the only interior lights were a dim red.

On a clear night when operating less than a mile off the coast, the moon had both positive and negative effects. On the positive side, it made the sprint to our battle station much easier; on the negative side, it possibly made us a somewhat more visible target for enemy shore batteries. It probably goes without saying, we preferred overcast conditions. A destroyer is only 376 feet in length with a beam less than 40 feet. I mention this because I'm confident the vast majority of the crew could navigate bow to stern blindfolded. When underway, the feel of the wind on your face, coupled with the sound of the sea, made navigating the main deck much easier. During the first month, most NGFS missions were well after sunset. When called to GQ, I never saw a sailor use a lifeline or bulkhead rail to find his way fore or aft. The exception being if the seas were excessively rough and turbulent.

We reduced speed as we approached our station. Weather wise, we had a thick, cloudy overhead and the air was heavy. For whatever reason, the night seemed darker than normal. Regardless of the direction you faced, everything appeared the same. The only sound that could be heard was the hull cutting through the water. While the exterior of the ship was quiet, the ship's interior was alive and vibrant as each crew member settled into their assigned GQ position. As they did, a different type of edginess fell over the ship, an edginess best defined as a bit of anxiety, rather than concern. We were moments away from putting our years of training to the test.

Before going any further and for the reader to fully understand what we're about to discuss, I'd like to correct some misinformation I've come across published in articles or heard in videos. In every case, it was apparent that the authors or presenters lacked an understanding of naval protocol and practices.

Let's start with the statement or report that a naval destroyer responded to a Marine's mayday call. This statement is completely inaccurate and false. Naval ships only respond to and execute orders as directed from command. Every mission assignment came along with an authenticating element that confirmed it was issued by command. It also included a means of authenticating we were communicating with a "friendly" serviceperson. If the enemy thought or believed a ship would respond to a mayday call, they would have every warship off the coast of Vietnam chasing phantom missions from Dong Ha down to Ca Mau.

Next is the matter of shutting down our engines when tied up in a port within a combat zone. Again, this is more misinformation presented by someone unfamiliar or unaware of naval procedures. Let me explain why such an action would not only be unsafe for the crew but delay us from responding to any form of emergency. When the boilers on a Fletcher-class destroyer were shut down, they had to be heated slowly to prevent warping. This overall cycle took approximately three hours. The reason it took so long is because the boilers were required to generate steam at 650 psi (pounds per square inch), and super-heated to 850 degrees Fahrenheit. During the month we were assigned as Da Nang harbor defense ship, our boilers always remained online. This allowed us to get underway at moment's notice if we came under attack or were ordered to respond to emergencies involving either the Marines or UDTs.

Another erroneous statement involved the claim of "weighing anchor." For the same reason as mentioned above, weighing the anchors could significantly delay the ship's ability of getting underway. With the anchors and chain links weighing in excess of 20,000 pounds, weighing anchor was a relatively slow process. It typically took a Fletcher-class destroyer between 30 minutes to an hour to weigh anchor. The actual time was influenced by the length of the chain link and depth of the water. For this reason, when entering Da Nang harbor, we always tied up to a mooring buoy. By doing so, we could get underway within minutes in an emergency situation.

Finally, also involving our anchors, it was stated that once we arrived on station, we had to drop anchor before commencing naval gunfire operations. This statement is completely false. If we dropped anchor prior to firing, we would become a fixed target for the enemy's shore batteries. Instead, whenever we commenced NGFS missions, we were always underway and cruising in a random zigzag pattern. By doing so, our ship became a much more difficult target for enemy field artillery. As a reminder, whenever we conducted NGFS missions, we operated in a darkened-ship condition. The only time we exposed ourselves to the enemy was when the guns fired. Our fire-control system or GFCS (gun fire control system), was capable of locking on and firing at multiple targets, at subsonic speeds, all while underway.

Getting back to the mission; let me mention up front, this first mission revealed a bit of tweaking would be necessary for future missions. For me personally, I would be notified or awakened about 15 minutes prior to calling the crew to general quarters. This would allow a sufficient amount of time to establish communications and authenticate the identity of the Marine spotter, prior to our arrival on station. This authentication process was never taught in NGFS class or used during drills off San Clemente. Authentication was necessary to ensure the spotter wasn't an English-speaking enemy, who may be attempting to call for or direct naval gunfire on friendly forces. This verification step was added to the NGFS sequence at the same time we were released to conduct NGFS missions.

The authentication process began with the use of a highly classified book containing multiple pages of numbers—I'd estimate the book contained more than 50 pages of nothing but page after page of numbers. A copy of this publication was in the possession of the ship's NGFS coordinator and the Marine spotter. Using a coded message, the spotter was challenged to go to a specific page, followed by a specific line number counted down from the top. Finally, the spotter would be requested to provide a string of numbers from a position within the line. This group of digits would vary between 14 and 18 numbers in length. As you can imagine, establishing communications and completing this process took up valuable time. Completing the verification sequence before arriving on station became critical. It could very well be the difference between a successful and failed mission, or life and death.

This mission began three days after Washington authorized the Navy to commence NGFS operations. As we were approaching our station, I established communications with the spotter by repeatedly transmitting, "Broken Arrow One Four Echo, this is Buckboard over." Part of all mission orders included the spotter's call sign; in this case "Broken Arrow 1-4 E." When using a letter in the military, the serviceman always referenced the military alphabet or military phonetic alphabet, so "E" becomes "Echo." Also, the 1-4 isn't referred to as "fourteen," but rather as "one four," so, it's "Broken Arrow One Four Echo." An overview of the mission indicated we would be firing illumination shells, followed by high-explosive rounds, for "harassment and interdiction."

This became a frequently used description for many missions. As you will see, this is only one of the many "missions of opportunity" uncovered by the Marines during our assignment in Vietnam. In my 11-plus consecutive months, serving in Vietnam on board two different destroyers, the first month as Da Nang harbor defense ship was far and away the most intense, active, demanding, dangerous, and challenging. All others were dwarfed by comparison.

Following the authentication phase, the actual mission began and continued as follows:

Buckboard: "Ready! Over."

Broken Arrow 1-4 Echo: "Coordinates X-1223, Y-5647; one-gun, main armament, illumination round, at my command, will adjust, over!"

As we began the process of converting the spotter's coordinates from magnetic to true bearing, entering the data into our fire-control system, and loading an illumination round in one of the 5-inch gun chamber, I repeated to the spotter:

Buckboard: "Roger Broken Arrow One Four Echo, Coordinates X-1223, Y-5647; one-gun, main armament, illumination round, at my command, will adjust, out."

As I received word a computer solution had been reached, an illumination round was loaded, and we were prepared to fire. I transmitted:

Buckboard: "Ready, over."

Broken Arrow 1-4 Echo: "Ready, break, fire, over!"

Buckboard: "Fire, out!"

I heard the gun fire, which could also be heard and felt throughout the ship.

Buckboard: "SHOT."

This notified spotter that he had an incoming round. After observing the location of the illumination round, he made an adjustment to improve the accuracy of our gunfire on the target:

Broken Arrow 1-4 Echo: "Left 50, up 100, over."

With this adjustment, we began the process of recalculating the firing solution as I repeated:

Buckboard: "Roger, Left 50, up 100, out."

I received word the computer solution had been reached and a second illumination round loaded. I said:

Buckboard: "Ready, over."

Broken Arrow 1-4 Echo: "Ready, break, fire, over!"

Buckboard: "Fire, out!"

Again, after hearing the gun fire, I said:

Buckboard: "SHOT!"

Broken Arrow 1-4 Echo confirmed the second illumination round exploded directly over the target by saying:

Broken Arrow 1-4 Echo: "Four guns, main armament, 24 rounds, high explosive, fuse quick, fire for effect!"

Buckboard: "Roger Broken Arrow One Four Echo, four guns, main armament, high explosive, fuse quick, 24 rounds, fire for effect, out."

Within a second following the completion of my transmission, all hell broke loose; all four guns erupted, each firing a 55-pound, high-explosive projectile. This was the first time since World War II that all four guns fired simultaneously and continued firing multiple shells. As each series of rounds left the gun barrels, the sound, the rattling, the vibration throughout the entire ship, were incredible. It felt as if the ammunition magazines had exploded, or as if we'd been struck by a torpedo. The impact of four guns firing simultaneously was just that powerful. Because we were firing from a broadside profile, the recoil caused this 2,100-ton ship to move more than a foot in the opposite direction. After firing about half of the requested rounds, the spotter said:

Broken Arrow 1-4 Echo: "Fire one illumination round!"

This round was necessary to observe the effectiveness of our firing and to verify whether any additional adjustments were necessary.

Buckboard: "Fire one illumination round, out!"

We frequently included illumination rounds when firing a large number of shells; however, only one gun is instructed to fire the illumination round. My acknowledgement of the spotter's request was sufficient for him to realize they will be coming in short order. Because all four guns were firing, it was impossible to differentiate the firing of a HE round from an illumination round.

While we'll be discussing this activity in much greater detail later, this is a typical example of the conservation between the Marine on the ground and our ship.

During this first mission, the Marine spotter's response to our initial firing was completely unexpected. However, similar reactions were repeated when operating with an inexperienced Marine spotter. Upon receiving the fire for effect request and seconds after the four HE rounds exploded, I clearly heard the spotter broadcast "HOLY SHIT!" Not believing my ears I replied with, "Repeat, I say again, repeat!" And his reply was shocking; it was completely unexpected.

Recalling training exercises off San Clemente Island, ships fired on coordinates and areas that had been attacked by every type of weapon imaginable. And this constant bombardment went on year after year, for decades. In addition to being attacked by a variety of warships, the area also came under assault by aircraft, field artillery, and troop incursions. The region had become nothing more than a barren, razed, and decimated land mass.

This was the first time the spotter observed four airburst (proximity fuse) shells, detonating simultaneously in an actual combat environment. In response to my "repeat, I say again repeat," he replied, "When the shells exploded over the target, it defoliated every tree under its coverage. The trees were instantaneously transformed from summer to winter. There were several VC lookouts positioned in the trees and they fell as well."

What the spotter had observed was the devastating destructive power of a naval destroyer. We fired airburst rounds from our main armament, the 5-inch gun mounts. Each of the high-explosive shells weighed 55 pounds. The propulsion part of the shell, called the casing, is independent of the warhead. In a handheld firearm, the bullet head and the powder cartridge are one piece. With a 5-inch shell, these two components (warhead and casing) are completely independent. Each 5-inch shell contained 4,000 fragments of specially designed and manufactured razor-sharp shrapnel pieces (aka shell fragments). What the spotter witnessed was each airburst delivering 16,000 (4,000 fragments per shell × 4 rounds) pieces of shrapnel, with each fragment traveling at 2,600 to 3,000 feet per second. This could be the equivalent of 16,000 rounds of bullets simultaneously being fired on a target in an omnidirectional or umbrella-like fashion. The delivery and coverage of shrapnel was repeated every time another group of shells was fired.

This was the first time the Viet Cong witnessed the devastating firepower of a U.S. destroyer. When the Viet Cong realized what they were up against, it immediately became urgent for them to step up any plans of capturing the harbor. They had to accomplish this goal before the United States mobilized additional ships and Marines.

Returning once again to the mission, after firing the illumination shell, the spotter transmitted:

Broken Arrow 1-4 Echo: "Buckboard, *cease fire*, I repeat, *cease fire*, over."

I confirmed the request by saying:

Buckboard: "Roger Broken Arrow One Four Echo, Cease Fire, I repeat Cease Fire, out."

As I confirmed the request, the gun mounts were notified and immediately fell silent. But let me be clear with the word "silent"; while the sound of gunfire could no longer be heard or felt, I can assure you the ringing in our ears couldn't have been louder.

Within minutes after the ceasefire, the spotter transmitted:

Broken Arrow 1-4 Echo: "Buckboard this is Broken Arrow One Four Echo, new target coordinates."

And the NGFS sequence began once again.

As with the previous target, once our illumination round and single HE round found their mark, we received a release from the spotter: "Four guns, main armament, high explosive, fuse quick, 16 rounds, fire for effect." I confirmed the spotter's request and we again opened fire on a Viet Cong position. During the next several hours, ceasefire instructions, followed by revised coordinates of new targets, were received, computed, and fire for effect requests received. By the time the last ceasefire was received, we had fired approximately 80 to 100 rounds of high-explosive rounds and 25 illumination shells. While the entire crew was curious about the effectiveness of our effort, many were wondering what held this old bucket of bolts together. So, this is what is meant by the phrase "shiver me timbers." If the beating the hull took, while pitching and rolling during rough seas didn't crack every weld, then firing four guns broadside for more than an hour certainly must have. The continual punishment this ship endured during NGFS missions increased the crew's absolute adoration, love, and respect for this remarkable greyhound of the sea. After all this pounding, her unyielding hull provided the crew with a safety shield, not unlike that an infant feels in its mother's protecting arms. Is this why sailors refer to their ship as "she," or in the female gender? I always thought this love was more related to the love a sailor shared with his girlfriend or wife back home. But as we completed our first firing mission, I knew I had to revisit or rethink this thought or logic, while being so thankful "the old girl" kept us safe.

Shortly after the last ceasefire, we received a mission summary stating there were a "significant" number of enemy casualties," along with the destruction of vehicles and supplies. Oh, remember I mentioned earlier there were a half dozen or so small watercraft or gunboats that might present a minor threat? Well, that threat had been completely and permanently eliminated. Following the ceasefire, we remained on station for several more hours. We did so as a precaution, ensuring enemy forces didn't return to attack the Marines or attempt to recover any weapons or supplies. We were released and returned to Da Nang harbor around 0300. Excellent, we had a few hours of rest before resuming our patrol duties.

As a reminder, the crew was put on a port and starboard schedule prior to the ship arriving in Da Nang. Being on this type of schedule was demanding, to say the least. But when including time spent during general quarters, many shipmates were on duty for more than 18 hours in a 24-hour period. Even the remaining six "off" hours may have been divided into segments. The captain and officers quickly realized this schedule was likely to become the norm. With this possibly, they became concerned about the impact it may have on the crew's performance. Almost immediately, they took this into consideration by adjusting the watch composition and schedules. The crew members essential to our patrolling operations were assigned the 0800 to 2000 watch, whereas those critical to NGFS missions were assigned to the 2000 to 0800 watch.

Our crew, being an exceptional group of professional sailors, became concerned with the welfare and safety of every other shipmate, as well as the ship. When one of the watches was disproportionately impacted by a mission or event, the off-duty shipmates pitched in and relieved them. In many instances, if the watches weren't balanced by the crew, a sailor could easily have served well in excess of 18 continuous hours on duty. By balancing the hours, each watch had approximately the same number of off hours to recover. It was the 0800 to 2000 watch that felt the most impact. During the patrolling and boarding activity, the 0800 to 2000 watch accomplished their assignment without the ship being called to general quarters. So, it was normally the 2000 to 0800 watch who reported early or remained longer on duty. It's how you would expect a band of brothers to operate: *all for one and one for all!*

You may have noticed, at the onset of the mission, the spotter provided us with the target's coordinates but relatively little about its identity. While this may have been the case, it changed as we—the Marine spotters and the ship—gained more experience and began working closer together. Early on the spotter and I followed the exact protocol taught and implemented during NGFS training. Once we had a few missions under our belt, the working relationship between the Marine base, spotters, and the ship increased. With the *Stoddard* being the only ship providing NGFS at the time, along the entire coast of Vietnam, the Marines and our ship began working closer as a team. With most of our missions being windows of opportunity, a more descriptive dialog developed; this was especially the case as it applied to the identity of the target. But once we completed our Da Nang harbor assignment and began working with different spotters, our interface was precisely as had been taught in NGFS training, meaning the dialog and sharing of information was minimal. It became a matter of a request for gunfire support, firing the number of shells requested, receiving a ceasefire, and moving on. I can honestly say, once we left Da Nang it was unlikely we communicated or supported the same spotter more than once.

Throughout my time in Vietnam, many of missions in these earliest of stages of the war were an order of magnitude more dangerous than later ones. Now that's not to say we ever gave less than 100 percent. But there were times, knowing our Marine or our UDT brothers were facing dreadful odds, that caused our adrenaline to flow to off the chart levels. This rush created an even more intense focus or effort, as it may very well be the difference between life and death. I can emphatically state, life and death situations were never considered nor accepted as the norm. Let me use an example to explain how the crew responded and were able to manage the stress and dynamics involving a dire situation.

When presented with a difficult situation, the captain may give the order for the ship to proceed at "all ahead full." This may sound like a reference to a ship's top speed. However, during an absolute emergency, he may give the order to proceed at "all ahead flank." Flank speed pulls out all the stops. While it is faster, it uses an incredible amount of energy and could only be maintained for a relatively short period of time.

Possibly a better example may be our gun mounts. The 5-inch gun crews could fire each gun at a rate of 15 rounds per minute. Firing at or above this rate for an extended period is extraordinarily strenuous and demanding of both the gun crew and equipment; in fact, it may even create a dangerous situation. Such extended firing may cause the mount to overheat, causing a round to "cook off" or explode prematurely in the barrel. So, while in emergency situations it was essential the guns fire at a rate exceeding their maximum designed rate, they should not do so for a prolonged period. Hopefully, this explained how the crew was able to react when confronted with a desperate or dire situation.

It had been a very long and trying day and an even longer evening; it left the crew exhausted. When the ship was released to return to the harbor, the crew not on duty headed toward their bunks for some well-deserved sleep. On this day, the 2000 to 0800 watch in CIC had already been on duty for an extended period. In an attempt to balance watch times, we were relieved and given four hours off to catch a few zzzs. With the temperature averaging over 85 degrees Fahrenheit and the humidity exceeding 80 percent, coupled with the lack of air conditioning, the crew resorted to sleeping in just their underwear. To be more accurate, most of the crew even removed their T-shirts. I mention this because following our first mission, and as we crawled into our bunks, we were immediately greeted with a completely unexpected guest, no, bombshell!

Recalling our NGFS training missions off San Clemente Island, we generally fired only one gun until we were guided on target. Once on target and receiving the release to fire for effect, the exercise ended. Once or twice, upon receiving the fire for effect release, we fired an additional round, but never more than one from one gun. While our first mission followed the same protocol, the end result was so different. In the end, we fired approximately 100 rounds of HE projectiles from our four main guns, plus the illumination rounds. These four 5-inch guns hadn't been fired simultaneously since World War II; the *Stoddard* had not been called upon to conduct any shore bombardment missions during the Korean War. Firing all four guns shook, rattled, and vibrated the ship violently. This vibration caused small particles of fiberglass insulation dust to fall from the overhead and coat everything below. The instant a sailor hit his bunk, fiberglass dust covered every inch of his exposed skin. It was unbelievably and annoyingly itchy; it was impossible to sleep. Being exhausted required an immediate response from the crew. Within minutes after hitting the rack, every sailor began stripping and heading for the showers. The demand for water was so great, each man could only spend enough time to get a quick rinse before getting out (or being yanked out) of the shower. The crew was exhausted and there was no way they were about to clean the sleeping quarters at 0330. Instead, the majority of the crew decided to sleep on the main deck. Sleeping on a steel deck up against a steel bulkhead is less than comfortable, but in all honesty, I don't recall hearing even one complaint. Well, maybe a little bitching about the unexpected dust.

Following the fiberglass episode, showering was on everyone's mind and fresh water became even more of a premium. To protect this "valuable asset," several times when it rained the first thought was to strip, grab a bar soap, wet down, soap up, and rinse. There were a few times that, when not on a mission, if the captain or OOD saw a rain squall he would immediately head in its direction. It gave those who were not on duty a shot at some well-deserved hygiene. Although the monsoon season in Da Nang normally began in September, with the second half of July being relatively close, it rained quite frequently. As a result, rain squalls became a form of hygiene and entertainment.

Photo taken mid-1965, when the *Stoddard* had just come through a rain squall to provide a little hygiene for the crew. (Author's collection)

There was a short period of time when we ran low on bars of soap. To cope with this shortage, the crew began using shaving cream with which to shower. I'm sure you can imagine how a bunch of mature sailors reacted to such a tempting situation. You can be assured it was something to witness. Just think about a bunch of fun-loving sailors, running around bare-ass naked in the rain, each armed with a can of Barbasol shaving cream. It quickly became our newest form of R&R. Hey, no one got hurt and we all deserved a little time to unwind; even if only for a few minutes. And it also had a positive effect on our hygiene.

In an attempt to manage the fiberglass insulation issue, we began using our sheets as protective barriers against the dust. After a night of NGFS, while returning to the harbor, crew members not on duty cleaned the overheads, bulkheads, and decks in the sleeping quarters. Just before getting into his rack, each sailor would carefully fold up his sheet, carry it up to the main deck, and shake off as much dust as possible. Sailors who had top racks, closest to the overhead, suffered the most. Over time, the volume of dust began to lessen, but it was always present following NGFS missions. Eventually, the crew began sleeping on a bare mattress, with the "clean side" facing down toward the canvas bottom and a sheet over it. Before lying down, the sailor removed the sheet and flipped the mattress to expose the clean side.

Following almost every NGFS mission, it was common to see crew members sleeping on the ship's decks. With the monsoon season rapidly approaching, rain became a normal and almost daily event. The crew sleeping on the deck may have been awoken when the rain started, but just as quickly fell back to sleep. Now you may feel this was a hardship, but consider just how efficient it was: sleeping, showering, and washing your skivvies simultaneously. Now that's the true definition of multitasking.

Patrolling and searching watercraft around the harbor during the day, while conducting NGFS during the night, kept us extremely busy. It was this way throughout our assignment as Da Nang harbor defense ship. The only change was to the length of time devoted to NGFS missions, which was constantly on the rise.

***

Normally, my 12-hour watch began after dusk and ended at 0800. But on July 20 or 21, because of the length of time spent at GQ, our watch remained on duty for an additional three hours or until 1100. This would allow the port watch (0800 to 2000) additional time to catch up on some well-deserved sleep before another long night. Since being assigned as Da Nang harbor defense ship, it was one of the few times I was in CIC during our daily patrolling, harbor surveillance, and boarding operations.

As we were returning to Da Nang, an unidentified blip showed up on our surface search radar. The contact was 11 miles to our east and less than 20 miles off the coast. Following normal protocol, we reported it to the Bridge and informed them it was on a westerly course, speed 10 knots, with a CPA (closest point of approach) of four miles. The Bridge acknowledged the skunk and requested we track it and report any changes. As we were tracking it, the skunk continued on a westerly heading, but it was apparent they were making frequent course and speed changes; changes that coincided with our movements.

We began to suspect it was a much smaller ship or craft; one that could see us but wanted to remain out of our visual range. We reported the skunk's unusual movements to the Bridge and recommended we test our theory by changing course in their direction to observe their reaction. The Bridge concurred and we made a sharp 90-degree turn. After a few minutes we observed and reported that the skunk had made a similar course correction. Being suspicious of the skunk's latest maneuver, the captain asked for a course and speed to intercept it approximately five miles off the coast. We provided a course and speed to comply with the captain's request. As we came about to our new course, we could hear and feel the urgency as we increased to full speed. The crew loved steaming ahead at full speed; it created a beautiful rooster tail in the wake, while dark smoke spewed out of both stacks. It also came with the awareness of an abrupt change in our schedule.

Almost immediately, the skunk realized we had changed course and were heading in their direction. They immediately began to take countermeasures by changing to a course that would take them further out to sea. We closed the distance from the skunk, as it finally came within visual range from the Bridge. The craft was an oversized junk, less than 100 feet in length. While a Fletcher-class destroyer may not be a cigarette boat, it certainly could outrun a junk. We continued tracking the skunk, feeding the Bridge its course, speed, and distance from the ship. After closing to within a hundred yards, and after several hand gestures failed to gain their attention, the crew on the .50-caliber machine guns fired warning shots across the junk's bow. This firing wasn't in response to anything they had done but to simply express we meant business and that they should cut their engines.

Normally, we had a South Vietnamese officer on board to act as a translator. Because we were returning to Da Nang from a night mission, he wouldn't be coming on board until we returned to the harbor. After having conducted numerous boarding operations, the boarding party felt comfortable they could use some basic Vietnamese words, coupled with several unsophisticated hand gestures, to communicate our intent to board and search the vessel.

As the boarding party was being lowered into a small dinghy, I stepped outside and noticed the crew on the junk had assembled on the main deck. They had done so with their hands over their heads. Every member of our boarding team was armed, some with .45-caliber handguns and others with semi-automatic rifles. Still, their response kind of surprised me. My initial thought was they must have contraband on board and were surrendering. But as I looked around, I noticed the crews on the .50-caliber machine guns and 20-millimeter AA guns had their weapons trained in their general direction. I recall thinking, "Good move, boys." Suddenly, I felt their reaction was entirely appropriate.

The inspection took the better part of an hour. I was amazed by how thoroughly proficient and professional the boarding team were in performing their duty. This was a no-nonsense team; they opened and inventoried every container on board and compared the contents against the bills of lading. By the time they completed their search, I'm confident they knew the color and manufacturer of the crews' underwear; they were just that thorough. In the end, the junk was deemed to be clean and allowed to proceed. Being my first experience in stopping and searching a vessel flying a foreign flag, I was pleased with the outcome. I later learned about 25 percent of the time that some form of contraband or suspicious cargo was uncovered. These goods were either removed, brought on board, or dumped overboard. If any weapons or munitions were found, the hands of the crew were bound behind their back and, as prisoners, were secured to a permanent structure on their vessel. Under our control, the watercraft was taken to a dock just north of Da Nang and turned over to the South Vietnamese military. This exchange usually took place several hundred yards off the coast. To date, this occurred only a few times.

In later conversations with the South Vietnamese officer, I learned all of the weapons captured on such searches became the property of the South Vietnamese and were reissued to their troops. Per an agreement with the U.S. military, each was marked to show it was taken from an enemy soldier and reassigned to a South Vietnamese soldier. This was an important identification characteristic, especially when a South Vietnamese soldier was being interviewed or detained by U.S. or South Vietnamese forces. Without this marking, the captured individual, sometimes in uniform and other times in more traditional attire, was assumed to be a member of the resistance or opposition. Not every enemy came from North Vietnam; many members of the resistance were born and raised in the South but became conditioned, eventually sympathizing with the North.

These individuals became part of a communist guerrilla movement, better known as the Viet Cong. The Viet Cong were supporters of the communist National Liberation Front and sought to conquer and unify North and South Vietnam into one communist state. From conversations with many Marines, I was informed the South Vietnamese frequently tried to play both ends against the middle. The vast majority of South Vietnamese were extremely poor; poor in the sense of poverty beyond anything the typical American could ever comprehend. The South Vietnamese elite, U.S. forces, and North Vietnamese/VC were well aware of this unfortunate situation. In order to gain intelligence or cooperation from the locals, both sides exploited this condition by offering them food and drink. In turn, the locals would pledge their alliance and cooperation to whichever party made the last offering. Not to mention, they may have "worked" with the Viet Cong because they feared the physical consequences of refusing.

During one of my visits to the base, a Marine provided an excellent example of this. One morning, a combined group of South Vietnamese soldiers and Marines entered a village on the outskirts of Da Nang. They met with several locals who acted as spokespersons for the entire village. After an hour or so, using food and drink as a reward, they were able to obtain some very important intelligence. Later that afternoon, they returned to clarify a few matters associated with their earlier visit. Upon arriving, they observed a significant number of Viet Cong soldiers. Knowing they were outnumbered, they returned to their base. Shortly after nightfall, the Marines returned with reinforcements and, after coming under fire, neutralized a large contingent of VC soldiers just outside of the village. A post-mission inspection revealed a variety of VC weapons and ammunition. Most interesting however, several Chinese nationals were among the casualties. Apparently, in the early stages of the Vietnam War, it was common to find Chinese soldiers among the battle casualties. Wanting to avoid a war with China, the United States more or less downplayed or failed to publish these findings.

Returning to our patrolling and searching assignment, I found the experience unique. I remained on duty until the junk was well out of range. The ending was less than exciting, but it did leave me with a different respect and admiration for the ship's board and search team. It was so interesting to watch a group of young, fun-loving kids—many in their late teens—executing their duty and responsibility with the intensity and experience of a professional. Throughout the encounter they remained focused on their mission and performed it to perfection. I was once again reminded just how proud and fortunate I was to be a shipmate of such an extraordinary crew.

***

The exact events of the sequence described below or the dates on which they occurred may be less than accurate. Also, the timing between missions may have been more condensed than presented below. For instance, I've struggled remembering whether the second attack along the Cu De River occurred before or after the attack on the Esso fuel storage farm. From a timing perspective, it may have happened following the attack on the Esso farm. I've attempted to keep them in some semblance of chronological order. However, and most importantly, I've outlined the major missions and battles conducted during our assignment as Da Nang harbor defense ship. As you shall see, the unexpected frequency of these encounters impacted the crew both mentally and physically. As mentioned earlier, future encounters or battles could not measure up to what we experienced that first month.

Being the very earliest stages of the war, we quickly learned neither the U.S./South Vietnamese or the North Vietnamese/Viet Cong were fully aware of the others' intention or capabilities. And if you ask why, simply put, this is when the tension in South Vietnam was elevated to a war-like level. While our first NGFS mission was on July 18, 1965, years later I learned that because the Marines stationed in Da Nang were the only U.S. combat forces in South Vietnam, the *Stoddard* was the first United States naval warship to conduct an NGFS mission or fire a round in Vietnam.

The Marines mobilized in Da Nang in March 1965 were the first mobilization of U.S. combat forces. Their orders were to protect and defend Da Nang harbor and airfield from being taken over and controlled by the Viet Cong. By the end of March, nearly 5,000 Marines were at Da Nang, including two infantry battalions, two helicopter squadrons, along with supply and logistics units. In April the U.S. government agreed to deploy more Marines to Vietnam and to permit those at Da Nang to engage in counterinsurgency operations. These additional troops began to be mobilized in late July 1965.

In the first several months, after the additional troops mobilized, report after report confirmed a rapid buildup of enemy forces was ongoing. Resulting from this rapid buildup, in mid-summer the Marines began moving their cantonment at Da Nang. This also increased their area of responsibility (AOR) to include the Viet Cong-infested villages primarily to the south.

To manage this continuing increase in Viet Cong troop numbers in and around Da Nang, now estimated to be in the range of 15,000, the Marines needed additional firepower in the area. On July 15, 1965, to meet this need, Washington assigned the *Stoddard* as Da Nang harbor defense ship and authorized the Navy to conduct naval gunfire missions. From the date of this release, it took the Marines only a few days to ramp up and develop a plan to effectively use this "new" tactical weapon.

Although the Viet Cong were being aggressively attacked, reports continued to reflect the rapid buildup of enemy troops was continuing. These reports stated the largest concentrations were observed south of Da Nang. The assignment and responsibility of retaining and protecting this extremely valuable asset fell squarely on the shoulders of the 3rd Marine Division, the UDTs, and the men on board the *Stoddard*. With the war in its infancy (referred to as a "police action" by the media at this time), it became clear the Viet Cong were not about to give up the harbor without a fight. In very short order, aware they were severely outnumbered by enemy forces, the Marines knew this growing threat had to be tracked, analyzed, and effectively confronted and neutralized.

CHAPTER 17

Ever See a Greyhound Madder Than Hell?

> To find us, you must be good; to catch us, you must be fast; to beat us, you must be kidding!
>
> UNKNOWN

As we continued with our NGFS missions, our interaction with this special ops team remained infrequent. Up to this point, our interaction had been limited to the evening they removed the bridge and trestle north of Da Nang harbor. Our involvement was to act as their ferry. Frequently, after getting underway, we would transport them to a predesignated location. Once we reached their drop-off point, we would lower their craft into the water and they would disappear into the night. We went about our business and on most days, they seemed to reappear the following morning. During the time they used our ship as an operating platform, we knew when they departed the ship; however, I can only recall a few times seeing them return. As you can imagine, in many ways, it bordered upon being downright eerie. But this would all change in just a few days.

For several nights following our first NGFS missions, the Marines reported observing significant movements of Viet Cong troops. These movements were primarily along roads inland of the harbor. In these earliest stages of the war, due to a limited U.S. presence, it was relatively easy for the enemy to move troops, as well as small arms, from the south toward the north and vice versa. They did so in a rather stealthy fashion, mostly through the landscape and vegetation. However, it was far more difficult to move vehicles, larger weapons, and sizable shipments of supplies without utilizing the roads. Being the "invading force," the Viet Cong had to address and accept the risk associated with operating in the open. The risk was necessary to strengthen and position their forces in preparation for an all-out attack on the base or the nearby Esso fuel storage tank farm (officially the Lien Chieu Fuel Depot), located at Lien Chieu (see map below).

After commencing NGFS operations, we regularly interacted with numerous Marine spotters on evening missions. The sole objective of these missions, which could better be defined as "skirmishes or clashes" rather than "battles," was intended to show our military presence and strength. It was also intended to prevent or deter the movement of large pieces of equipment, weapons, and ammunition. At this time, the Marines' field of operation was quite restrictive. It was limited to their compound

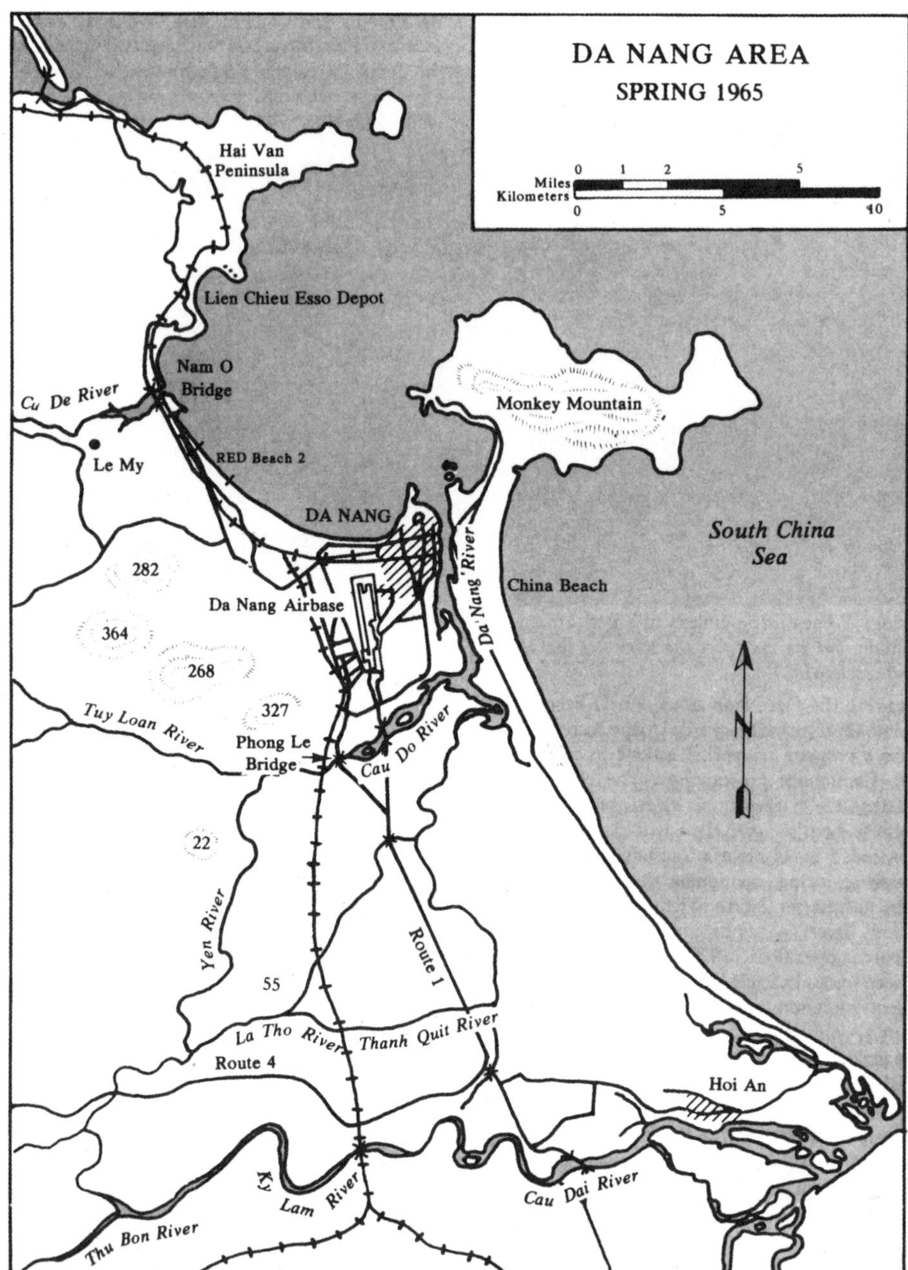

The Da Nang area, spring 1965. This chart shows Da Nang harbor as well as the location of three major battles: two of which occurred where the Cu De River meets the South China Sea, and the other where the Esso fuel tank farm is (called "Lien Chieu Esso Depot" on this chart), just north of the Cu De River. (History and Museums Division, USMC)

and the region immediately surrounding Da Nang. They were isolated by rivers to the north and south, mountains to the west, and the South China Sea to the East. Such a minimal operational area convinced senior staff the enemy was using a much longer route to achieve their equipment, troop movements and mobilization goals. It was generally believed the VC found a degree of success traveling through the mountains west of the harbor. With limited U.S. forces, only the port and airfield area could be effectively watched, guarded, and protected. This was the primary reason that impeding the less-travelled roads was essential to the Marines' safety, and, what we believed to be one of the UDT's primary objectives. Destroying the bridges along the secondary roads impeded the Viet Cong's movements, including large weapons and ammunition.

This action slowed their progress and kept them somewhat at bay. Although we were never privy to the UDT's assignments, we assumed they were focusing the majority of their time on destroying the rarely used bridges and river crossings. Unquestionably, they were more than capable of successfully executing such missions. This strategy limited and reduced the enemy's ability to freely move about. However, it seemed to have little impact on their ultimate goal of mobilizing troops, attacking, and controlling the Da Nang region. This rapid buildup of enemy forces could only be described as fast track. Along with the increase in troops came the concern larger equipment and weapons were likely being smuggled into the region.

In addition to our destroyer, the Marines also utilized their air wing (MAW), a wing that consisted of helicopter gunships. While the armament on these aircraft was generally limited, they were effective because of the chopper crews themselves. And as you'll see a little later, these Marine crews were absolutely fearless. The base also housed several large cannons; however, they were much less flexible than the ship-mounted artillery. These assets were stationary weapons and only effective on targets to the south. Also, the volume of vegetation in the region became troublesome; it had to be reduced or cleared to increase the Marines' safety. This was accomplished by means of "controlled burns," coupled with the spraying of large quantities of Agent Orange.

Agent Orange is a potent and effective herbicide. This defoliant was frequently sprayed by U.S. military forces during the Vietnam War. It was very effective in eliminating dense vegetation and ground cover. Eradicating vegetation made traveling, as well as the assembly of North Vietnamese and Viet Cong troops, much more difficult. During one application the aircraft crew either began spraying too soon or the wind possibly shifted. Either way, the end result was the same: an herbicidal chemical cloud was blown in the direction of the ship. The mist of this nasty-smelling chemical covered the ship, causing coughing, burning, and eye irritation. Those affected immediately headed for the showers. In the future, I would replay this event over and over in my mind, each time I underwent surgery for various forms of skin cancer.

On July 21, 1965, following nights of multiple lengthy NGFS missions, our magazines began running low on ammunition, with our illumination rounds almost depleted. We needed to resupply our munitions. Being in the early stages of the war, it was impossible for the Navy to have predicted or foreseen the frequency or length of missions. Time and experience would reveal most attacks would be conducted well after sunset. I recall overhearing an officer mention the number of illumination rounds we'd be receiving during ammunition replenishment would more than double our original allotment.

During the evening hours of July 21, we received orders to rendezvous with an ammunition supply ship the following day. Since we began our patrolling assignment, the volume of marine traffic entering Da Nang harbor had dropped significantly. There were a number of factors contributing to the reduction in boat and ship traffic entering Da Nang harbor. These included the *Stoddard*'s searching of watercraft entering the harbor, as well as the Marines and South Vietnamese conducting port inspections of goods being delivered. Once the enemy realized we were patrolling the harbor, they realized they had to find an alternate means of delivering supplies and weapons into the region. It was believed the enemy carefully tracked our every movement. Also, our surveillance of marine traffic may have made local ship crews uncomfortable when approached by a warship. To continue showing our presence and monitoring marine traffic, the USS *Craig* (DD-885) was temporarily assigned this duty. It's important to point out, with the release to conduct NGFS less than a week earlier, the *Craig*'s ammunition magazines had not been increased to wartime levels. Also, from a command perspective, there was minimal concern that a large enemy attack was imminent. With every previous mission occurring well after dark, command was confident the *Stoddard* could replenish her magazines and return to the harbor before nightfall. Once the *Stoddard* was back on station, the *Craig* would be released and return to Yankee Station. At the time, the USS *Independence* (CVA-62) task force was located approximately 150 miles off the coast of South Vietnam.

The following morning, July 22, according to plan, we departed Da Nang and headed south. In a few hours, we would be rendezvousing with an ammunition supply ship some 50 miles off the coast. When we pulled alongside the supply ship, we transferred several sacks of the crew's mail. Although we didn't receive any mail in return, we were pleased our mail would begin its journey to our loved ones and friends stateside. The most important element of this mail transfer was the confirmation we were safe and healthy.

It may come as a surprise but heading out to sea and meeting up with the ammunition ship seemed to have replenished the crew's mental health as well. The captain, being sensitive to the needs of his crew, gave the men not directly involved in the UNREP time off from the war. This allowed part of the crew a few hours to unwind and rest. As we headed out and returned, the men off duty took advantage of the opportunity to recover from the war, if only for a few hours. Some sailors used the time to catch up on sleep, while others just sat along the main deck relaxing. The only time the 1MC came alive was to announce that "the smoking lamp was out,"

Replenishment of ammunition off the coast of Da Nang in 1965. (*STODDARD '65*/the USS *Stoddard* 1965 cruise book, unofficial U.S. Navy publication)

as we came alongside the supply ship. Once alongside, we began highlining skid after skid of high explosive and illumination rounds of ammunition. The captain's actions during the UNREP operation were somewhat abnormal when compared to naval protocol. Much like GQ, every man was assigned a post during UNREP activities. But these times were different in so many ways. While the captain allowed those not directly involved with the transfer to stand down, he did so with the understanding they were to remain clear of the port side of the ship (the side facing the ammunition supply ship).

Once the loading of ammunition was completed, we pulled away and settled in on a westerly course. Shortly thereafter, the 1MC came alive to announce that "the smoking lamp is lit." This was followed with a message: "The ship will remain in the harbor for the evening." And the crew's response would be as expected: wait, this means we're being given the night off, right? Can this be true? Are you kidding me? Did I hear that right? Oh my God, this is just what we needed! Was it really too good to be true? Well, of course it was!

The crew was quite content, as we headed back in the direction of the harbor. Even the weather and seas were cooperating. The weather was tolerable from both a temperature and humidity perspective, and the sea relatively calm and quiet.

Life was good! It was pleasantly quiet; the only sounds were the water striking the ship's hull and the hum of the engines. It quickly became evident the crew was beginning to unwind, as they enjoyed the relative stillness of the day. Those off duty relieved the 0800 to 2000 watch, so they could enjoy a little mindfulness time as well.

Late in the afternoon, continuing our westerly course, land slowly began to appear on the horizon. A visit to CIC wasn't necessary to confirm the identity of the approaching terrain. At first the land mass appeared to be black or a dark gray in color; as we got closer, the color changed to more of a vibrant Kelly green. Incredibly, the entire coast appeared to be laid-back and tranquil. As we continued our approach, it was difficult to comprehend how such a beautiful place could be so violent, so cruel, so hostile. Regardless, "welcome home!" To most, this probably sounds like a few sessions with "Dr. Looney Tunes" were in order, but for the crew the last few hours were refreshing and revitalizing. Just knowing, we could breathe without being interrupted by war seemed to briefly loosen the anchor around the crew's neck.

With dusk approaching and being just 10 or 15 miles south of Da Nang, every sailor's thoughts were focused on how to take advantage of our brief respite. As we continued approaching Da Nang harbor, this tantalizing thought was unexpectedly interrupted with the sound and feel of a sudden surge in the engine's rpm. Initially, I thought we were about to search a junk or vessel before entering the harbor. As I looked forward, I saw a radar striker running in our direction; hmmm, another rather abysmal sign. When he arrived, I was told to report immediately to CIC. Immediately the thought of a short breather from the war began to fade and be replaced with a "you have to be friggin' kidding me" moment. But as I look back, even before we completed the change in course, the entire crew was mentally and physically back on track and well prepared to handle whatever was developing. In the end, I can assure you every crew member thanked God we had just replenished our ammunition. Also, for the past 10 or so hours we'd been afforded a brief period of relaxation and quietness; it allowed us to begin feeling human once again.

As I was heading up to CIC, I heard the engine's rpm increasing to levels I'd never heard before. With the captain putting the pedal to the metal, dark plumes of smoke began pouring out of both stacks. Arriving in CIC, I was informed that moments ago we received orders to change course and head north at flank speed.

As we came about to our new course, I learned a squad of Marines may be facing what could only be described as an extremely dire situation. While guarding a bridge on the south side of the Cu De River, they heard what they believed to be a large contingent of Viet Cong forces assembling on the north side. We were given orders to precede as quickly as possible to a location just north of Da Nang. This is an area where the Cu De River flows into the South China Sea. As we steamed ahead, it was believed the contingent of Viet Cong troops greatly outnumbered the Marines platoon. The troops were apparently assembling on the north side, about three-quarters of a mile from the Cu De River Bridge. From the communication, with the volume of noise coming from the area, it was apparent the enemy was unaware of the Marines' presence. Days earlier an intelligence report suggested the VC may eventually attempt to capture this area. This location contained an ESSO aviation fuel storage tank farm (Lien Chieu Esso Depot). To make matters worse, rather than attacking the fuel storage farm, the VCs may intend to cross the Cu De River Bridge and attack the Marine base.

The bridge over the Cu De River was along a major route and was a very important asset to the Marine air wing. The Esso tank farm on the north side of the bridge contained a number of fuel storage tanks. The largest tank contained between 1.5 and 2 million gallons of aviation fuel. This fuel farm was used by the Marines for their vehicles and helicopter squadron. As a point of interest, this vital fuel storage tank farm was the only reason the Cu De River Bridge remained in place.

A second message informed us the *Craig* (call sign Assassin) was closest and had been dispatched to the Cu De River area. The *Craig* would be the first to arrive. The *Craig* reported it had an adequate number of high-explosive rounds in her magazine but was critically short on illumination shells. As it approached the coast, Assassin made contact with and authenticated the identity of the Marine spotter ("Apache"). Normally, upon arrival the *Craig* would have taken a very aggressive posture and quickly begin the process of neutralizing the threat. However, with it being after sunset and being critically low on illumination rounds, it had to reevaluate if this was the best strategy or tactic. A major factor in the *Craig*'s analysis was determining if it had a sufficient quantity of illumination rounds to allow the spotter to keep a visual track of the enemy movements. Remember, at this juncture, it was believed the Viet Cong were unaware of the Marines' presence and were over a half mile from either the Cu De River Bridge or entrance to the Esso fuel storage tank farm.

With this being the case, the *Craig*, in conjunction with the Marine spotter, concluded being critically low on illumination shells may impact the overall success of the mission. Knowing the *Stoddard* was rapidly approaching, it decided to delay firing for effect until we could get within range. The plan was to hold the Viet Cong at bay until we were able to take up position and illuminate the target area. On the other hand, if the enemy began their attack, the *Craig* would respond accordingly. Their primary concern was allowing the Marine squad to keep visual tabs on the enemy's forces. If the enemy's goal was to cross the bridge, their forces would have a direct route to attack the Marine base.

As the enemy forces continued to assemble, Assassin and the Marine spotter initiated a plan to manage the situation. The strategy was to maximize the usage of the *Craig*'s high-explosive ammunition. Rather than attacking the enemy directly, they decided to concentrate their gunfire on a position on the northern side of the bridge. This area included entrances to both the bridge and the tank farm. Knowing we would be on station shortly, rather than firing any illumination rounds, which were running low, the *Craig*'s strategy was to fire one 5-inch HE round randomly at sporadic intervals. This would prevent enemy forces from approaching and crossing the bridge or attacking the ESSO fuel storage facility. From the enemy's perspective, the rounds would be detonating a distance away and not working in their direction. Over the last few days, we had been involved in a number of random firings. The shells were fired at areas believed to contain enemy forces and intended to keep them on their toes, restrict their sleep, and make it difficult to relax (harassment and interdiction).

The plan turned out to be sheer brilliance on the part of Assassin and Apache; it was the key in reversing an absolutely dire situation and turning it into a successful mission. As a point of reference, if the VC showed any signs of crossing the bridge, Assassin was prepared to defend the Marines by destroying the bridge.

Within minutes after changing course, the *Stoddard*'s 60,000 shp (shaft horsepower) takes the ship past full speed and reaches flank speed. As we headed in a northerly direction, the old tin can began shaking and quivering violently. This made it feel like the *Stoddard* was just madder than hell. Suddenly, I heard sounds I'd never heard before and began wondering if the old bucket of bolts may come apart at the seams. But it just kept on steaming; it was on a mission and, by God, there was no way of stopping her.

While at flank speed, I established communications and began the authentication process with the *Craig*. We used the exact same procedure as used with Marine spotters. Assassin immediately showed it was fully prepared for a mass firing mission (mass firing is the firing of two or more ships on one target, with both ships using the computer solution from one of the ships). At the conclusion of the authentication process, Assassin immediately provided the computer solution from her fire-control (FC) system, and we entered the data into our FC computer equally as fast. The fire-control systems on both ships were locked in on the exact same position or coordinates. Our physical position would be slightly north of the *Craig*'s, so our FC system would tweak the data to meet our specific needs and position. As a reminder, these FC systems were so sophisticated they adjusted the firing data differently to compensate for the distance between the 51- and 54-gun mounts (front and rear mounts).

Once the authentication phase was behind us, we learned the severity of the mission. A platoon of Marines found themselves facing what could only be described as a catastrophic situation. Based upon data later provided by the spotter, the VC

Stacking expended shell casings from the 54 mount (the gun closest to the fantail) following a night of supporting a UDT mission. (Author's collection)

outnumbered the Marines by at least 20 to 1 (approximately 400 to 500 versus 20). In the simplest of terms, this squad was in deep, deep shit.

Feeling a bit edgy, I began thinking back to my training in NGFS, realizing I had to once again mentally remain in control of my emotions and thoughts. The Navy had trained me for such a situation; so, as with the earlier mission with the UDTs, my focus was completely on the mission. However, my last conversation with Gunny ran through my mind. I thought, "Gunny, you can be assured, we'll do our absolute best and then some."

Being miles from our rendezvous position, I tried replaying my training by recalling similar challenges during NGFS school. However, my thoughts were interrupted by Assassin. He requested confirmation we had sufficient quantities of illumination and HE rounds in our magazines. I'm confident both Assassin and Apache were relieved to learn we were "loaded for bear," returning from replenishing our munitions.

After coming about to a northerly course, we eventually identified Assassin on our surface radar screen. We confirmed our station would have us in a position in front of and on the port side of her bow. The goal of the Marine spotter and of both ships was to eliminate the threat of the upcoming enemy attack, as quickly and efficiently as possible. With that said, once Assassin provided us with their computer solution, we were fully prepared and ready to participate in the mission. In essence, Assassin acted as our spotter. Up to this point, the enemy was still assembling; they hadn't shown any signs of moving in the direction of either the bridge or tank farm. This afforded us the opportunity of arriving on station to maximize the impact of the upcoming mass firing mission.

As we approached our station we reduced speed, entering the area in darkened-ship protocol, a condition being employed by Assassin as well. As we pulled ahead of the *Craig*, we advised them our mission speed would be under 5 knots. After receiving the *Craig*'s acknowledgment, we confirmed to Assassin and Apache we were on station and ready. Within seconds, Apache released us to fire two illumination rounds on the targeted area coordinates provided by Assassin. By the time they exploded, the same mounts were reloaded with a second round of illumination shells. As reality set in, with Apache realizing just how badly they were outnumbered, he provided a major adjustment to coincide with the troops' actual location. The enemy troops were located on a plain about half a mile west of the bridge entrance.

Both ships immediately entered Apache's yardage adjustment. As soon as a FC solution was reached, and with Apache's release, a second group of illumination rounds were fired. As they illuminated the area, Apache reported the illumination rounds "lit up the entire area like Times Square," and released both ships to "fire for effect." Just seconds following his release, both ships began firing all 10 guns (the *Stoddard* had four 5-inch guns and the *Craig*, a Gearing-class destroyer, had six).

With Apache's spot-on accuracy, the enemy forces felt the full impact of 10 rounds of high-explosive, fuse-quick shells being delivered in an umbrella-like manner on target. This initial round of 10 HE shells delivered approximately 40,000 fragments of shrapnel (10 guns × 4,000 pieces per shell = 40,000), blanketing the entire area. As the shells detonated over the targeted area, Apache reported the impact was "absolutely devastating," with "more than half of the VC troops dropping with the burst of the opening salvos." Even before Apache provided the impact of the first 10 shells, a second and third group of shells were fired. As the remaining enemy troops attempted to evacuate the area, Apache adjusted and readjusted the firing coordinates. Both ships entered the spotter's (Apache's) adjustments into their FC systems simultaneously and continued firing.

When a ceasefire was called, each ship had fired in excess of 40 rounds of high-explosive shells, with the *Stoddard* occasionally firing an illumination round. Apache reported the target had been completely "neutralized" with "no visual movement" observed on the battlefield. This battle concluded without an injury or loss of life to any of our Marine brothers; thank God! Suddenly, Gunny crossed my mind once again; if he only knew, he would be so proud of the entire team's performance.

After receiving the ceasefire order, the *Craig* was released and headed out to sea to return to her prior assignment. As a precaution, we remained on station for the remainder of the evening to "clean up" any remaining targets or issues.

This photo and the one below show expended powder casings on the *Stoddard* following an NGFS mission. The expended casings were saved and returned so that they could be refilled and reused. (Author's collection)

On July 25, 1965, by means of a news release, the commander in chief, U.S. Pacific Fleet confirmed this July 22, 1965 Cu De River battle to the wire services. The following is the news release memorandum that was issued and printed in newspapers throughout the nation:

USS STODDARD (DD-566)
FPO, SAN FRANCISCO 96601

MEMORANDUM

From: Commanding Officer

To: All hands

Subj: News Release

Commander in Chief, U.S. Pacific Fleet promulgated the following on 25 July 1965 for release to the wire service:

- TWO 7TH FLEET DESTROYERS CHALKED UP A FIRST IN THE IN-COUNTRY OPERATIONS THURSDAY NIGHT (JULY22 [*sic*]), WHEN THE USS STODDARD AND THE USS JOHN R. CRAIG JOINED FORCES IN A MASS FIRE MISSION AGAINST A VIET CONG CONCENTRATION IN THE I CORP AREA OF THE REPUBLIC OF VIETNAM. MASS FIRING IS THE FIRING OF TWO OR MORE SHIPS ON ONE TARGET, WITH ONE SHIP USING THE COMPUTER SOLUTIONS OF THE OTHER. THE SHIPS FIRED OVER 40 ROUNDS OF FIVE-INCH HIGH [*sic*] EXPLOSIVES INTO THE TARGET, A SUSPECTED VIET CONG ASSEMBLY AREA IN THE CA DE SONG RIVER, ABOUT EIGHT MILES FROM THE DA NANG HARBOR.
- IMMEDIATE EVALUATION OF THE DAMAGE WAS NOT AVAILABLE, BUT A SPOTTER REPORTED "VERY EFFECTIVE IMPACT ON THE TARGET." WEATHER IN THE AREA WAS CLEAR, NO RETURN FIRE FROM THE BEACH WAS REPORTED DURING THE ONE HOUR MISSION. THIS WAS THE FOURTH NIGHT IN SUCCESSION THAT STODDARD HAS CONDUCTED SHORE BOMBARDMENT FROM THE DA NANG HARBOR. SHE HAS FIRED A TOTAL OF 281 ROUNDS DURING THESE MISSIONS. STODDARD'S COMMANDING OFFICER IS CDR. CHARLES K. PRESGROVE OF CHULA VISTA, CALIFORNIA. CRAIG IS COMMANDED BY CDR. J.K. JOBE.

R.J. BACKES
By direction

Commander C. K. Presgrove's July 24 letter to the friends and family of *Stoddard's* crew mentioned operations:

> After a week's stay in Hong Kong, with a paycheck to spend and early liberty for all, we left on 14 July for our turn at Viet Nam duty. Since the 15th (this is a magical date that concerns us all—the 15th we became eligible for Federal Income Tax exclusion for July!) the *STODDARD* has participated in coastal surveillance operations, and recently has been the sole destroyer responsible for the harbor defense of Da Nang, South Vietnam. Da Nang, the site of the second largest airfield in South Vietnam, is located in the northern part of the Country about forty miles from the North Viet Nam border. Da Nang is extremely important in the overall U.S. effort to keep free the people of South Viet Nam [*sic*]. By day we have patrolled the entrance and coastline area of Da Nang against penetration by the Viet Cong and North Vietnamese. In fact, just a few days ago our boarding party headed by LTJG Jim CHAPPEL, our new Operations Officer, actually boarded and searched a suspected junk. The past four nights we have conducted shore bombardment against Viet Cong troop movements.

On the same day that the captain wrote to our loved ones, the XO circulated this "Plan of the Day" to the crew:

USS STODDARD (DD-566)
PLAN OF THE DAY
SATURDAY, 24 JULY 1965

DUTY YN:GRABIEC,SA [*sic*] DUTY MAA: FORD, EN1 DUTY DIV: "R"

CARRY OUT THE REGULAR AT SEA ROUTINE WITH THE FOLLOWING EXCEPTIONS:
0745—Muster on Station
1300—Ropeyarn Sunday

ANNOUNCEMENTS:

1. The following was released to Hawaiian Media at 200915Z. "The 2400-ton U.S. Navy destroyer USS FRANK KNOX (DD-742) while operating in the South China Sea ran aground on a coral reef seven- and one-half miles [*sic*] south west of Pratas Island Saturday, July 18, at 0300 local time. Prates Island is located 165 miles southeast of Hong Kong and approximately 240 miles south west of Taiwan. The auxiliary ships MUNSEE, COPA, GRAPPLE and MANOPAC steamed to the aid of FRANK KNOX and are conducting salvage operations. The exact extent of damage to the KNOX has not been determined. There are no personnel injuries to date.
2. The crew is commended for your outstanding performance during the past few days. Thursday night for the fourth night in succession we fired shore bombardment at Viet Cong troops in support of the 3rd Marine division. A total of 281 rounds have been fired since being assigned to Da Nang defense on 16 July 1965. The following is a summary of targets and results:

19 July	Target 1: 12 rounds illumination of an enemy position
	Target 2: 100 rounds explosive on an area target for harassment and interdiction.
20 July	Target 1 and 2: 28 rounds illumination of suspected enemy movements. 3. [*sic*]
24 July	Target 1: 25 rounds on suspected enemy movement for harassment.
	Target 2: 23 rounds on enemy movement
	Target 3: 13 rounds on enemy movement
	Target 4: 9 rounds on enemy movement
	Target 5: 12 rounds on enemy movement
	Target 6: 12 rounds on enemy movement
	Target 7: 10 rounds on enemy movement
	Target 8: 13 rounds on enemy movement
22 July	40 rounds on a suspected enemy area by mass firing with CRAIG

3. The Marine spotters reported that all firings were effective

RJ BACKES
LCDR, USN
EXECUTIVE OFFICER

CHAPTER 18

Looking Forward to a Solid Hour of Uninterrupted Sleep

At sea, I learned how little a person needs, not how much.

ROBIN LEE GRAHAM

With the war in its infancy and the Marines having somewhat limited intelligence about the enemy's size or movements, it was widely believed the Viet Cong may be in the early stages of preparing a major offensive attack. If the enemy's offensive attack was successful, the Viet Cong would control Da Nang harbor, the airfield, and the ESSO fuel storage depot, along with the surrounding real estate.

To counter a potential attack, the United States implemented tactics intended to weaken the Viet Cong buildup in the region. As time passed, it became apparent we were up against a much larger and more determined enemy. By observing and analyzing the reports, specifically the buildup of Viet Cong troops and their movements in the region, the Navy took immediate action. This action involved significantly increasing in the number of ammunition supply ships in the region, assigning more destroyers to conduct NGFS missions, as well as increasing the number of air attacks. But as you can imagine, this acceleration, which could more accurately be described as the redeployment of military assets, took time before showing any measurable results. With limited naval resources in the region, the crews would frequently be on duty in excess of 16 hours a day. The question was, how long could this go on before the crews began showing signs of breaking?

While the Navy was working on a solution, the Marines assigned to Da Nang and their primary artillery, the *Stoddard*, had to confront and manage the situation to the best of their abilities. In less than a month, the Navy effectively and conclusively implemented tactical changes and addressed and resolved every issue. This change in strategy resulted in a noticeable increase in the number of warships off the coast. The redistribution of military assets resulted in ships operating at their maximum effectiveness, as they began attacking enemy positions around the clock. Once in place, there was never another concern about running low on inventory or munitions. It was a relief knowing such a powerful, committed force was supporting our effort.

However, before the Navy could implement the deployment of these naval assets, the *Stoddard* crew began to feel the impact of the long hours. Continuing with our harbor monitoring, we realized a significant uptick in both the volume and

The *Stoddard* setting sail to begin patrolling operations following another night of NGFS, circa July 1965. This photo shows the aftermath of a late-night mission. Note the smoke coming from the shore to the right of the Vietnamese junk. (Author's collection)

duration of NGFS nightly missions. This around the clock duty began having a negative impact on the crew, with fatigue becoming apparent throughout the ship. Officially, we may have been on 12-hour shifts, but when including the added hours at general quarters, there were times we were on duty for near 18 hours per day. This constant engagement quickly began taking its toll on sailors "off duty." They struggled to relax, as the ship was constantly changing course and speed, with frequent announcements blaring over the 1MC.

Being so exhausted, you might think a sailor could sleep through just about anything, but that was not the case. Every sailor slept with one eye open, not knowing when the 1MC would come alive with the call to general quarters.

Signs of fatigue included: sailors forgoing meals to catch a few extra minutes of sleep; and rather than showering and sleeping in their bunks, many elected to wear the same clothes for a few days and sleep along the main deck. While I never witnessed any physical exchanges, it became obvious the crew was becoming irritable, even in the way they were responding to one another; smiling and laughing became a memory. It was like having a run of beautiful weather, suddenly replaced with more than a week of cold, cloudy, gloomy, rainy weather. With the gloomy "weather" continuing, each day was becoming more miserable than the previous.

Forecasting the sheer volume and length of combat missions was not only unrealistic, it was impossible. With that in mind, coupled with limited resources and assets available, only so much can be handled. As a result, neither the Navy nor the captain could have forecasted the demands or impact our assignment would have on the crew. Demands included being on duty well beyond the scheduled 12 hours, a condition that may last for days on end. But the long hours experienced by the majority of the crew couldn't be compared to the physical beating the gun mount crews were enduring. For these men, the frequency and duration of GQ resulted in pure, unadulterated punishment. To provide some relief to these men, sailors from other classifications pitched in to help where and whenever possible. Examples include moving shell casings and projectiles between forward and aft gun mounts, the stacking of expended shell casings, etc.

Following days and nights of what seemed to be never-ending missions, the captain and his officers realized fatigue was raising its ugly head and becoming problematic. They were concerned it would have a negative impact on the crew's performance. It required the captain's immediate attention and quickly became a top priority. Let me offer up an example of how the captain and his staff officers reacted when they realized the crew had reached this level of exhaustion.

Let me begin by saying, and this may sound a bit off the wall, as time passed exhaustion became almost addictive; something you craved or needed. Exhaustion was being confused with doing a good day's work. At the end of the day, if you lacked the feeling of overwhelming lassitude, you questioned whether you had given your all. Fatigue became like vodka to an alcoholic or heroine to a drug addict. And much like excessive alcohol or drugs, it began to take its toll. This example reflects the concern shown by the captain and his staff.

As mentioned, CIC is the nerve center of all combat operations; during GQ it's crowded, bustling with activity, and on the noisy side. During GQ every sailor assigned to CIC was focused on his area of expertise; there wasn't time for discussing events that were occurring or had occurred. At the time, the 2000 to 0800 starboard watch had been on duty for more than 14 continuous hours. Following the latest mission, the port watch remained on duty and gave us a three-hour break. Following a rather long mission, ending after 0300, three or four of us were on the fantail talking and enjoying a smoke before turning in. Our discussion centered on the feedback from the Marine spotter; confirmation on how well the gun mount crews had performed. One of the radarmen was filling us in on how, minutes into the mission, the ship came under attack from enemy shore batteries. He continued by praising how the men manning our 20- and 40-millimeter AA guns instantaneously engaged and neutralized the threat.

As we were discussing the gun crews' performance, the XO approaches and sternly asks, "Shouldn't you be in your racks? You really need to get some sleep, so you're clearheaded for our next mission. Now come on guys, get with it!" We weren't sure whether to respond with "Aye, aye, sir!" or "but Mom, can't we stay up just a little bit longer?" It was the one and only time I ever heard this or anything similar from an officer. Even as we retold the story, other sailors struggled with the exchange as well. On the other hand, we fully understood his reasoning. We were part of his crew, and he recognized the long and wearisome hours may have an adverse effect on our performance. Our job was to perform at our highest level, and his job was to ensure we did; it became a toss-up over who had the more difficult task.

Once the captain became aware of the issue, he was committed to managing and relieving the situation. Over the 1MC he acknowledged the long hours and complimented the crew on their stamina and work, while promising to find a solution. Just knowing he recognized and understood the crew was struggling acted as a relief to some extent. With the captain's promise, we knew there was light at the end of the tunnel, only this time it wouldn't be coming in the form of an oncoming train. This was typical of our captain and clearly explained why the crew held him in such high esteem. We respected him because he respected us. Straightaway, we learned the captain opened discussions with the Marine base commander. Just speculating there may be a stress-relieving possibility in the works was a relief. Actually, to some extent, it began to ease our minds. We were confident his effort would result in some form of relief. It's difficult to explain how the anticipation of relief alone was energizing, exciting, and comforting. Yet, we didn't have any false expectations. We understood downtown Da Nang was off the table; it was anything other than a safe port of call. It was unlikely we would be heading to another country or port, as neither the Navy nor the Marines could afford our absence for more than a few hours; no more than the time it took to refuel or rearm.

Soon after, rumor had it, the captain was "negotiating" with the Marine commander for the crew to spend a few hours on one of the local beaches. This beach would be within the confines of Da Nang Marine Base. The Marine base commander liked the idea so much, he decided to include his Marines as well. Years later, I learned the beach was used by every branch of the military for R&R throughout the duration of the war.

Shortly thereafter, we returned to Da Nang after completing a night mission. Before beginning our patrol duties, several boatloads of sailors were transported from the ship to "China Beach," in Da Nang harbor. I recall it as being one of the most beautiful beaches I've ever visited. The overall beach ran for more than 20 miles along the coast of the South China Sea. However, for safety reasons, we were confined to a relatively small area within the limits of the base. Regardless of size, it was perfect for R&R, although it did have a few unusual quirks. The "safe area" was marked off by handmade red posts, less than a quarter mile apart along the shore. There were more than 200 Marines and sailors enjoying the white sandy beaches and the crystal-clear water, as heavily armed guards stood watch, and three Huey helicopters hovered overhead. Within minutes after arriving, the security guards seemed to blend into the landscape. We were there to enjoy ourselves, and by God that's exactly what we did! After several hours we returned to the ship and relieved our shipmates.

This continued in short spurts over a three- or four-day period, until the entire crew had a chance to kick back just a bit. During this R&R, the ship maintained the port and starboard watches. While half of the crew remained on watch, a quarter was transported to the beach, and a quarter remained on board. Those remaining on board were allowed to relax or catch a few hours of sleep. I would be remiss not to mention that while on the beach each sailor was given two bottles of ice-cold beer (low alcohol; I believe it was referred to as "near beer," but it tasted damn good!). When they broke out the beer, I thought the guys were going to burst into tears. What an absolutely sensational day, and if I recall correctly, we did it a second time during our assignment. But like all vacation days, it had to come to an end. It was time to get back to work, so let the war resume!

CHAPTER 19

Huey and a Few Good Men

It follows then as certain as that night succeeds the day, that without a decisive naval force we can do nothing definitive, and with it, everything honorable and glorious.

PRESIDENT GEORGE WASHINGTON

For the next few nights, we continued providing NGFS to the 3rd Marine Division while learning the Viet Cong were continuing their rapid buildup of troops. With the continued buildup of enemy forces, the region north of the Cu De River Bridge remained of extreme concern. This area has always been the focus of concern; it's in the vicinity where Highway 1A and the railroad converged. It's the primary route from Da Nang to all points north leading up to the border with North Vietnam.

One of the Marines whom I frequently interfaced with mentioned the senior staff were acutely aware of and troubled by the pace at which the enemy was increasing troops in the region. Every Marine and sailor was confident the Navy was working tirelessly to increase U.S. troops and equipment to confront this buildup. Yet, at the same time, we were aware of the Herculean effort necessary to reassign and mobilize the assets necessary to lessen or alleviate the threat. Each night we were called upon to provide hours of NGFS for Marine spotters. The majority of these missions were along the roads and paths both south of the Han River and west of the Cu De River Bridge. In addition to our nightly efforts, the Marines deployed Echo, Foxtrot, and Hotel companies to engage the Viet Cong. Yet the overall effort yielded minimal success. It was around this time when it became abundantly clear that the Viet Cong had very little regard for human life. The increase in missions resulted in a significant uptick in VC casualties; nevertheless, the scuttlebutt always suggested the number of enemy troops continuing to rise.

As time passed, confidence grew that the VC were preparing to mount a major offensive attack. The Navy and Marines were aware that in order to achieve their ultimate goal, the VC had to engage and ultimately defeat the 3rd Marine Division. During one of our trips to the Marine base, Lt. Bower was requested to attend an impromptu meeting. He mentioned I was the NGFS communicator for the ship, which allowed me to attend as well. The meeting consisted of a handful of Marines of different ranks, along with the two of us.

At the meeting, a junior Marine reminded us the Viet Cong were still on the move; even though the *Stoddard* fired over 200 high-explosive rounds, several Marine companies engaged them along a road, and they were also attacked by the Marine air wing. It was confirmed these combined efforts failed to slow the progress of the Viet Cong's troop buildup or impede their movement. The Viet Cong continued moving from the southern part of Da Nang north to beyond the Cu De River Bridge. It was suspected, within this region, the VC were assembling forces for an attack. The Marines also suspected the Viet Cong were beginning to assemble in smaller groups of troops under the cover of the trees and vegetation. Where was Agent Orange when you really needed it? The Marines reported that although the troop numbers were on the rise, the type or style of weapon observed, post encounter and inspection, remained the same. They failed to see weapons larger than handheld weapons and rifles in or around the fallen troops.

Another alarming observation was the report that came out of the area near the village of Hoa Minh, where the villagers reported seeing a large contingent of VC, which also included accounts some might be Chinese. Once again, it was believed the Chinese were primarily engaged in the training of troops and became collateral damage during several intense battles.

The sudden heavy buildup and training of enemy troops was thought to be a strategic change on the part of the VC. More than likely, it was initiated when the VC realized the United States was more than "guarding" the harbor; the Marines intended to control, defend, and protect Da Nang, along with the surrounding area. This recognition began as early as when the 3rd Marine Division landed and continued as additional U.S. forces mobilized. Their awareness may have peaked when the *Stoddard* was assigned to assist and support the Marines in their effort. It probably became more problematic after the enemy experienced the awesome firepower of a destroyer's guns against field forces. These developments may have required an immediate and major change in the VC's strategy. Unless they acted swiftly and decisively, it was likely they would permanently lose Da Nang.

At the same time, the Marines realized they were confined within a designated area; the Han River Bridge to the south, the Cu De River Bridge to the north, the Annamite mountain range to the west, and the South China Sea to the east. This meant that crossing either one of or both bridges gave an attacking force a clear and unobstructed path directly to the Marine base. The unknown question was how many VC troops were in the area to engage the Marines. Some unsubstantiated reports suggested there were 10,000–14,000 VC troops within the region.

While the Marines had installed large, fixed artillery facing the southern portion of the compound, they had little field artillery facing northward. Only a sizable field of brine and marsh separated the Marine base from the Cu De River Bridge. With the reported buildup of enemy troops, the Marines continued to post a squad at each bridge crossing. The Marines were fully aware that if they lost either bridge, the overall outcome and their survival would be questionable. But this brought about a second question: if the Viet Cong were building up forces to attack the Marine base, they'd require more than handheld weapons and rifles to support such an all-out assault. But where would such an armament come from?

Well, the answer was simple. They were most likely coming from the North and being smuggled into the area via an infrequently used means or route. If the Marines uncovered how the enemy was moving large pieces of artillery they could prevent, delay, and minimize the effectiveness of an all-out attack. After a brief discussion, it was ruled out that such weapons were being smuggled in by sea. We were confident every vessel large enough to carry heavy equipment and supplies was being stopped and thoroughly searched before reaching the coast. This led the Marines to suspect it was being smuggled in via rail or truck. Part of the question was answered a few days later when a window-of-opportunity mission was uncovered by the Marines.

***

Several days after the Cu De River battle, we returned to the harbor after completing our surveillance assignment. The South Vietnamese officer had just departed the ship when we received an urgent message. The message directed us to proceed to a location about halfway between Da Nang harbor and the border with North Vietnam.

The request mentioned a squadron of Marine helicopters coming upon a heavily guarded VC position or installation. According to the wire, when the choppers reduced altitude to get a better view, a small group of VC soldiers opened fire. As the Marines were preparing to return fire, the group retreated into what appeared as a casemate, carved into the side of a hill. Once the troops were inside, the rounds fired from the Marines' machine guns had little effect on what was believed to be a fortified entranceway. Fortunately, the entryway was facing in the direction of the South China Sea, which would allow us to participate in eliminating the threat. With concern over a possible attack, coupled with the knowledge that the VC must have fortified the compound for a reason, we were ordered to provide the firepower to render the compound inoperable or preferably destroyed.

Dusk had reached its final stage as we got underway and settled in on a northerly course. I was on the fantail when I heard and felt the screws come alive, as the engines began cranking up to full speed. I headed up to CIC and learned of the mission. I put on my headset and 10 or 15 minutes later was communicating with "Steel Rain." Steel Rain was the lead of three Marine helicopters involved in the mission. After completing the authentication protocol, the pilot advised that a large group of VC soldiers with whom they'd engaged had retreated into a "bunker" built into the side of a butte. (The authentication process wasn't limited to NGFS missions. It was a part of the process whenever two or more "friendly forces" were communicating. This prevented the enemy from imitating a friendly force with misleading requests, information, or directives.)

After confirming we were steaming in his direction, with orders to destroy the bunker, the lead Marine pilot advised they had received orders to remain on station and be available to participate in the mission. It was during this conversation that we learned the three helicopters lacked a trained Marine spotter. While this meant the mission would be a bit more complicated and challenging, it didn't mean it would fail. A solution would be found. This compound could be part of a staging or storage area, one of the components contributing to the potential attack on the Da Nang Marine base.

With the initial request using the phrase "storage depot," it was likely the Marines had uncovered a VC cache of weapons, ammunition, and other supplies. Regardless, whatever was being stored inside this fortified compound was of significant importance to the enemy and required our immediate attention. With our arrival well after nightfall, the area would be void of any light; the view from the ship would be utter darkness. Most importantly, the mission would lack the invaluable input of a trained Marine spotter.

As mentioned earlier, the maps associated with NGFS usually contained extraordinary detail. However, being a hidden compound, its physical location would not have been recorded on any maps. Upon receiving the assignment, we took a close look at the map. We were trying to determine if a warehouse or a similar structure was present in the area. If such an object was shown on the map where the X and Y coordinates would be readily available, the mission would be a walk in the park.

Knowing the Hueys lacked a trained spotter, we were confident any plan of attack would involve both the ship and the Marine helicopters. We had less than half an hour before arriving on station. Within this time, we had to develop a strategy along with a means of executing it. It didn't appear to be an overly complicated mission; the most important element was calculating the distance and bearing between the target and the ship. Once this data was available, the mission would be over in two or three sweeps of the radar. We were equally confident the firepower on the *Stoddard* was more than adequate to destroy the entrance of any fortified bunker.

The first decision was eliminating any idea of positioning a Marine in the area of the bunker. It was taken off the table because it presented too many risks, safety issues, and unknowns to justify further discussion. As the planning discussions continued, we were steaming to a position just off the coast from where the bunker was located. The water depths of the coastline were checked and they verified there would be an adequate amount of water beneath the hull, even at low tide.

At the captain's request, an open line was set up between the Bridge and CIC. This was requested so he could participate in the brainstorming phase of the mission. It was agreed that any and all plans would include the use of illumination rounds. And we took into consideration that its use comes with the liability of alerting enemy forces that more destructive weapons are likely to be forthcoming. We assumed the enemy's compound was designed to include multiple entrances and exits. The use of illuminating rounds had to be immediately followed by a series of accurately fired shells to destroy the reinforced entry. This would also include a barrage of high-explosive ammunition to ignite its contents. In other words, the bunker was more or less a fireworks display and it was our job to light the fuse.

During the attack, we would employ every weapon capable of reaching the target. If the mission went as planned, within a minute or two after the illumination rounds exploded, the bunker would be nothing more than another wartime memory. Knowing the bunker was close to the coast, we intended to use night-vision/range-finding binoculars. After firing the illuminations rounds, we would use these binoculars to calculate the relative bearing and distance to the target. Later they would be used to make the necessary gunfire adjustments. The main concern with this plan was whether we could get close enough and whether there'd be sufficient light to get an unobstructed view of the compound from the Bridge. Both were necessary to collect accurate data.

For the next 15 or 20 minutes, we discussed a number of scenarios before deciding upon the one that seemed to offer the highest likelihood of success and provided the least amount of risk. Under our plan, as we arrived on station, two of the Marine helicopters would take up positions on the northern and southern side of the hill holding the bunker. This would provide us with a rough idea of how far inland the compound was located from the shore. From this basic information, we would plot that position on our map and enter it as the data point into our fire-control system. When the helicopters maneuvered out of the danger zone, we would fire the illumination rounds. Once the targeted area was illuminated, all three Marine Hueys would fire on the fortified entrance. By observing the sparks, we could determine the exact bearing and get a better reading on the distance to the compound entrance. While the Marines continued to fire on the entryway, we would calculate an accurate bearing and range to the compound, enter the data in our fire-control system, reach a firing solution, and open fire with our 5-inch main armament. If we were close enough, we intended to employ our 40- and our 20-millimeter AA guns as well. The 20-millimeter gun had an effective firing range just under a mile. If we had a catapult to launch our depth charges far enough, they would have been included in the plan. It may redefine the definition of a mass firing mission.

The key to the success of this plan was whether we could get close enough to have an unobstructed view of the compound. Of course, we needed a backup plan for if we ran into unanticipated obstacles that might threaten the mission's success. Discussions continued and a decision was made; if we were unable to destroy the bunker, we would release the helicopters to return to their base. Simultaneously, we would go through the channels to request immediate air support from the carrier group. At the time, the carrier task force was operating several hundred miles offshore. We would remain on station until the attack aircraft arrived. Once in the area, we would fire a group of illumination rounds to provide the pilots with a clear view of the bunker. We were confident the senior staff on the carrier were aware of the situation and concerned over a potential offensive attack against the Marines.

As we were approaching the area, we informed the Marine helicopters of Phase 1 of our plan and they immediately responded with their support.

With the CIC officer's permission, I stepped outside to grab a breath of fresh air. Off in the distance, I could see the Marine helicopters firing on the target area. Remember, it was after nightfall and the area was absolutely pitch-black. Visually, I could clearly see the Hueys engaging the enemy, and it was a unique experience. The Hueys were firing tracer rounds, which gave the appearance of a line of light dashes. These dashes seemed to bend or arc as they found their way on target. They were firing on a location where ground fire was coming from. Up to this point, I wasn't aware the Marines continued to engage the enemy prior to our arrival.

Just a little more than a mile from our desired position, I took one last drag on a cigarette, flipped the butt overboard, and headed back into CIC. I put my headset on and informed Steel Rain we were approximately a mile from station. Steel Rain questioned our location, as he was unable to visually see a ship. I informed him we were under a mile from his location and tracking all three Hueys both visually and on radar. We would commence the mission within minutes.

Based upon observing the firing from the helicopters, we became more confident the bunker would soon become history. If our plan of attack was executed as designed, the compound would become a memory in about the time it takes a sailor to polish off a cold bottle beer following a month at sea. We confirmed we were in position and ready to fire the illumination round.

As we arrived on station, we estimated the distance and the bearing that dissected the two attacking helicopters. This data was immediately entered into the fire-control system. We reported we were ready to fire, as the chief skillfully vectored the helicopters to a safe position. He requested they remain there until the illumination round exploded. Once our radars confirmed they were no longer in harm's way, we fired the illumination round. I reported the shells were en route and to standby. As they ignited, one of the pilots yelled, "Holy shit, there's the entrance clear as day." Within seconds, all three Hueys opened fire on the compound entrance. Equally as fast, we realized our first obstacle raised its ugly head. There was a small mound or hill impeding or obstructing our view of the entrance to the compound. This hill had an adverse effect on our ability to obtain an accurate bearing and distance to the target. Shit, would this be the first mission we were unable to complete? With the captain's approval, I notified the Marines of the obstruction and informed them we'd be turning to our fallback plan. They would be released to return to their base and we would request air support from command.

The Marines just weren't going to have any of this fallback nonsense. Steel Rain transmitted, "There must have been instances you fired on targets that were not within your line of vision, similar to this situation." I informed him we did it all the time, but it always involved a trained Marine spotter who provided the target's coordinates and gunfire adjustments. With this data, we could calculate the direction and distance from the ship and enter it into our fire-control system. After firing the first salvo, the spotter would adjust our fire to close in on the target.

The next transmission was one I would remember for the rest of my life. The frequency comes alive with, "Fuck that, this bunker has to go!"

Steel Rain continued, "If I hover over its entrance, would you be able to get the bearing and distance to the target? One that would allow you to take it out?"

In all honesty, I had no idea how to respond. This request was extraordinarily dangerous. It was like asking a Marine to stand on the top of the compound and wave a light or flag in order to get the necessary firing data. Think about it, this junior Marine was willing to put his life on the line for every Marine stationed at the Da Nang base. It probably goes without saying, but you could hear a pin drop in CIC.

After what seemed to be an eternity, the silence was broken as the captain interrupted and entered the conversation: "This is the captain speaking, tell him it's achievable, however; he may have to direct our fire." As I exhaled, I mentally thanked "God" for making such a difficult decision. I informed Steel Rain of the captain's response, including the likelihood of having them participate in adjusting our gunfire. Then the thought crossed my mind, "Can this really be done, is it doable, or is this Marine willing to go too far out on a limb?" Are we willing to let him risk his life, when we were relatively confident the carrier task force commander would support our request? Is the risk–reward at least in balance? I hardly got the words out when Steel Rain responded with, "OK, let's do it!" And we're off to the races!

While the choppers were moving to a holding position, we began maneuvering offshore in an effort to improve or achieve a more favorable angle or shell trajectory. The captain adjusted the ship's position a bit more south in hopes of improving the angle to increase the likelihood of hitting the target. His insight and decision-making skills were the reasons why he was not only a great and caring man but an absolutely brilliant captain.

As we were repositioning, I explained to Steel Rain his role in the NGFS portion of the mission. We would fire several illumination rounds so he could move into position and hover directly above the compound's entrance. When his movement stopped, we would record the bearing and range from the compound. After obtaining the data, he would be released to clear the area to a location offshore. Following the choppers being vectored safely offshore, we would fire an illumination round which would immediately be followed with a salvo of a high-explosive rounds from our 5-inch guns. When he observed the HE shell explode, he would be required to estimate the yardage to the target in two directions; first, right to left and then, up and down. The right to left were the yards horizontal with the shoreline, whereas the up and down were the yards leading inland to or from the shoreline. As an example, if he observed the shell exploded south of the target by 50 yards and 75 yards beyond it, he would say (originating from a perspective from the shoreline), "Right 50, Down 75." Almost instantaneously he acknowledged he fully understood. It was always so rewarding working with Marines; they're savvy and void of any bullshit!

For safety reasons, we reiterated to the volunteer pilot that he was to remain at a safe distance from the bunker. He was to remain there until we fired the illumination round and lit up the area. Once the round exploded, the pilot would fly in the direction of the bunker, taking a route that would provide the least amount of risk, and hover directly over it for about five or six seconds. We would track him on our radars and realize he was over the target when his movement stopped. Some five or six seconds would be more than enough time to obtain the required data to satisfy the needs of the systems. After which, he would be instructed to depart the area as quickly and safely as possible. The Bridge would also attempt to use high-powered binoculars, as confirmation of the bearing and range.

Once we confirmed Steel Rain was in a safe location, we fired two illumination rounds. As the Bridge reported the area was illuminated, we watched as one of the helicopters began moving in the direction of the targeted area. The radarman on the radar read the chopper's bearing and range following every sweep on the scope; the gun-mounted radars were also locked onto the Huey.

In 20 to 30 seconds, the blip on the scope remained stationary, indicting he was hovering over the compound. We collected the data and began feeding it into our fire-control system. The chopper remained in its hovering position for well under the six-second estimate. With a nod from the CIC officer, I was so relieved to transmit: "Steel Rain, clear the area, I repeat, clear the area, Buckboard out!"

Within seconds after I finished my transmission, we received word the 51 mount was ready to fire and keyed the mike, "Steel Rain, standby, we are ready to fire." Upon confirming the Huey had cleared the firing area, was in a safe location, and with the captain's permission, we fired one HE round.

As I heard the gun fire, I broadcasted, "Shot fired!"

Now it was all up to Steel Rain to provide an accurate adjustment. After 15 or 20 seconds, the frequency came alive:

"You need to move south about 75 yards and about the same inland."

OK, it wasn't exact but we fully understand his instructions. We made the adjustment, and informed Steel Rain we were ready to fire a second salvo; he acknowledged the transmission. This went on a few more times. Finally, we received an adjustment:

"This is Steel Rain, the bunker is about 15 yards to the south."

That was close enough, we were basically on target, and we could take it from here. We'll continually adjust our firing to blanket the entire area with gunfire. At this point, the Bridge reported they had a visual on the location where the last round had exploded. This was incredible; knowing the compound may be within eyesight was a game changer; it meant we could employ multiple weapons in our fire for effect bunker attack.

We instructed all three Hueys to clear the area and head out to sea, well away from the impact zone. Once they were clear, we loaded one gun with an illumination round and the other three 5-inch guns with high explosives. The 40-millimeter AA were instructed fire to the left of where the last round had exploded.

Within seconds, after notifying Bridge and the Hueys to stand by, we fired the illumination round, followed by firing for effect; the 5-inch guns commenced firing HE rounds, along with the 40-millimeter guns. Several minutes passed, with the better part of 16 to 20 rounds being fired, without results. The firing data was slightly adjusted with each salvo. So far, we'd been unsuccessful in hitting the target, but I can assure you there wasn't the slightest thought to cease the firing. The noise of the rapid firing 40-millimeter guns, as well as the percussion originating from the 5-inch guns, was being carved into the memory of every sailor on board; it was an entirely new experience. To break the tension in the air, I recall the chief suggesting we consider rolling the depth charges, and his timing couldn't have been better.

Seconds later, the fuse was lit and had ignited the fireworks display. To this day I have never heard anything that even came even remotely close to the sound of the explosions that erupted. Every man on board heard and felt the impact of the eruptions, with many of us thinking the entire hill must have been leveled. The reaction of every sailor on board and the Marines in the helicopters said it all; it was just utter euphoria, jubilation, elation. The explosions were so intense, the helicopters repositioned themselves a few hundred yards further out to sea. But the excitement in their voices and dialog said it all. Steel Rain continually shouted into his mike:

"We got it, we got it, we got the God damn bunker!"

And he was absolutely right, "We got the God damn bunker," but it wouldn't have been possible without his fearlessness, bravery, and excellent input, combined with an extraordinary gun crew, who pulled out all the stops to make it happen.

As the explosions continued, the CIC officer encouraged a few men at a time to step outside to witness our success. When it was my turn, as I stepped out my mouth must have dropped. Over the years, I have been fortunate enough to have personally attended the 4th of July Macy's firework display over the Hudson River. Those displays paled in comparison to what I was witnessing from both a visual and audio perspective. It was positively mind-blowing and staggering. Almost immediately, I thought about my Uncle John's description of the fireworks display after learning the Japanese had surrendered at the end of World War II. I wondered if it was anything like what I was witnessing. The scene was almost indescribable; it seemed like the whole area was ablaze. But it was the men's faces that really told the whole story. They were waving their hands in the air and yelling in a joyous and celebratory manner.

For days, the only discussion on board centered around the crew's individual spin on the events of that mission. The definition of camaraderie could have been redefined as "the mutual trust, respect, friendship, and jubilation, among the sailors on board the *Stoddard* and the Marines in three Hueys, one July evening in Vietnam." It just doesn't get any better, or does it?

But our excitement may have been dwarfed by the concern that fell over much of the Marine base. Suddenly, there were more questions than answers. How many of these fortified compounds were in the area? How many large weapons were being stored? And how were they being smuggled into the region? One concern was eliminated, but it spawned any number of new ones.

***

We continued providing NGFS to the 3rd Marine Division. Intelligence reports continued to confirm the strengthening and buildup of Viet Cong troops in the area; this was especially the case to the north of the Cu De River Bridge. With Da Nang being 40 miles south of the border with North Vietnam, it was likely troops, weapons, and ammunition were being smuggled in from this region. To narrow it down, the area where Highway 1A and the railroad converged offered an excellent route between the Quang Tri Province and Da Nang. It was relatively isolated, provided overland or rail transportation opportunities and, resulting from a limited fighting force, was subjected to minimal surveillance by the Marines.

Throughout July 1965, the number of missions increased substantially. This increase impacted the *Stoddard*, the Marine ground forces, and their air wing. Each night these three "weapons" consistently dueled with the Viet Cong. The encounters took place along the roads and paths leading from the Han River Bridge northward toward the Cu De River Bridge. A detailed analysis concluded the encounters were having "marginal success" slowing down or reducing the enemy troop buildup. After nights of only limited success, according to my Marine contacts, confidence rose the VC were only weeks or possibly even days away from staging a major offensive. If the enemy waited much longer, the buildup of U.S. forces may prevent them from defeating the Marines and retaking control of the Da Nang harbor and airfield.

As we were wrapping up things following a visit to the Marine base, Lt. Bower was once again asked to attend an impromptu briefing. I was known to the Marines by now, as well as my involvement in NGFS, so no one questioned my entering the room. As with previous meetings, we joined a handful of Marines of different ranks around a small table. A junior Marine recapped what was widely known: although enemy forces were being engaged daily by the *Stoddard*, Marine ground forces, and air wing, the Viet Cong were on the move and their numbers continued to increase. At best, the three groups may have slowed down the VC's movements, and even that may have been an overly optimistic point of view.

The Marine continued his update by mentioning a reported troop buildup coming out from the village of Hoa Minh. Unquestionably, large shipments of weapons and supplies had to be transported into the area via rail or truck. The credibility of this theory was proven with the destruction of the storage bunker. Immediately following its destruction, it became imperative that more assets be committed to learning more about the enemy's movement of equipment and other supplies. The more the Marines understood the enemy's assets and intentions, the easier it would be to develop a strategy to counter their offensive.

One of the higher priorities was uncovering the Viet Cong's sources, means, methods, and contents of shipments being smuggled in from the North. It was suspected the storage areas were more than likely to be north of Da Nang. If stored south, the incoming shipments would have to pass close to Da Nang, making them far more complex, dangerous, and increasing the likelihood of them being detected by the Marines. Knowing the UDTs on board were free to move about the region, coupled with the knowledge we occasionally dropped them off north of Da Nang, Lt. Bower suggested discussing the matter with them. Soon thereafter, we learned a meeting between the UDTs and the Marines had taken place. As you would expect, no one from the *Stoddard* was in attendance. While we may not have been invited to the meeting, in short order we became involved in its outcome.

Some time had passed when the UDTs requested a meeting on the fantail. They opened up the meeting by mentioning that, with command's approval, they'd agreed to participate in a rather unusual mission. It turned out to be quite unorthodox; they'd received orders to prepare for a mission with an "unknown target, description, or location." Their goal was to find out if, how, when, and where the VC was moving troops, large pieces of military hardware, and munitions into the region. After careful analysis they identified two possible or likely routes leading from the North. Neither of these routes were under any regular surveillance by U.S. forces, with each running along the 40-mile stretch close to the border with the North.

Because of the unknowns, we were assigned to provide NGFS to support the UDT as needed. The plan divided the UDTs into two squads, one of which would be stationed at a location where two major roads intersected. The other would be stationed about three-quarters of a mile south, where a railroad switch was located. This switch was capable of diverting a freight train in the direction of Da Nang.

Potentially, two UDT spotters could be requesting NGFS simultaneously. To reduce the authentication time, each would have their own call sign. The team positioned to the north would be "Desoto R" (Desoto Romeo; the "R" designating the "Railroad" spotter), and the other "Kodiak H" (Kodiak Hotel; the "H" designating the "Highway" spotter). The UDT leader would be attached to Kodiak H. For authentication purposes, the following would apply:

Desoto R: "Buckboard, this Desoto Romeo, do you have the Tokens? Over."

Buckboard: "This is Buckboard, I do, they're in the jungle, the mighty jungle. Over."

Desoto R: "This is Desoto Romeo, Roger, The Lion Sleeps Tonight, coordinates __________ or standby."

Kodiak H: "Buckboard, this Kodiak Hotel, the shot heard round the world, over."

Buckboard: "This is Buckboard, Bobby Thompson a true Giant, over."

Kodiak H: "This is Kodiak Hotel, poor Ralph Blanca, Coordinates or Standby."

Again, if there were any ambiguities whatsoever, we would revert back to the normal authentication process.

At the conclusion of the meeting, we were advised this mission would commence the following evening. This may sound unusual, but the UDTs suggested the mission may be delayed if the weather was clear. Understandably, they preferred a light drizzle, especially during the first phase. Apparently, they were already operating in the area, however they would have to mobilize additional equipment and supplies for an extended stay. The rain would allow them to move easier and cover their tracks. The mission was scheduled to last a week but may be extended. For the *Stoddard*, waiting would be a major element in the mission and, for the crew, a godsend; it might provide a bit of rest or downtime. There would be limited activity unless the UDTs uncovered a shipment of VC weapons or met up with a company of enemy troops.

Later the same day, we were advised our participation would involve a specific number of hours each evening. The initial time frame was from 2200 to 0300, with additional transit time allotted for arriving on station. This time frame was selected because it was assumed the enemy had to cross the border, reach its destination, unload the weapons or goods, and return to the Northern border between nightfall and daybreak.

Taking into consideration the condition of the roads (rough by U.S. standards) and the location selected by the UDTs, the enemy had an overall window of approximately four hours to complete their work. It was believed these shipments would involve either unmarked railroad cars or truck containers. It was decided a 30-minute cushion would be added: 30 minutes on either side.

The mission would begin when the UDT group was dropped off at a predetermined location: one they selected to coincide with their other assignment. For several evenings, after participating in shortened NGFS missions, we would get underway and cruise at full speed to arrive at our station close to 2200. Each night after arriving on station, we sailed up and down the coast, covering a corridor about 10,000 yards in length (five nautical miles). As long as the communication frequency remained silent, the crew was allowed to remain at a stand-down state of general quarters. Mentally it was what the crew needed; it allowed time for them to clear their head or even write a few letters home. Because of the nature of the assignment distance, the UDT crew did not return to the ship each day. We assumed they hunkered down in the area during daylight, returning to their other duties and surveillance operations after nightfall.

We continued this pattern for a few evenings. Once on station, we continued sailing in the same corridor off the coast for the remainder of the night. The sailors in CIC were aware the frequency would remain silent, unless the UDTs needed our support.

I'm relatively confident there were daily communications between the UDT crew and Command; however, we were not included in the loop. There was a suggestion of broadcasting the message "on station" when we arrived each evening. Knowing the UDTs would only activate their radio when needed, the idea was immediately shelved. Our daily routine became as normal as weighing anchor. We got underway and provided NGFS for the 3rd Marines before heading north to cruise along the corridor some 3,000 yards off the coast. While we lacked direct communications or dialog with the UDTs, we knew Command would update us if there were any changes that impacted our involvement. Regardless, not hearing any radio communications or updates became a bit nerve-wracking. To ensure the equipment was functioning properly, I requested Burl Roads, the ET on duty in CIC, to check out the gear and double check we were dialed into the correct frequency. Roads confirmed all was in order.

Let me build upon that for a second, the Navy must have invested heavily into the design and manufacturing of the highest-quality radio equipment. The radio transmitters and receivers operated 24/7, and I can honestly say, I'm unable to recall even the slightest problem with the system. It goes without saying, there were radiomen and ETs stationed nearby to ensure all lines remained open and operating properly. The overall performance of all electronics was flawless and as close to perfection as one could imagine. I'm confident it was the ETs' preventative maintenance program in port that paid off in spades when we were at sea.

Let me also add, we had emergency backup networks and frequencies for a number of reasons. Yet I'm unable to remember even once missing a message or any communication resulting from faulty equipment. Even the headset I used during NGFS missions had a defined service life expectancy, expressed in hours of operation. I was provided with a new headset at regular intervals. Occasionally when operating stateside, we'd pick up a transmission on a frequency from an unknown source; one not attached to our task force. When this occurred, the flagship would transmit a classified message changing to an alternate frequency, but even these adjustments were few and far between.

The overall preventive maintenance program practically eliminated equipment failures. If they did occur, the crew was so well trained that corrective action would be immediate, with the issue usually resolved within minutes. While generally rare, the most major failure seemed to center around one of the evaporators. Evaporators are used for converting salt water into fresh water. When the salt water was heated to a boiling point, the steam was captured and condensed, producing fresh water. The salt in the water is not carried over in the steam. The failure of one of the evaporators meant all of the fresh water produced by the other unit would be committed to the operation of the four oil-fired boilers. For the most part, it was usually back online the same day. As addressed earlier, when an evaporator repair was projected to take longer than a day, the officer of the deck (OOD) kept an eye open for a rain squall.

As mentioned, these squalls became the crew's "shower" and were necessary for maintaining proper hygiene until the repair was completed.

Back to the mission. Early in the assignment, as we were providing NGFS, we encountered an unusual amount of enemy resistance from a position to the south. The resistance involved what appeared to be a large shore battery firing in our direction. The battery was so far away that the shells fell harmlessly into the South China Sea. Visually, the enemy could not see the ship; we assumed they must have been firing in the direction of the fireballs, created when a round left a gun mount. The firing was so brief, the ship's radars were unable to accurately identify the shore battery's precise location. The belief that a major offensive attack by the VC was highly probable caused a high sensitivity to any and all field artillery. We notified our spotter and included the approximate coordinates of the weapons. He passed the information on to command.

Shortly thereafter we received a cease-fire order from the spotter, got underway, and set a northerly course. As we were coming about, we learned the Marine spotter was ordered to investigate the reported shore battery. We were directed to remain on station and support his assignment. This order meant we would be arriving late to the region under surveillance by the UDT crew. In approximately 30–45 minutes, the spotter located a nest of enemy artillery and provided the coordinates for their removal. Following a single gunfire adjustment, the nest was neutralized by a barrage of gunfire, and we were steaming to our UDT designated rendezvous point. Although we were still miles from our normal station at the time, if a situation developed, we were within range to support the needs of the UDT team. We arrived off the coast close to midnight and began our slow zigzag maneuver.

At this juncture, many of the crew began to feel somewhat disappointed and questioned if our time was being wasted. It was precious time; time that could be more constructively used to combat a strengthening enemy or catch a bit more sleep. As a reminder, throughout the mission we remained in a "stand down" level of General Quarters. Our CIC officer mentioned the probability that the shipments of supplies were being randomly scheduled, rather than occurring every night or on a regular basis. And while the shipments may be infrequent, more than likely they were of considerable size.

On the second or third day, we received orders that Command was extending the length of the UDT mission. Like every previous night, the radio frequency remained silent.

For several more days, as the Marines identified new enemy movements in the region, we continued providing NGFS before steaming to the coastal corridor. With the increase in NGFS missions, we began arriving on station closer to 2300 than 2200, returning to Da Nang per the original plan.

However, everything changed when we were less than a week into the mission. At around 0130, the network line came alive:

"Buckboard, this is Desoto Romeo, do you have the Tokens, over?"

My heart rate, along with the heart rate of every sailor within earshot of this transmission, increased. I felt the adrenaline beginning to kick in. Could this be it? I responded:

"This is Buckboard, I do, they're in the jungle, the mighty jungle, over."

As the ship's crew was called to GQ:

Desoto R: "This is Desoto Romeo, Roger, The Lion Sleeps Tonight. Kodiak Hotel, *do you copy?* Over."

Kodiak H: "Roger Desoto, Buckboard this is Kodiak Hotel, the shot heard round the world, over."

OK, this was never discussed as part of the authentication process, but we all understood Desoto wanted to address both the *Stoddard* and the other UDT unit simultaneously. Great move, Desoto! I responded:

"This is Buckboard, Bobby Thompson, a true Giant, over."

"Roger, this is Kodiak Hotel, poor Ralph Blanca, over to Desoto."

"Buckboard, Kodiak, this is Desoto, loud sounds of truck engines off in the distance and closing, coordinates X-2314, Y-8434, one-gun, main armament, illumination round, at my command, will adjust. Fire for effect will be continuously firing two guns, main armament, high explosive, fuse quick, over."

Hmm, why only two guns?

Buckboard: "This is Buckboard, coordinates X-2314, Y-8434, one-gun, main armament, illumination round, at my command, will adjust. Fire for effect will be continuously firing two guns, main armament, high explosive, fuse quick, over."

Desoto R: "Believe we have a convoy, Kodiak shift positions, provide Buckboard with road coordinates in your area, you will be the first to engage the lead vehicle. Buckboard do you copy and understand?"

Buckboard: "This is Buckboard, Roger, understand! Ready for additional coordinates, over."

Desoto R: "Buckboard, Kodiak, this is Desoto; Kodiak will provide coordinates and I want one gun, main armament, illumination at Kodiak's command, will adjust. Fire for effect will be continuous firing of two guns main armament, high explosive, fuse quick. Buckboard, I want continuous firing with the two guns for Kodiak to slowly be adjusted from south to north and Desoto's guns slowly adjusted from the north to the south. I repeat, the first salvo for both positions will be an illumination shell for adjustment, over!"

As I was repeating Desoto's mission request and data, I, along with everyone in CIC and most on the Bridge, immediately understood Desoto's plan; it was brief but abundantly clear. He was asking us to prepare to fire upon what he believed to be a convoy of trucks carrying VC troops, weapons, equipment, ammunition, and other supplies. To maximize the effect or impact of the gunfire, the team would be providing coordinates at two separate locations, initially a mile or so apart. The actual distance was dependent upon the number of vehicles and length of the convoy. If that wasn't shrewd enough, he intended for us to open fire with two 5-inch guns aimed toward the lead vehicle and the other two pointed toward the vehicle at the end of the convoy. Once we opened fire, we would slowly adjust the fire-control system to allow the shells to shift from both ends toward the center of the convoy. The plan was simply mindboggling, off the chain, brilliant! To the best of my knowledge, it may have been a first; it was unlike anything covered in NGFS school, performed during practice missions, or from prior experience.

As I'm repeating Desoto's instructions, the captain calls CIC and inquires if the request is achievable. Unquestionably, our fire-control system was designed to contest multiple targets simultaneously; executing this request would be a no-brainer for this ship, the equipment, or its crew. For clarification, as with all missions we were using the same NGFS map as the spotters. A detailed layout of road was clearly shown on the map. Once the spotters made their adjustment and we were locked on both targets, we could easily adjust or recalculate the coordinates along the road (direct fire). We were also confident that if the airbursts began to drift off target, the UDT spotters would provide an adjustment.

However, the captain's request may have caught Lt. Bower a bit off guard, as he responded with, "Sir, I don't believe it's ever been done before." To which the captain replied, "My question is, can it be done? I'd like an answer and I'd like it now!" Lieutenant Bower said he'd get back to him momentarily, to which the captain said, "Get on it and I mean get on it now!" Holy shit, hearing the captain's tone of voice made me wonder if a whole bunch of sailors were about to soil their skivvies; this was absolutely unprecedented.

There wasn't much of a discussion; we all knew it was very doable and marveled at the sheer genius of the idea. In a matter of seconds, the captain was given confirmation it was viable and implementation of the plan was underway. After some thought, I was more than confident the captain was more than aware we had the capability of performing the mission; it was nothing more than the captain's way of confirming we were all operating on the same page.

The night was pitch black, not a light or shadow could be seen in any direction. In our favor was the sea and weather; the sea was calm, with the temperature and humidity tolerable. Also, both the air and surface radars were clear of any skunks or bogeys. We were physically located less than 1,500 yards off the coast.

The radarman, over sound-powered phones connected with the Bridge, heard the captain give the orders to keep a lookout for any signs of lights or headlights coming from the north. We later learned we were not the only ones operating under the condition known as darkened ship; well, in the enemy's case "semi-darkened truck."

A few minutes later the circuit once again came to life as Kodak's team arrived at their position:

"Buckboard, this is Kodiak." He went on to provide the road coordinates in his area.

We locked these coordinates into our fire-control system and awaited Kodiak's release to fire. This release would be given when the enemy's vehicles entered the targeted zone. After repeating the NGFS data, I transmitted:

"Desoto, this is Buckboard, did you copy?"

Desoto R: "Roger, copied."

From this range, it would be rather easy to immobilize the lead truck. It may have been a different matter if the enemy used a rail system. On the other hand, if an unscheduled shipment was being made by rail, we assumed the UDT would have set explosives to derail the locomotive or lead cars. It would not have surprised me if both UDT crews set explosives on the roadway to prevent any of the vehicles from escaping by destroying the lead and end trucks.

At this point, we had already loaded one illumination round in the forward and aft gun mounts; the other two guns were also ready to fire, each loaded with a high-explosive round. From the first contact with Desoto until we were ready to fire on both targets, we had a maximum of 15 minutes. This included the time required for Kodiak to relocate from the railroad tracks to the roadway and provide the applicable coordinates. Upon being informed the rounds were loaded, I notified the spotters:

"Desoto, Kodiak, this is Buckboard, ready over."

Both replied, "Ready, out."

We were confident Command had confirmed the South Vietnamese military was not expecting any truck shipments from regions to the north of Da Nang. We were equally confident that Desoto would verify the truck convoy contained enemy troops, military weapons, equipment, and supplies as best he could. It was believed any shipment of weapons would consist of more than crates of small arms, rifles, or handheld weapons. In order to stage a major offensive, the VC required shipments of large pieces of artillery; artillery large enough to provide massive destructive power to maximize casualties.

Unless the mission was terminated by Desoto, the next communication would come from Kodiak in the form of a release to commence firing. In the interim, it was time to just sit and wait, unquestionably the absolute hardest part of any battle. No further communications were necessary; Desoto and Kodiak were professional and experienced warriors with an upmost degree of confidence in each other's talents and capabilities. With that in mind, I wasn't expecting any notification as the convoy approached and passed the position held by Desoto. And I was equally confident both spotters had taken up positions which gave them the widest view of the road and the targeted area.

It was just after 0200 when the radio headset came to life.

"Buckboard, this is Kodiak, fire, over."

And so it began, as I repeated, "This is Buckboard, fire out."

When I heard the round leaving our aft gun mount, and knowing a high-explosive round would be loaded before the illumination round even detonated, my reply was simply the word "shot." Kodiak immediately knew he had an incoming round. Seconds later, Kodiak replied with an adjustment, followed by "fire for effect," releasing us to begin continually firing two of our 5-inch guns at the lead vehicles of the convoy. After firing less than 10 rounds, we began to slowly adjust our firing to the north, toward the center of the convoy. Prior to receiving the release to fire, we decided the adjustments would be made in 100-yard intervals, thus overlapping previously fired rounds by a minimum of 50 yards.

Almost immediately, we began hearing the impact and effectiveness of our firing, and the news didn't come from Kodiak but rather from the Bridge. They reported witnessing numerous large explosions, with fireballs igniting the entire area.

About 10 minutes later the frequency came alive once again:

"This is Desoto, fire."

Because both forward mounts were firing continuous rounds of HE shells, we asked the gun mount to notify us when the illumination round was fired. That happened seconds after the release, to which I transmitted, "Desoto, shot."

A few seconds passed and the illumination round detonated. Immediately, Desoto provided a rather large adjustment south from the original coordinates. This was actually expected; Kodiak ordered us to fire when the forward-most vehicles arrived at the preset coordinates, whereas Desoto adjusted his target coordinates to coincide with the position of the last vehicles. By destroying the first and last several vehicles, it created sufficient wreckage to prevent those in the middle from fleeing.

After firing a second round at Desoto's adjusted coordinates, Desoto made a minor adjustment and ended with, "Fire for effect, two guns main armament, over." After repeating the adjusted firing data, I continued with "fire for effect, two guns main armament, out." Once again, our forward guns began firing while slowly making 100-yard incremental adjustments to the south. For the better part of an hour, not a minute passed without a sizeable explosion and fireball. As the firing closed in on the middle of the convoy, the Bridge reported a large stretch of land appeared to be ablaze. As time passed, the frequency of explosions began to lessen. Finally, the Bridge reported that it appeared all four guns were firing within the same area. This was confirmation the fore and aft mounts had reached their objective and were essentially firing at the center of the convoy. At the request of the Bridge, I asked Desoto:

"Should we continue firing on these coordinates?"

Desoto: "Buckboard, this is Desoto, we still see movement, standby, do you copy Kodiak?"

Kodiak: "We also see movement, standby, over."

I began pondering the definition of "movement"; did he see the movement of enemy troops, or were vehicles still operational? As if it really mattered.

Within minutes we were provided with revised firing coordinates by both spotters and similar adjustments were made for about another half hour. Finally, we received the ceasefire order from Kodiak and less than 10 minutes later, a ceasefire from Desoto.

This was followed by Desoto advising that both teams remain on station until daybreak. At the break of day, they would inspect the wreckage to insure all the vehicles, artillery, and supplies were destroyed or rendered unusable. Desoto requested we remain off the coast to provide any cleanup firing or additional support if necessary. The Bridge, hearing the request, contacted Command and a few minutes later confirmed we'd remain on station as requested. Command was a team of Navy professionals, a team responsible for the scheduling of all activities within the region. It was against Navy policy for any ship to arrive, remain on, or depart from a station without the knowledge of and permission from Command. Part of a mission's description usually included when to engage and disengage. If any changes were necessary, they could only be made and authorized by Command.

We changed course and proceeded to operate about two miles offshore for the rest of the night. The crew remained at GQ stations, but in a stand-down condition. However, the order to stand down only applied to specific crew members. Two of the 5-inch gun mounts, one fore and aft, remained at GQ. The stand-down order also included most key functions including the Bridge, CIC, radio control room, engine room, etc. In almost all cases, these functions were manned by the starboard watch crew (2000 to 0800). The rest of the men were given a little time to unwind; all the while knowing all hell could break loose at a moment's notice. After a short break, the men on watch were temporally relieved to get a bite to eat, hit the head, and grab a "fresh" cup of stale coffee.

When it was my turn, I was in awe stepping onto the main deck. I observed a huge strip of land burning. It was difficult to comprehend exactly how much destruction we had caused. Unexpectedly, I recalled the spotter's reaction the first time we fired a few weeks ago: It was like the landscape was instantly transformed from summer into winter. Mentally, I was picturing the entire area leveled, including its color. As it burned, it almost appeared the entire region was being transformed to black and white. Continuing to inspect our evening's work, there was a relatively large explosion in the northern end of the fire zone. Suddenly, I was struck with concern over the UDT's safety. I briefly thought of returning to CIC to confirm no one was injured or affected by the explosion. However, common sense suggested otherwise.

As the morning broke, the fires began to die down, but smoke continued to rise from the area. I was hoping Kodiak and Desoto were in the final stages of their inspection. We suspected local residents would be showing up to salvage anything that appeared to be useable. We were confident the UDTs possessed sufficient qualities of explosives to destroy any equipment that may have survived the attack. About 30 minutes after sunrise, between 10 to 15 explosions could be seen and heard radiating from the area. That was clever; rather than destroying any useable equipment as they came across it, they set timed explosives to eliminate them simultaneously. The explosions most likely occurred after the team exited the area. From the size and number of explosions, I was confident a survey of the wreckage would confirm the equipment was no longer operational or salvageable.

Following a rather large explosion, the radio frequency came alive:

"Buckboard, this is Desoto, mission completed and you are released, over."

"This is Buckboard, Roger mission completed and we are released, out."

Those words were followed by a deep sigh of relief as we changed course and headed "home." We had sailed less than two miles when the ship began slowing down. I returned to CIC to learn the UDT crew requested a "ride home." As their boat pulled alongside and a rope ladder dropped, the UDT unceremoniously saluted the OOD as they stepped onto the main deck. Once on board, they nodded to the crew members closest to the rope ladder and headed for the showers; it was all in a day's work. And to expand on that just a bit and dispense with any thoughts this mission was any different, not a single word was exchanged with the crew. It was void of any post-mission critique, comments about the smoothness of the evening's events, or mention of what was destroyed, not even a "screw you." No one on board had a need to know anything more about the mission. Most importantly, we later learned that the UDTs passed all relevant data onto Command and the Marine base. While this particular mission may have ended, a very important question remained: what was the final destination for the shipment?

CHAPTER 20

The Imperialist Ship *Stoddard*

Late the same afternoon, Lt. Bower and I headed over to the base to pick up the latest maps and charts; these would involve an area north of Da Nang closer to the border with North Vietnam. Shortly after our arrival, Lt. Bower was asked to attend an impromptu meeting. Earlier, the Marines reported there was an area to the south where a large contingent of enemy troops may be assembling. He thought this may be the topic.

Upon entering the room, a senior-level Marine advised the primary reason for the meeting was to discuss continuing concerns following the previous night's mission. He offered a bit more information about the battle, including that there were no enemy survivors and a sizeable amount of artillery and ammunition had been destroyed. But the overall report was quite unsettling. There were many questions and few answers pertaining to the volume of weapons, artillery, and ammunition that may have been previously smuggled into the area, as well as about their whereabouts.

He stated all routes and trails leading toward Da Nang would be monitored around the clock. This would be accomplished through additional air surveillance and advanced scouting forces on the ground. We assumed the Marines had mobilized additional troops in Da Nang. In addition, the removal of assets, such as bridges and trestles not part of the U.S.–South Vietnamese long-term strategic plan, would be accelerated. To be perfectly honest, with the *Stoddard* lacking any sort of an identified role in the plan, I'm uncertain of its success. We presumed our attendance was to notify us of the likelihood that NGFS missions would be conducted further from Da Nang. Returning to the ship, Lt. Bower mentioned the possibility of increased daytime NGFS missions. Such a change in plans would impact our patrolling and searching assignment. If this were the case, we were confident Command had plans to ensure this important activity continued.

From the tone of the meeting, it was obvious the base remained extremely concerned a VC major offensive attack was eminent. Assuming this concern was accurate, Command and the Marines were aware of two major but opposing factors that were in play. First, the Navy was actively and expeditiously advancing the buildup of fighting forces and other assets in the Da Nang region. This buildup would thwart any future attempts to attack the compound and likely reduce the Viet Cong's presence in the region. Second, in order to take control of Da Nang harbor and airfield, the VC would have to kill every American and South Vietnamese fighter in the region.

As we exited the room and were heading back to the dock, we ran into one of the Marines I met during the "day at beach" event. I immediately noticed he was grinning from ear to ear. He began the conversation with, "So, how does it feel to be famous, no, infamous." In my most eloquent military language I asked, "What the fuck are you talking about?"

He continued, "Wait, are you saying you haven't listened to the great rock and roll music being played on the North Vietnamese propaganda channel?" Seeing a blank expression on my face, he began to realize I hadn't a clue what he was talking about. He began telling me about a station based in North Vietnam that played American music from the late 1950s and early 1960s. I'm talking "our" music, the good music, well before the British invasion with such groups as the Beatles, the Hollies, the Zombies, and, of course, the Rolling Stones. I'm talking about the Coasters, the Five Satins, the Drifters, or Buddy Holly and the Crickets; you know, the really great music!

He continued to say that during the previous night's broadcast, their notorious announcer, Hanoi Hanna, referenced the *Stoddard* during her propaganda rant. To be honest, I thought this Marine was busting my stones. From his reaction, I became a believer. I was sold on the story when he offered to provide the frequency of the broadcast. As we were returning to the ship, I mentioned this little gem to Lt. Bower. At first, he found it to be a bit funny or possibly even unsettling. However, by the time we pulled alongside the ship, he had a change of heart. Rather than being unsettling, he began thinking it actually may have some positive roots; it could be something we "needed," and mentioned his intent to discuss it with others.

The following day, Lt. Bower stopped in CIC and asked if I could record Hanoi Hanna's broadcast on the ECM (electronic countermeasures) equipment. I responded "absolutely," mentioning any radarman could record it. He asked me to record it and to keep it just between us for the time being. I wondered what he had up his sleeve. I had already mentioned it to a few close shipmates, and they thought it was comical and interesting. Assuming the ECM equipment was available, I intended to record it ASAP. It wasn't exactly rocket science to record the program. It was as simple as setting up a tape and scheduling it to record a specific frequency, at a predetermine time, for a specific time period.

The following evening, as I assumed my 2000 to 0800 watch, I scheduled a tape to record the frequency provided by the Marine. I set it up to record at a slightly slower speed; this way the tape would run longer, with no impact on the quality of the recording. It could easily record most of the 12-hour watch. The Marine mentioned her show only aired in the evening and the timing fluctuated from night to night. My plan was to remove the tape from the ECM gear at the end of the watch.

The evening was relatively slow. We participated in an NGFS mission beginning around 0200. We fired a half-dozen rounds for harassment rather than effect. The Marines advised there were groups of VC troops scattered throughout the area. The sound of a 5-inch airburst round would keep their attention and be very disquieting. By spreading the gunfire over a rather wide area, it would prevent the entire area from resting comfortably. Being at GQ limited any interest or awareness the ECM equipment was even recording. Following the stand-down from GQ, one of the ET's mentioned the ECM gear was activated. I told him I had turned it on to erase an old tape, one to be used if we were called upon to perform any coastal electronic surveillance. For the record, if such a recording was ordered, a new tape would have been used. But it answered his question and the conversation ended,

At the end of the watch, I removed the tape, made my way to the radar equipment room, loaded it into the playback device, rewound it and pressed "play." This super-heterodyne receiver allowed the operator to fast forward through a tape and stop at even the weakest of signals. It was so sophisticated that it would automatically stop and back up to a position before the signal. In less than five minutes I covered more than three hours of the recording. Approximately halfway through the third-hour period, the machine came to a screeching halt and backed up to where the sound originated. Suddenly, a woman's voice could be heard in my headset. I carefully listened to every word she spoke. However, due to her strong accent, trying to understand her was quite challenging. Rather than talking in complete sentences, she spoke more by means of broken words. My main focus remained: would she once again mention the *Stoddard*? After a few minutes of ranting, she began playing, "Tonight, Tonight" by the Mello-Kings, a much-welcomed sound for some weary ears. Following another propaganda rant, up comes "Tear Drops" by Lee Andrews and the Hearts; could this woman know I was listening? These were two of my favorite songs; if this was Hanoi Hannah, I loved her.

Not knowing the length of her broadcast and before going any further, I stopped the tape and visited the mess deck to grab a little grub. It was probably the Marine version of SOS (or Shit-on-a-Shingle, also known as creamed chipped beef on toast) which used ground beef. It was one of my favorite breakfast meals. I enjoyed it as much as the chipped beef in a cream sauce on toast (shit-on-a-shingle, Navy style). I also enjoyed the reconstituted powdered eggs but was never a fan of powdered milk.

Following breakfast, rather than heading toward OI Division crew quarters, I decided to return to the radar equipment room and continue listening to the tape. After notifying CIC of my whereabouts, I lay down on the rubber mat covering the floor and put my headset back on. After more anti-American rhetoric, up comes "Angel Baby" by Rosie and the Originals; and the hits keep on coming. But I was tired and before the middle of the song drifted off into sleep. When I woke, only the sound of static could be heard on the headset. Looking at the time, I realized her show lasted about 30 minutes. Subsequently, I learned she recorded and broadcast as many as three shows a day.

I rewound the tape to the beginning of the show and began listening once again. I have to admit, the sound of a woman's voice in my headset, regardless of the accent, was unusually comforting. I carefully listened to every word, rewinding the tape when her accent caused a problem. Frequently, she mentioned her broadcast was intended "for all American servicemen within range of the signal." Every show opened by focusing on "all the wonderful things that were happening back in America." She always mentioned how the troops were missing out on so much back home, while reminding us how our "fellow Americans opposed the government's decision to attack the Vietnamese people."

Years later, I learned many veterans felt each word in her narrative was well orchestrated and her presentation flawless. As my experience was of her first broadcasts, I found them to be quite the opposite. I felt they could be better described as unscripted rants. Possibly her "show," accent, and pronunciation of English words, matured over the years. For me, though I struggled to understand her speech, it was generally coherent. Regardless, I still liked the sound of a female's voice, loved the music she played, and laughed at her attempt to be relevant or "cool." She did so by using the latest expressions or slang; it seemed every other word was "GI" this or "GI" that. Her shows always began and concluded with a message questioning the legitimacy of our "invasion" into her "beloved country." This was followed by how our "Marines were ruthlessly killing civilians, women and children." And unless we stopped immediately and left their shores, we would be "slaughtered like pigs." Not the best message to hear before turning in. Most of her messages were less than amusing; better yet, they were quite disturbing. But once you realized it was propaganda, you tuned out her rhetoric, sat back, and enjoyed the music.

During every broadcast, she found a way of addressing particular military units. Once again, such references seemed extremely creepy. As an example, she may say "this next song is dedicated to all the Marines, in the 3rd Marine Division, in Da Nang." It was her way of saying, if she knew your location, so did the North Vietnamese and Viet Cong. But rather than having a negative impact on morale, I would argue it had the exact opposite effect. While being odd or strange, it eventually became a form of notoriety.

About halfway through the broadcast, she said, "This is for all the lonely sailors, who miss their loved ones and family, on the Imperialist ship *Stoddard* anchored in Da Nang harbor." Her announcement ended with the playing of "The End of the World" by Skeeter Davis. Oh my God, we hit the jackpot, bingo, utopia! The Marine was right, we had been identified and recognized as a true threat to the VC. It was likely the *Stoddard* was entered into the record books as the first U.S. Navy vessel to achieve this recognition, distinction, and "notoriety." We were referenced by Hanoi Hannah; it doesn't get much cooler! While I was excited to mention my findings to Lt. Bower, it could wait. Getting some sleep was an order of magnitude more urgent.

Around 1400 hours, I found Lt. Bower and told him the recording produced gold. After explaining the contents of the tape, I told him it was all set up for him to listen. He asked me to join him, so we headed up to the radar equipment room. Before putting on the headset, I cautioned him about the propaganda rhetoric. He pressed play and listened to the entire broadcast. I could tell from his facial expressions, and the number of times he rewound the tape, he was struggling with her accent. In the end, he liked most of what he heard. He believed the recording would be received and enjoyed by the entire crew, believing it may be a morale booster. He wanted others to hear it, so I set it up to begin about a minute before the charming Miss Hannah "honored" the *Stoddard.*

As with many evenings, we were requested to fire half a dozen rounds for harassment at "Charlie." The rounds were randomly fired in 10- to 25-minute intervals. After receiving a cease-fire," Lt. Bower mentioned the propaganda tape would be played for the crew. It would be played during lunch or dinner on the mess deck. He mentioned he'd spoken to the chief and requested the ECM equipment record Hanoi Hannah's future broadcasts. Of course, this only applied if the ECM equipment wasn't needed for official business.

To save time, ET Burl Roads used the same setup he used for playing the San Diego rock and roll tapes. The propaganda tapes became a hit, with many crew members sticking around to enjoy an extra cup of caffeine or a glass of "bug juice" (aka Kool-Aid) while listening to some great music. There was always excitement when a new tape was recorded and played. During the broadcasts, the crew clapped and shouted whenever the *Stoddard* received our well-deserved recognition. They also booed the propaganda she continued to serve up. From a morale perspective, it was an overwhelming success. With the mobilization of U.S. troops in South Vietnam still in its earliest stages, we received frequent recognition. During our assignment as Da Nang harbor defense ship, more than half of her broadcasts mentioned the "Imperial Ship *Stoddard*." For the entire crew, it was much like a badge of honor.

The Cu De River Bridge: The Sequel

With the successes realized at the Cu De River battle, the destruction of the weapons storage bunker and now the truck convoy, we thought there may be a lull in the number of missions. However, the buildup of VC troops continued, but rather than assembling in large groups, they were scattered though out the region in small clusters, and further from the harbor. Instead of being at general quarters half the night, we were assigned missions that generally ended shortly after midnight. This allowed the port watch (0800 to 2000) to catch a few extra hours of sleep.

I overheard the OOD ask the Vietnamese officer his opinion on the string of Viet Cong losses and defeats experienced by the enemy. His belief paralleled the American assessment of the situation. He agreed our recent victories had more than likely hastened or motivated the Viet Cong to expedite their plans of taking control of Da Nang. He suspected the Viet Cong realized these defeats would continue unless they took a more aggressive posture. Indisputably, the United States was aware of the situation and additional military assets were beginning to arrive. The destruction of the weapons storage compound and truck convoy proved the U.S. forces shifted from a defensive posture to one focused on a more offensive approach. Allowing the United States to continue the buildup of troops and weapons while increasing the number of warships in coastal waters might prevent the possibility of the VC retaking Da Nang.

Following the most recent battle, the crew seemed refreshed and it appeared they'd returned to some degree of normalcy (whatever that meant). Walking along the main deck revealed the majority of sailors had more spring in their step and generally appeared less tense. Most of the crew were able to take regular showers, along with three or four hours of uninterrupted sleep. Of course, the question was: how long would it last?

As July wound down, my Marine contacts suggested the number of VC troops continued to rise. I recall one of the Marines questioning the accuracy of earlier reports. He suggested the increase in surveillance may be distorting recent enemy troop reports. Regardless, the only recourse for the Marines was to assume the worst and prepare accordingly. Since the attack on July 22 near the Cu De River Bridge, there hadn't been a major encounter with enemy troops. Most of the action could be defined as skirmishes rather than battles. However, the Marines continued with preparations to counter any offensive attack.

It was believed the internal VC reconnaissance reports must have been distressing to their Command. Regardless of troop size, they were defeated at every battle when up against U.S. forces. The Marines and sailors were well aware that the loss of the Da Nang airfield and the port would have a devastating impact on our overall war effort. However, as this cat and mouse game continued to evolve, I wondered if the cat was aware it was stalking an American Raptor.

While there were signs the buildup of enemy troops continued, there were also signs the Navy had already taken and would take further proactive measures to prevent or lessen the threat of an enemy attack. Several additional destroyers were assigned to the region and they began patrolling along the coast, both north and south of Da Nang. As mentioned earlier, I'm confident the Marines increased their troop numbers in Da Nang as well. Another telltale sign was when we received orders to immediately replenish our munitions from an ammunition supply ship. It was at a time when our magazines were just over half of capacity. Rather than a rendezvous point 50 miles off the coast, the rearmament took place a few miles beyond the horizon.

While the signs suggested an attack may be imminent, the unknowns remained unanswered. How, when, and from where would the assault be launched? Another unknown was the type, size, and amount of weaponry to be used during the offensive. We were confident an invasion by air or sea was unlikely. Rather than assembling troops as a regiment or division, the VC seemed to be mobilizing troops in smaller units. Reports provided by local villages confirmed a sharp troop increase in the region. If they intended to launch the attack by means of an overwhelming influx of troops, it probably meant it would be initiated from the north. This region was being closely watched by the Marines. Every battle reconfirmed the North Vietnamese and Viet Cong had little to no regard for human life. This being the case, a substantial loss of life was inconsequential in achieving their ultimate goal.

As the sun was setting one evening somewhere in late July to early August, a few of us were on the fantail talking and enjoying a smoke. The conversation centered on what the next few hours may have in store for us. The ship was underway and less than 2,000 yards from dropping off the UDTs, south of Da Nang harbor. Suddenly, the hum and vibrations associated with an increase in power could be felt as the engines came alive. A quick glance revealed a dark plume of smoke pouring out of each of the stacks. We were rapidly picking up speed, as the engines cranked up to all ahead full.

Looking forward, it was apparent the UDTs were preparing for a rapid departure from the ship. We began wondering what task they'd been assigned and whether we would be involved. Too many unanswered questions; it was time to head up to CIC to get the straight skinny.

As the UDTs departed the ship, the rpm of the engines immediately increased and we began making a hard turn to starboard. Watching and feeling a 376-foot destroyer in a hard turn is a sight to behold. Moments after completing the course change, it was back up to full speed and heading in a northerly direction. As expected, the rooster tail was absolutely spectacular. But the captain wasn't putting on a show for the crew; something was up and apparently did not involve UDTs.

The sun had just set behind the mountains as several of us arrived and entered CIC. As we passed through the pocket door the chief said, "Marines are reporting another possible assembly of VC troops and equipment on the north side of the Cu De River Bridge." He continued, "Command has instructed us to head up to the area ASAP and meet up with the USS *Tyler Henry* (DD-891), call sign 'Silver Eagle'." We also learned the captain intended to call GQ shortly, so the three of us who had the 2000 to 0800 watch remained in CIC. When we were within range, I established communications with Silver Eagle and we authenticated our identities. By this time, the captain had cranked the old tin can up to flank speed and we would be on station within 13 or 14 minutes.

While there were likely many similarities to the first battle of the Cu De River Bridge, there would also be an equal number of differences. We would likely have a different spotter, the second destroyer was different, plus the area or plain on the north side of the bridge was substantially larger. This increase in open area resulted from the earlier battle, along with several applications of Agent Orange. The larger open area had a positive effect on both sides. From the VC perspective, especially during nighttime operations, the added space made it more convenient to mobilize a larger contingent of troops and equipment. It also made it easier to move men and heavy artillery. On the other hand, when we fired the illumination rounds, it provided the spotter a much clearer and larger viewing area to observe the enemy forces, weapons, and movements.

We would arrive on station five to seven minutes ahead of the *Tyler Henry*. We established communications with the Marine spotter, call sign "Night Fury E (Echo)," and authenticated his identity. At the captain's direction, I briefly suggested a strategy for the mission with Night Fury E. Naturally, it paralleled the brilliant approach used by Assassin and Apache at the first Cu De River Bridge battle. I explained the intent was to hold off firing until both ships were on station and in position. This approach would allow for the maximum coverage and impact on the mobilizing yet unsuspecting enemy troops.

To shorten the overall response time, it was suggested that, with Night Fury E's approval, both ships would enter the coordinates for the entrance to the north side of the Cu De River Bridge before arriving on station. Unless instructed differently, upon Night Fury E's release, both ships would fire an illumination round on the entrance coordinates. Night Fury E would provide adjustments, culminating with a release to fire for effect. With this release, both destroyers would commence firing high-explosive fuse-quick rounds from their main armament.

Without any further discussion, the spotter understood and bought into the plan. As I said before, it's so easy and rewarding to work with the Marines. Following our brief conversation, there wasn't the slightest bit of doubt the Marine spotter was as prepared and up to speed for the mission. It was as if we had been discussing the strategy for hours.

Silver Eagle overheard the conversation, but to ensure we were operating on the same page, the two captains discussed the mass firing directly. As we were closing in on our station, we entered the coordinates of the north side of the bridge into our fire-control system. Operating in the condition of darkened ship, both ships would arrive on station in a stealthy manner. This way, the enemy would be completely unaware of our presence until the illumination rounds exploded. Based upon the blips on the surface search radar, the *Tyler Henry* was already well within striking distance.

After general quarters was called, the chief explained the specifics of the plan to everyone in CIC. Immediately, everyone understood and concurred the plan was excellent and provided the highest degree of success. The only caveat, which could have immediately negated the plan, focused on the Marines' safety. During the discussion with Night Fury E, I mentioned that if at any time the spotter felt

"Charlie" was showing signs of crossing the bridge, the plan would be scrapped and, under his direction, both ships would open fire on the Cu De River Bridge. Although the bridge was an important asset for the base, if the Marines and base were in danger, the bridge would become the primary target. While never mentioned or suggested, I wondered if the Marines had set explosives to destroy the bridge if the VC attempted to cross it.

With the *Tyler Henry* reporting they were on station, both ships confirmed illumination shells had been loaded into their main armament, with their fire-control systems locked on the northern side of bridge. To be more accurate, minutes before Silver Eagle arrived on station, the captains decided the illumination firing coordinates for the *Tyler Henry* would be about 200 yards further inland. This minor adjustment was passed onto Night Fury E. This was intended to light up the entire plain, where the spotter believed the VC were assembling for their attack. At the same time, we wanted to deliver our most potent blow.

With both ships reporting as being on station, I notified Night Fury E we were prepared to fire:

"Night Fury E, this is Buckboard, Ready, over."

Night Fury E acknowledged the message with "Roger," followed by a few seconds' delay before transmitting:

"Buckboard, Silver Eagle, this is Night Fury Echo, fire, over!"

In as much as we had made the first contact, I simply said, "This is Buckboard, Roger, fire out; did you copy Silver Eagle, over?"

Silver Eagle confirmed receipt of the message and moments later the mounts fired the illumination rounds, and I broadcasted, "Shot!" A second later, Silver Eagle confirmed their rounds were also en route. Upon firing the illumination rounds, both ships reloaded their combined eight-gun mounts with high-explosive fuse-quick shells, just awaiting Night Fury's E adjustment. In well under a minute, Night Fury E provided a major adjustment and continued with:

"This is it! this is the offensive, the plain is covered with VC troops and armament; fire main armament, high explosive, fuse quick, continuous fire, FIRE FOR EFFECT, I REPEAT, FIRE FOR EFFECT!"

As Night Fury E was providing the adjustment, you could hear and feel the urgency and stress in his voice, which was perfectly understandable, yet troubling. As I was repeating Night Fury's instructions, I notified our gunnery officer that we were released to commence firing. As he was releasing the mounts, I couldn't help wondering if the Viet Cong heard from Fate. This thought came to mind because they were about to be schooled why attacking our Marines was not only a mistake, but the beginning of an enormous shitstorm. Over the last several months the VC had witnessed the awesome power generated by Operation *Rolling Thunder*, and now they were about to feel the impact of the "lightning" imbedded within this "storm"! The first groups of shells were fired, followed by a second and a third, all fired in rapid succession. God bless the extraordinary teams of men who manned our gun mounts.

Almost immediately, Night Fury E reported the initial salvos were on target, and the remaining enemy troops began dispersing in all directions. Being well trained, he regained his composure and began targeting troops attempting to retreat into the wooded area. In doing so, he adjusted our firing over the entrance to the woods, favoring the edge and first several hundred feet into the wooded area. Our mission was to neutralize, weaken, or break the will of a very determined enemy, as well as destroying all of his armament. Accomplishing this objective would send a very strong message to Hanoi: Da Nang was ours, "now stay the hell off our lawn!" Well, it turns out they learned our lesson, before offering up a bit of their own!

Fortunately, the remaining enemy troops failed to show any further interest in moving in the direction of either the aviation fuel storage tank farm or the Cu De River Bridge. Their only concern was survival by evacuating the area ASAP and finding cover. This worked in our favor; it reduced concern over the safety of the Marines as both ships continued to engage the enemy. As they were fleeing, Night Fury E continued to adjust the gunfire focusing on all the vacating troops. He had Silver Eagle's firing on the troops closer to the South China Sea and the *Stoddard*'s on those headed inland.

Almost immediately following our initial airburst rounds, the Bridge reported several shore batteries opened fire in our general direction. Immediately our AA guns opened up with a barrage of rapid fire, eliminating the threat in short order. While other destroyers may have excellent gun crews, I'm confident none were better than ours. It must have been mind-blowing to watch, as the tracers from the AA guns found their way on target. I recalled watching the Marine Hueys firing on the ammunition bunker and how the tracer rounds seemed to find their target.

Less than an hour into the mission, the opposing forces were reduced by more than 90 percent. To give the gun crews a rest, and with the approval of the spotter, the *Tyler Henry* and *Stoddard* began alternating fire from two mounts per ship. With periodic adjustments by Night Fury E, we continued to fire for about another 30 minutes. Finally, Night Fury E reported the lack of movement on the plain and called a ceasefire.

As Da Nang harbor defense ship, we remained on station to assist the spotter if needed and the *Tyler Henry* was released to return to her previous assignment. For the next few hours, we occasionally fired an illumination round and Night Fury E continued reporting the plain remained quiet.

After several hours, and with all remaining quiet, the spotter began showing signs of wanting to cross the bridge to evaluate the effectiveness of the mission. At the orders of the captain, I suggested any surveillance or similar activities be delayed until after sunrise. The risk of putting an American life in danger was just too high. What if one or more of the enemy troops survived and remained in the shadows, hoping to ambush a Marine or group of Marines? What could be gained by not waiting a few hours? Evaluating the effectiveness of the battle should be conducted after sunrise. This would give the Marines a chance to scour the area by air before setting boot on the battlefield.

As morning broke, a squadron of Hueys arrived to conduct a post-mission evaluation and critique. You may wonder why the Marine air wing wasn't ordered to engage the enemy earlier. Besides being after nightfall, the biggest concern was safety. With eight airburst rounds exploding every few seconds, there was concern over one of the choppers being struck by shrapnel. Plus, the frequent adjustments to our firing coordinates would have put them in danger. Another was the element of surprise. Remember the Marine air wing consisted of helicopters armed with a .50-caliber machine gun and possibly some short-range rockets. The combination of the two destroyers firing a total of eight 5-inch guns delivered an umbrella-like field of 32,000 pieces of shrapnel, showering the target. And this devastating power was repeated with the firing of each group of shells.

The arrival of the helicopters also came along with our release from the mission. They began circling the area prior to landing, as we changed course in the direction of Da Nang harbor. A short time later we arrived in port. As we neared our normal mooring area, I noticed the UDTs, were "patiently" (ahum) awaiting our return. It was one of the few times I witnessed them boarding the ship following an evening's activities. Once the UDTs, and the South Vietnamese officer were on board, we got underway.

As I walked along the starboard side of the ship, I passed the UDTs along the main deck. This time I was confident they were wondering why our return had been delayed. But now it was my turn; as we passed, I simply acknowledged their presence by nodding. OK, maybe I threw in a bit of a smile. I'm probably mistaken, but I'd like to think my silence and smug look thoroughly pissed them off in more of a ball-busting fashion. This isn't meant to show impertinence in any form. There wasn't anyone on board who had more respect and admiration for this extraordinarily brave team than I; it was just a spirited element of our relationship.

After completing our patrolling duties, we returned to Da Nang in the late afternoon. Almost immediately, Lt. Bower and I headed over to the Marine base. Over the last several weeks a number of our navigational charts had become somewhat tattered, contained more than one coffee stain, and needed to be replaced. Earlier in the day, we were notified the replacement charts had arrived at the base. As we entered the Marines' main building, we were greeted with "thanks and well done," by several Marines. This simple acknowledgement sent a kind of chill up my spine; it was completely unexpected and unnecessary. After all, we were just doing our job.

We learned the enemy casualty count exceeded 700, with a large cache of weapons of various types and sizes being destroyed. The small arms salvaged from the battle would be turned over to the South Vietnamese forces. Any large artillery that survived the battle was destroyed by the Marines during the post-mission evaluation inspection. One of the Marines I normally interfaced with indicated no prisoners were taken, and it was unlikely many survived the intense gunfire. He also mentioned that they believed the mission had effectively destroyed an entire Viet Cong battalion or regiment. Hopefully, this victory would persuade the VC against mounting any further offensive attacks and ease, or lessen, some of the pressure on the Marines. By easing or lessening, I don't mean letting their guard down. The recent defeats should act as further proof the Marines were the most powerful force in the region: "DON'T TREAD ON ME!" And the best part was, the Marines' strength would increase substantially in the coming weeks and months.

Prior to departing the ship, the captain directed Lt. Bower to pass on his sentiments or evaluation concerning the performance of the young Marine spotter. Under extremely difficult conditions and stress, he executed his duties professionally and in an exemplary fashion. He immediately picked up and contributed to the plan of attack and effectively directed and adjusted the gunfire for both ships. As a matter of record, there was a short period when he directed the gunfire independently for each ship. While his performance was flawless, this degree of professionalism wasn't unusual. In fact, it was the norm with every Marine spotter I had the privilege of communicating with.

The Marines attached to the Da Nang base, as well as every sailor on board the *Tyler Henry* and *Stoddard*, were pleased with the results of this second battle of the Cu De River Bridge. However, it wasn't time to get overly cocky. From such an overwhelming defeat, there was a general belief that the VC were likely to retaliate in some way. While never publicized, the list of casualties did suggest a few may have been Chinese regulars. President Johnson, along with Congress, remained very sensitive to any involvement of the Chinese. Publicizing the loss of Chinese lives may force the Chinese to respond in some fashion. As a result, the Cu De River battles had very limited press coverage. Politics aside, the VC encountered significant losses of both troops and weapons. Years later, it was revealed that the battles of the Cu De River Bridge were likely the first major U.S. victories in the Vietnam War. Regardless of the politics, both missions were successful in the most positive and important way. There weren't any injuries or loss of American lives; every Marine and sailor lived to fight another fight. Circumstances aside, it just doesn't get any better!

CHAPTER 21

Just When You Learn War Is a Bitch, It Has Puppies!

As we entered August 1965, we continued our daily operations, including shuttling the UDTs up and down the coast. Although we delivered a series of major blows to the enemy, the level of readiness in and around Da Nang harbor remained at its highest levels. Marines mentioned enemy movements continued as they were receiving more specific or detailed data. More than likely, a major contributing factor may have been the increase in the number of Marine patrols; patrols more than doubled and covered a much broader area. The number of helicopters grew exponentially as well and operated around the clock.

When we arrived on July 15, it was common to have a Marine helicopter operating within our field of vision. However, following the second Cu De River battle, flights increased to six or seven choppers in the air at any given time, patrolling a much larger area around the base. During daylight hours they flew at low altitudes, 50 feet or so above the treetops; we suspected they were trying to draw fire to expose enemy positions. For safety reasons, the helicopters flew at much higher altitudes following sunset. During my 2000 to 0800 watch, we tracked the Hueys' paths on our radar and maintained an open frequency with the Marine pilots. Whenever we observed or picked up anything considered unusual or suspicious, we would simultaneously report it to the Bridge and, if appropriate, to the choppers.

As a point of interest, prior to the second battle of the Cu De River Bridge, it was rare to engage the enemy during daylight hours. The VC showed a definite preference for operating within the shadows and darkness of night. But in recent weeks, they'd become more aggressive during daylight hours. The *Stoddard*, following direction from the Marines, responded accordingly.

Since the second Cu De River Bridge battle, when not involved in a specific mission or assignment, we maintained a zigzag course close to the shoreline. Our course was determined more by the depths of the water than the distance from the land. We covered an area about 10 miles to the north and south of the harbor. For security reasons, commercial ships or boats were banned from nighttime entry into the port. In support of these orders, the Navy stationed several additional destroyers just beyond the horizon of Da Nang harbor. These destroyers prevented any size of watercraft from approaching the harbor between dusk and dawn. When called upon, they were also available to support NGFS missions. The radars showed they were strategically positioned to allow their surface search radars to overlap the coverage. They reacted to each and every skunk that attempted to enter the area. I recall one report of an oversized rowboat being stopped, searched, and prevented from breaching the evening's blockade.

A few nights passed and all remained relatively quiet, though the definition of "quiet" in a combat zone is much different than when operating in friendlier waters. Following the latest Cu De River Bridge battle, we continued to interact with the Marine's Echo, Foxtrot, and Hotel companies by engaging and harassing enemy troops operating within the area. This was a norm since we began providing NGFS. The primary difference was that the number of enemy troops was still on the rise, but they were located in areas further from Da Nang, and the increase seemed to be at a slower pace. It appeared the VC realized Da Nang would remain in our control, as they seemed to focus their effort on other objectives. In addition, with increased reconnaissance, the enemy was unlikely to launch another large-scale offensive attack without our advance knowledge.

On August 5, 1965, much like many previous evenings, the UDTs departed the ship at a location just north of Da Nang. When the UDT craft was at a safe distance from the ship, we increased speed and continued on a northerly course for another six miles. We were about 12 miles from Da Nang when we reversed course in a southerly direction.

A quick check suggested we had a mission-free night. To be clear, many of our evenings began in a similar fashion but quickly changed based upon windows of opportunity uncovered by the Marines. With the exception of the mission involving the convoy of trucks, pre-planned missions were rare. With the Vietnam War still in its infancy, the Marines were just beginning to learn of Charlie's location and movements. The vast majority of our missions remained as windows of opportunity. A window of opportunity could best be defined as a fleeting time period during which a rare and desired action could be taken. These types of missions usually began with a Marine squad coming upon or visually observing enemy forces.

As we closed in on zero dark 30 (a very early hour before dawn, typically between 0000 and 0330), the Bridge requested a course change to take up a position 2,000 yards north of the Cu De River estuary. This was an area approximately a mile and half from where the river empties into the South China Sea. It's an area we knew very well. Could the VC be staging yet another offensive attack? I immediately asked the radarman on the surface search scope if any other destroyers were in the immediate area or heading in our direction. He confirmed that while there were several destroyers on the scope, none were heading in our direction. As requested, we provided the Bridge with a course recommendation, just as a radioman was delivering a message. But this message had a rather unusual tone. It simply ordered us to report to the position and await further instructions. This was highly unusual, as every prior mission included a rough description of the assignment and included the spotter's call sign. As mentioned, providing a call sign with the mission assignment allowed us to establish communications and authenticate the spotter's identity before arriving on station. But then again, after the last three weeks, nothing could or would surprise us.

At first, I wondered if a Marine squadron had spotted a contingent of enemy soldiers around the Cu De River Bridge. Then, as I took a closer look, I realized our assigned station was located to the north of the bridge, closer to the Esso fuel storage tank farm. As the ship came about to the new course, we felt the thrust of its engines as it passed all ahead full and approached flank speed. With the increase in speed, the *Stoddard* once again appeared angry as hell, as it began to vibrate violently. The vibration was quickly joined by frantic pitching and rolling. How much punishment could our "Steaming Demon" withstand before cracking? As you would expect, the atmosphere throughout the ship was always different when steaming at flank speed. The increase in speed always resulted in a rise in anxiety. It was then I realized, I hadn't felt this way lately. Over the last few days, the stress levels seemed to have lessened from prior weeks. It's quite possible this sudden feeling of anxiety resulting from the mission's unusual nature was experienced solely by the sailors in CIC.

At the time, only CIC and the Bridge were aware we had been assigned to what seemed to be a mysterious mission, one which must still be in its early development stage. How complicated or horrific could the mission be, if we were assigned before even a spotter? I'm confident the entire crew knew an emergency mission was developing but was unaware of its unusual nature or severity. As the ol' bucket of bolts continued to steam forward, the crew patiently waited for the sound of the boatswain's whistle calling them to general quarters.

We were less than four miles from our station when we received a message: we would be communicating with "Lobo." After reading the message, I hit the transmit button:

"Lobo, this is Buckboard, over!"

A half minute or so passes and I transmit:

"Lobo, Lobo, this is Buckboard, do you read me, over!"

As we arrived at our station, we still lacked a spotter with whom to communicate. It's funny how our minds work. Once again, I wondered if there was an equipment issue. Why wasn't Lobo answering? I continued:

"Lobo, Lobo this is Buckboard, do you read me, I repeat, do you read me, over?"

As I released the transmission button, I realized my voice had increased several decibels. Hmmm, can that actually help? I had to chuckle; as I looked around, I noticed others may be feeling the same way.

Seconds later I heard, "Buckboard, this is Lobo, Roger, I read you loud and clear, over."

As the Bridge realized we'd established communications with "Lobo," the sound to general quarters was announced throughout the ship.

Rather than waiting for my response to begin the authentication process, Lobo continued to broadcast with noticeable uneasiness in his voice. An uneasiness that quickly turned to a whisper:

"This is Lobo, do you have the Tokens?"

I immediately knew Lobo must be the UDT crew assigned to our ship, as I replied:

"They're in the jungle, the mighty jungle, over."

"The Lion Sleeps Tonight!"

"Roger this is Buckboard, ready, over."

I also thought, "Oh shit, this can't this be good, but just how bad is it?" As these thoughts crossed my mind, I said a quick prayer: "Please God, you have to watch over and protect this special group of men." We heard the report from the Bridge that "all men are present and accounted for." Every sailor was at their assigned battle station and ready to engage.

The view from the Bridge suggested all was quiet, yet when Lobo responded we knew their situation was far from being quiet:

"This is Lobo, an all-out attack on the ESSO fuel storage tank farm is underway."

This was followed by the most unusual request I would ever receive. After providing the coordinates, Lobo ended with:

"Four guns, main armament, high explosive, fuse quick, continuous fire, fire for effect; I repeat, fire for effect!"

As I was replying to his order, I was thinking that we're going right into "continuous fire, fire for effect," with four guns no less. No illumination rounds, no single gun, no adjustments, just a fire for effect? Everyone within earshot of the communication realized the UDTs must be facing a dire or catastrophic situation. But just how severe was this shitstorm? I couldn't comprehend anything worse than having our brothers come under attack! The question was whether we could reverse the impact of the attack and turn it completely around. We had done it before and, please God, let us do it again. Almost simultaneously, it hit all of us: "Son of a bitch, it's payback time!"

The Viet Cong, having realized they'd failed to retake Da Nang and the Marine base, were instead attempting to slow down our expansion by attacking the ESSO fuel storage tank farm.

As Lobo completed his transmission, the captain called down and impatiently stated, "You have my permission to fire when ready. What's taking so long, I want those guns active and I want them active now; God damn it, get with it!" We wanted to respond with, "We all feel the same urgency; you must understand the crew is doing everything humanly possible to enter the data into the fire-control system, position the artillery, load the shells, and fire the guns." But, instead, we responded with "Aye, aye, sir." We all realized his bite was nothing more than his way of expressing his sense of urgency. I can assure you, every sailor on board felt the urgency long before the captain said a word.

Seconds later the first round was fired from all four guns and I transmitted, "Shot!" I was expecting some kind of input from Lobo, but the frequency remained silent. After firing five or six salvos (20 to 24 rounds), I transmitted:

"Lobo, this is Buckboard, advise accuracy and impact of rounds fired, I repeat, advise accuracy and impact of rounds fired."

Though I didn't realize it at the time, the next broadcast from Lobo would be his last. He was yelling over the small arms firing that I could clearly hear in the background:

"Buckboard this is Lobo, THEY'RE ALL AROUND US, KEEP FIRING ON THE CURRENT COORDINATES AND SLOWLY MOVE INLAND, LOBO OUT!"

As I repeated Lobo's instructions, I once again asked our Lord, "Please help them find their way to safety, don't let it end this way, please allow them to return safely to the ship in the morning."

We continued firing and moments later the 1.5-million-gallon fuel storage tank exploded—no, erupted—into the largest fireball imaginable. Other smaller tank explosions soon followed. Being less than a mile from ground zero, the sound and force from the explosion could be heard and felt throughout the ship. Sometime later, one of the officers on the Bridge reported the percussion from the explosion caused the ship to shift starboard, while the heat from the explosion could be felt seconds later.

Based upon the timing between Lobo's final transmission and the explosion, reality began to set in. We realized it was unlikely anyone or anything within several hundred yards of the tank could have survived this horrific explosion. The blast not only created an unbelievable fireball but also showered the entire area with fuel. Fuel that quickly ignited. Comparing this explosion to the dropping of napalm was like comparing the flame of a candle to an entire forest fire; it was just that intense and powerful. It appeared the entire coast was burning. It wasn't until morning that its intensity began to diminish. Being unaware of the UDT's actual location in relation to the tank farm gave us hope our brothers were located a safe distance from the large storage tank. On the other hand, having heard Lobo's broadcast of "they are all around us," it remained very daunting and unnerving.

As instructed, we continued firing on the northern side of the ESSO fuel storage tank as we slowly shifted our field of fire inland. Every several minutes I would open the frequency and transmit, "Lobo, this is Buckboard, do you read me, over?" The firing and attempts to contact Lobo continued and even when, about an hour into the battle, the captain called a ceasefire, I felt it extremely important, no, urgent, to continue making every effort to reach Lobo. It was a feeling shared by every man in CIC and likely throughout the ship.

After reporting an update of the battle to Command, we received orders to remain in the area until 0600. This was more of a preventative measure. We were prepared

Photograph taken by the author the morning after the ESSO fuel storage farm attack, August 6, 1965, as he was leaving the area to return to Da Nang harbor. During the attack, the *Stoddard* was called in. It destroyed several of the larger fuel tanks, one of which held between 1.5 and 2 million gallons of aviation fuel. (Author's collection)

for the possibility of the enemy attempting to cross the Cu De River Bridge and attack the Marine base. Throughout the night an almost constant stream of Marine helicopters flew around the area, concerned Charlie may be regrouping.

As hour after hour passed, I continued trying to raise Lobo; there was nothing that could be said or done to stop me. And this was a feeling shared by everyone in CIC. Each time I transmitted, "Lobo, Lobo, do you read me, over," you could see every sailor listening intently, hoping to hear a reply. As the sun began to rise, the captain requested a course and speed to reach Da Nang at 0730.

After providing our recommendation, the CIC officer suggested it was possible Lobo encountered an equipment failure. Whether it was true or not was irrelevant. Just knowing there was still hope, regardless of how slim, was what mattered. About 10 minutes out from Da Nang, I made my final attempt to raise Lobo, but the frequency remained silent.

The 0800 to 2000 watch, who were dismissed from general quarters about two hours after the tank explosions, relieved us early so we could grab a bite to eat. Rather than heading down to the mess deck, several of us took off in the direction of the fantail, where we met up with a number of other shipmates. We were all there for one reason and one reason alone: to welcome the UDTs back on board. When the team arrived, it would be anything other than their normal re-boarding. I'm convinced we all felt, "Screw the need to know," and many of the other Navy protocols. Like it or not, every sailor present planned to give them a well-deserved hero's welcome. Unfortunately, we were dealing with Fate, and she was as unpredictable and temperamental as the sea. She listens to absolutely no one. I recall wondering about the relationship between Fate and God.

As mentioned before, besides CIC and the Bridge, my communications with the spotters were piped to numerous locations throughout the ship. Approaching the fantail, a number of sailors began asking us to confirm, or deny, the validity of a rumor that was circulating throughout the ship. It was a question everyone in CIC was also asking; especially following the last communications with Lobo. Based upon his final transmission, knowing the situation was likely impossible and their survival questionable, could Lobo have called for gunfire directly on their position?

We provided the group with our most honest and sincere answer. As with all missions, we had no knowledge of the spotter's physical position or location. All coordinates provided to the ship were in relation to target coordinates on a specific map. As with any rumor, once aired publicly, it was hard to contain.

A few days later, I heard the rumor suggesting one of our shells destroyed the fuel storage tank. Following the ceasefire, CIC conservatively estimated the closest our shells exploded from the tanks was in excess of 100 yards. The first five or six rounds were on coordinates closest to the fuel storage tank. In accordance with Lobo's final instruction, we fired a few more rounds on these coordinates before adjusting our firing inland and away from the tank farm.

When the South Vietnamese officer boarded the ship, and as we got underway, reality began to set in. Fear, concern, and anxiety were replaced with pain, sadness, and sorrow. As we began our departure from port, many of the sailors remaining on the fantail were silent as we said our final farewell to this brave team: our shipmates. In a manner seeming almost traditional, one of the deckhands stood under the 54-gun mount and began playing "Taps." I'm confident everyone present felt it was just what we needed and a most appropriate tribute. But with that said, have you ever seen a group of seasoned combatants looking up to the heavens with tears streaming down many of their faces? Well, I did, and it ain't pretty! To this day whenever I hear "Taps," I replay this moment in my memory and say a silent prayer for this remarkable group of men. They will always remain in my memory and be included in my prayers.

When a serviceperson takes the oath of service, he or she is well aware of the risk. American Legion National Commander Jimmie Foster once reminded a joint session of the House and Senate Veterans Affairs, "All who put on our nation's uniform make a commitment and in fact sign a blank check, payable to our country, for an amount up to and including their very lives." Every man or woman who has served understands this commitment; however, I can assure you when you lose one of your own, the hurt is dreadfully and indescribably painful. Think for a moment about just how much the previous evening impacted our entire crew. We all knew this group was using our ship as an operating platform, a haven from which to work. There was very little personal interaction between their team and our crew, yet the entire crew admired each of them and mourned their loss.

I had the sincere honor—no, privilege—of working with them on a few missions, and yet I didn't even know any of their names, only their call signs. Granted, they had a very complex or unusual relationship with the crew. You can ask, Were they ballbusters? Unquestionably! Were they arrogant? Absolutely! But they were still part of our crew, our family. Think about it this way, many of us have or had siblings that were arrogant and abrasive, but did we still love and respect them? Absolutely! The feeling was very similar here; while we may have been living our lives a bit differently, they were still our brothers and, as with any family member, we shall always love, support, and protect them forever.

Over the years, I visited the Vietnam Memorial Wall on numerous occasions. As I looked at the more than 58,000 names etched into the Wall, I realized Desoto's, Kodiak's, and Lobo's names are among them. At first, I wanted to personally honor these brave men individually, but then I thought maybe there's a better way. Having their names remain unknown would allow me to honor them, along with every service person whose name was engraved on that sacred Wall. It was then I realized each and every name engraved on the Wall is a Desoto, Kodiak, or Lobo in their own right; they all died while serving our country. Every name on the Wall is just as special and brave as the next.

It's one of the reasons you can always pick out a Vietnam veteran at the Wall. He or she is the one standing there facing the Wall, with a lonely stare or expression on their face, as tears run down their cheeks. And as you look at this grieving veteran, you can be assured their time in Vietnam was only part of their struggle. Coming home was equally as hard, maybe even harder.

I'll offer this example. After being in Vietnam from June 1965 through May 1966, I returned to Long Beach, CA, the home port of the *Samuel N. Moore*. Upon arrival and just outside the main gate, we were greeted with anti-military chants and anti-war protestors, courtesy of our fellow Americans. Being belittled and called horrific names by the unruly mob made us want to confront them physically. I hated each and every one of them with every fiber in my body. But rather than facing disciplinary action threatened by the Navy, I suggested a different route.

With much of the American public turning its back on us, we decided it was best to celebrate our return home, by visiting our friends south of the border. While Mexico was more than 100 miles south, I was confident we'd have a much better time there than if we remained in Long Beach. One of our shipmates had a vehicle stored in Long Beach. So, after changing into civvies, six of us jumped in the vehicle and headed south. When we crossed the border all the animosity and hatred remained on the U.S. side. We were greeted with open arms and encouraged to enjoy a few brews and laughs. I was utterly shocked by how many servicemen were in Tijuana that evening, an order of magnitude more than any earlier visit. I later learned we weren't the first to make the trip, nor the last, after returning from the war. For those returning to the Southern California area, it's exactly how many Vietnam veterans "celebrated" their return "home" to the United States.

Back to the war. After catching a few hours of shuteye, several of us headed up to the mess for a bite to eat. After finishing our meal, we ran into our CIC officer as he was leaving the wardroom. After exchanging a few pleasantries, he addressed what was on all of our minds: the fate of the UDTs. He mentioned the topic came up in the wardroom during lunch. One of the officers mentioned the impact it was having on the crew. He asked if the captain could shed any light on the team's fate. Lieutenant Bower explained that the captain had shared his thoughts and concern for the team, while stating he lacked any additional information to pass along to the crew.

The captain mentioned that when we had first been assigned as the first Da Nang harbor defense ship, the orders had mentioned a UDT unit would be assigned to and operate from our ship. These orders stated the UDTs would operate completely independent of the ship. Our involvement was limited to transporting them to various locations, so they could execute their missions. The orders also directed us to support them if or when required. Their missions would remain highly classified and would only be directed by Command. Their orders may include missions when they remain away from the ship for extended periods. At the conclusion of their assignment, they would depart as unceremoniously as when they arrived. In summary, there were three possibilities: they completed their mission in Da Nang and moved on, they we injured during the attack and transported to a medical facility for treatment, or they were lost during the battle.

This news may have left open a number of possibilities, but believing them was another matter. In the end, they "departed" that night in August and we never saw or heard about them again. From the crew's perspective, that was the hard reality. We had lost a group of brave and treasured shipmates. It was devastating.

We also realized, as tragic and heart-wrenching as it may be, the time had come to face the cold hard fact, to say a final prayer, and get back to work. As we departed Da Nang harbor, we refocused on our mission of supporting and protecting the brave Marines serving in and around Da Nang.

CHAPTER 22

Tạm Biệt Việt Nam[1]

A good Navy is not a provocation to war. It is the surest guaranty of peace.
PRESIDENT THEODORE ROOSEVELT

During daylight hours, the ol' "Steaming Demon" spent most of its time providing naval gunfire support (NGFS) to the Marines. However, it should be noted that most missions were noticeably shorter in duration. With our recent victories, the VC remained in the region, but their activity was dramatically reduced in the Da Nang area. This condition continued for the remainder of our assignment as Da Nang harbor defense ship.

During the second half of August 1965, we were released from Da Nang and set sail for the naval yard in Yokosuka, Japan. By this time, both the ship and crew were ready for some much-needed maintenance. When we were well out to sea, approximately 50 miles north of Da Nang, the crew was notified the ship would be returning to "normal operations." Most importantly, the port and starboard watches were discontinued as we returned to standing two 4-hour watches each day. That change alone had an enormous impact on the crew; it meant four less hours of watch per day, not to mention the relief from the additional hours spent at general quarters. It also answered a question I'd been pondering since we began NGFS operations: did the noise and vibration associated with the frequent firing of the guns impact our physical and emotional well-being? Well, I'm pleased to report it did not have any lasting effect. I believe much can be attributed to the joy and comradery shown by the crew.

After day or two at sea, most things appeared to have returned to "normal." Finally, there was time to just quietly sit back, relax, and hang out with your shipmates. And as each hour passed, this feeling grew from a kind of calmness into a party or celebration. As we were steaming toward the coast of Japan, a few sailors broke out their guitars and began playing them on the fantail. The word quickly spread throughout the ship, as the number of off duty shipmates increased: the "flash party" was on. Before long, the words to many of the classic songs were modified to reflect current conditions. I'll use the "Battle Hymn of the Republic" as an example:

1 Translates to, "Goodbye Vietnam."

> Mine eyes have seen misery of the coming of the draft,
> The day I burned my draft card was the day I got the shaft,
> I may cry, or bitch, or moan, or scream from now till evermore,
> Cause they stuck me on this destroyer and they sent me off to war.
>
> I had to leave my wife and kids, I guess the pain will pass,
> While it's God who owns my soul, it's the Navy who owns my ass,
> I may cry, or bitch, or moan, or scream from now till evermore,
> Cause they stuck me on this destroyer and they sent me off to war.
>
> Misery, misery, on the roam; God I wish that I were home,
> We dropped some bombs in Vietnam and then we left the scene,
> And we just keep steaming all along!

For the record, the Navy did not draft any sailors during the Vietnam War. And to top it off, the captain arranged to have steaks grilled on the fantail. And I can assure you, at that moment, each and every one of us thought life was pretty damn good.

We spent six days in port, with the majority of the time devoted to maintenance issues, limiting the time for liberty. Now wait, let's be honest—because time for liberty was limited, it took on a dual role. First, I'm confident every woman and barmaid local to Yokosuka was happy when we arrived and equally happy when the ship set sail and we'd gone, and second, we attempted to drink the city dry. Rumor had it—and it sounded quite reasonable—that as we departed port, the breweries in Japan added a third shift. But all was good as we departed Japan and were underway for some real R&R in Hong Kong.

Based upon the sheer number of messages we received, conditions had changed considerably for U.S. warships entering the Hong Kong harbor. Because of the United States' involvement in Vietnam, the Chinese filed protests with Britain, requesting U.S. warships be banned from entering the harbor. In an expeditious reply, the Brits denied this request. As a result, U.S. warships entering the harbor were met with challenges (i.e. signal lamps, small craft, etc.) from the Chinese mainland. As in the past, while more intense, challenges meant very little and were generally ignored. Once in Hong Kong, the city was as beautiful and as welcoming as always. I always enjoyed interacting with the people I met in Hong Kong. My first stop was to the Chinese restaurant along the waterfront.

As soon as I and a fellow sailor walked in, without exchanging more than a pleasant nod, my dear chef friend began preparing the dish. Come on, say it with me: "chicken chow mein, Cantonese style." It was far and away the best meal I'd had in well over a month. As I ate, I recalled a time we began running low on rations, but due to the increase and movement of VC troops we'd been unable to replenish our stores. As a result, we ran out of reconstituted milk for breakfast and replaced it with "bug juice" for our cereal. Hey, don't knock it until you've tried it; it really wasn't all that bad. The chow mein was sooooo good, I was tempted to order a second dish, but we were already late meeting up with a group of shipmates.

We found the majority of radarmen and ETs at the local bar we frequently patronized. It goes without saying, we painted the town red. No let me rephrase that—we painted the town every shade of red on the spectrum. Having a midnight curfew, we arrived at the dock just in time to catch the last launch back to the ship.

It was nearly 1100 the following morning when I woke up and realized we had a *great* time. This realization came from the foul odor in the sleeping area. It appeared to be a mixture of "that odor following a night of heavy drinking" smell, coupled with a mixture of aromas that made your eyes water. It was Sunday, so the mess deck was serving brunch, which is a much different meal in the Navy versus civilian life. It was believed to be made up of everything left over since last Sunday mixed together with powdered eggs and served with an overcooked mass referred to as meat. Having had difficulty getting my eyes to focus, I decided it might be best to remain on board and catch up on a few zzzs, so powdered eggs and the "meat thing" it would be. I was confident a second or third cup of coffee would cover up the nasty taste of the "meat." After washing up, I headed up to the mess deck. As I was walking along the main deck, I noticed the Mary Soo ladies were arriving. Let me tell you about this remarkable group of women.

Following long periods at sea, it almost became tradition for naval warships entering Hong Kong harbor to contract for the skills of the Mary Soo ladies. Prior to even dropping anchor, arrangements would have been made for Mary Soo to come aboard. This visit had the sole purpose of having her "ladies"—hardworking women who worked tirelessly—paint the entire exterior of the ship. To the best of my knowledge there was never an exchange of money. Her crew would paint the ship, including the masts, for a minimal "donation." The donation was the waste or garbage generated by the ship's mess.

With the majority of the crew on liberty and enjoying the food of Hong Kong, much of the galley's food was untouched and became waste. The Mary Soo girls would situate large containers next to the ship's trash cans. As the crew returned their trays for washing, they scraped the leftovers or scraps into these containers. This "waste" was later mixed with the food left over from the meal. After the last sailor left the mess deck, the Mary Soo ladies would pack up and carry their "earnings" off the ship. There was a running rumor; we may not have eaten the food on board, but later it was served in many of the Hong Kong restaurants.

Once the deal was struck, a small armada of junks would arrive and upward of 50 workers, mostly women, would board the ship and start painting. We provided the paint and they provided everything else. Instead of using paint brushes, they painted primarily with rags dipped in the paint. It was always a sight to watch them paint the masts. Part of their "performance" included painting the hull. They did so by crawling under the lifelines, dangling over the sides, while others painted upward from their junks.

The workers were dressed in ragged and nasty-looking paint clothes. They wore the typical Chinese conical straw hats to protect themselves from the sun. In their tattered and painted clothes, it was difficult to see what the Mary Soo girls actually looked like. Of course, there were rumors floating around that they were absolutely gorgeous. Regardless, from the way they worked, they had to be in great physical shape. Oh, one other unusual point about her ladies; you could be eliminating last evening's dinner when one of them would walk in and sit on the throne next to you. Even sailors found this activity distasteful and difficult to accept.

During one of my visits to Hong Kong, I mentioned this unique group of women to my favorite chef. He mentioned, the original Mary Soo ladies painted the ships as a means of covering the costs of running an orphanage. He wasn't sure if the original Mary Soo was still alive, but the "business" was still going strong. With the Navy so concerned about having anyone other than the assigned crew on its ships, this one exception began to make sense, and I hoped the story was true.

Other than a few watches and updating our navigational charts, the next few days were very easygoing and uneventful. The evening before getting underway, the chief left me a note to pull the charts for departing Hong Kong and meeting up with the *Independence* (call sign "Gun Train") at "Yankee Station." Yankee Station was a point or position, used by the U.S. Navy aircraft carriers from where they launched strikes in the Vietnam War. It was a location that would change based upon needs and conditions. All locations were usually 100-plus miles off the coast. When your primary weapon was jet fighters and bombers, it wasn't necessary to operate close to or within striking distance of the enemy's coastline. In this particular case, Yankee Station (officially called Point Yankee), was 145 miles east of Da Nang harbor. The following year it was relocated to the waters leading into the Gulf of Tonkin, but still 90 miles off the coast.

Just as we got underway from Hong Kong harbor, the captain gave us the parameters for reaching Yankee Station. A few minutes before the ship reached the open waters of the South China Sea, we provided the recommended course and speed. Traveling at 15 knots and assuming normal wind and sea conditions, we would arrive on station in just under 30 hours.

Late in the second half of August 1965, we reached the task force, with the flagship being the *Independence*. As we arrived, we were assigned a position on the outside perimeter of the task force. Regardless of how many times we joined a large task force, the spectacle of more than 15 warships operating in formation was a sight to behold. We learned the overall group consisted of an aircraft carrier, 12 destroyers, 2 cruisers, and 3 DLGs (Destroyer Leader Guided Missile).

Several days after joining the task force, and following the recovery of aircraft, we received orders to pull alongside the *Independence* for refueling (UNREP or Underway Replenishment). All aircraft carriers carried fuel on board to cover the needs of the ships operating within their group. This avoided weakening the perimeter's protection. Without this capability, when a destroyer began running low on fuel, it would have to breakaway to meet up with an oiler. However, we had just refueled the day before departing Hong Kong and probably had more fuel on board than many of the ships within the group. There had to be another reason we were topping off. As usual, CIC provided a course and speed to pull alongside gun train.

As we approached the carrier, the 1MC came alive to announce, "the smoking lamp is out" and state that the sailors associated with the Special Sea Detail were to muster at their assigned stations. Before long, we heard the gun line fire as the crew pulled over the messenger line. This line was used to connect the large fuel hoses between ships, as well as initiate a line of communications. UNREPs usually took about an hour, so the crew members involved with the operation had to remain vigilant at all times. If a problem developed, the refueling would be suspended and the ship would conduct an emergency breakaway. This would be performed as quickly as possible, without endangering any of the crew. This type of emergency breakaway is taught and practiced on board every naval vessel. During the entire operation, the replenishment ship stays on a constant course and speed. Based upon wind and sea conditions, it was the responsibility of the ship receiving the replenishment to adjust their course or speed to maintain a safe distance (approximately 150 feet and a predetermined speed, usually 15 knots).

The *Stoddard* coming alongside the starboard side of the aircraft carrier to refuel. It typically did so to refuel, take on stores, or transfer a piece of equipment. (Author's collection)

Photograph of the *Independence* taken from the *Stoddard*, fall 1965 in the South China Sea, several hundred miles off the coast of South Vietnam. The *Stoddard* pulled alongside to conduct UNREP operations. (Author's collection)

Following the UNREP and as we were breaking away, we received orders to remain within the inner circle of the task force and take up the plane guard position. This meant the carrier was about to begin flight operations. The Bridge requested a course and speed for taking the plane guard station, about 500 yards astern of Gun Train's port side. This maneuver is slightly more complicated than simply breaking away and returning to the perimeter. Instead of a direct course and speed, the calculation has to take into consideration the other vessels within the perimeter circle. Rather than conducting a 360-degree turn, we simply increased speed while breaking away from the carrier. Once we were clear, we reduced our speed and slowly drifted into position. Once the *Independence* passed, we increased speed and assumed the plane guard position.

Much of these movements resulted from exceptional nautical skills of our experienced captain. During the entire maneuver, CIC monitored ships within the perimeter while continually feeding the distance of the closest ships to the Bridge. The overall exercise took less than 10 minutes and went off without a hitch. For most on board, it was just another day at the office, but for me, after serving on a ship involved in a collision at sea, I may have been just a wee bit more uneasy operating at relatively close quarters.

It was midafternoon when the ship began flight operations, with Gun Train notifying the task force to change course directly into the wind. As discussed earlier, the speed of the wind across the flight deck coupled with the pressure of the catapult are the primary factors in determining the ship's required speed and direction for launching or recovering aircraft. Once the task force is on course and up to speed, flight operations would commence.

With my next watch still six hours away, I had the opportunity to watch the *Independence* launch its jet fighters and light bombers. I was absolutely fascinated hearing the jet engines revving up to full throttle, as the catapult engaged and the aircraft was propelled up to launch speed. But the best part was when the aircraft cleared the flight deck and briefly dipped below the elevation of the runway. Every time it left the flight deck, it appeared the plane was about to make a water landing. Then it would abruptly pull up and disappear into the distance. It was always a unique form of entertainment. During my enlistment, we frequently operated with aircraft carriers as they launched and recovered thousands of planes. Even with aircraft returning from combat missions, we never encountered an incident where the rescuing of a pilot became necessary. Once again, it was the extensive training that made this possible. When it came to studying and learning your trade, whether it be a sailor or an officer, we were required—no, expected—to give our all. There wasn't any room for hoodwinking when it came to completing the program or graduating; either the students met the Navy's strict standards and passed, or they failed!

***

After completing flight operations, we were directed to return to our perimeter position. During watch, the chief stopped by CIC to advise we had received orders to leave the task force and take up a position in the Gulf of Tonkin. Our assignment would be to act as a "watchdog." This is a term I'd never heard before and haven't heard of since. I think the chief may have made it up; however, as it turned out it was an excellent description of our new assignment.

The chief explained that beside enemy AA gunfire, the American jet fighters and bombers were encountering more and more SAM (surface-to-air missile) attacks. The SAM used by North Vietnam was a heat-seeking device, manufactured by the Soviet Union, whose accuracy was questionable at best. At launch, the missiles could be tracked at relatively high speeds. However, to extend their range during the flight, their speed was reduced seconds after becoming airborne. As a point of interest, many of our supersonic jet fighters were capable of outrunning most SAM missiles. In addition to outrunning the missiles, the jets also employed effective day and night antimissile devices and tactics.

During daytime missions, when a pilot was informed a SAM was in the air, he immediately changed course and headed in the direction of the sun. Shortly after completing the course change, he would briefly reduce thrust (to reduce the heat signature being emitted from the jet engines) and turn the aircraft as sharply as possible. He would execute a series of these sharp and abrupt turns in an effort to throw the missile off course. During these zigzag maneuvers, the pilot also increased speed by kicking in the afterburners as he cleared the area. In most cases, the SAMs locked on to the heat generated by the sun, ran out of fuel, and fell from the sky.

During night missions, when a jet fighter came under attack they would go vertical to avoid flying in the direction of the missile as they fired flares from the rear of the aircraft. The heat signature caused the SAM to lock onto the flares, throwing the missile off the targeted aircraft. Simultaneously, the pilot would execute a series of zigzag maneuvers and again, kick in the afterburners.

To combat the increase of SAM missiles, the Navy decided to station a series of destroyers in the Gulf of Tonkin. These ships were positioned off the coast of North Vietnam. The destroyers were assigned to keep an eye out (watchdog) for missile launches while assisting aircraft during their aerial attacks. As part of this assignment, we would also track and vector the friendly aircraft, keeping them informed if an enemy aircraft (bandit) appeared on our radar.

We operated relatively close to the North Vietnam coast. This location would allow us to quickly rescue a friendly pilot who had been shot down or who had to ditch his aircraft in the Gulf. The Navy positioned a chain of destroyers with similar assignments along much the coast of North Vietnam. From a navigational perspective, we would remain beyond the horizon of the North Vietnam coast until we were notified of a pending air strike. When notified, we would steam ahead at full speed to a position or station several miles off the coastline. We would arrive on station as the attack aircraft reached the area.

Another component of our assignment was to eliminate any coastal radar installations within our assigned region. This would be the type of mission referred to as direct fire, as it would be conducted without the input or guidance of a spotter. While we were prepared to execute this style of mission, we were never called upon to do so. For the next week or so, I spent a considerable amount of my "off time" in CIC observing the chief. It was amazing to watch as he meticulously coordinated and vectored the carrier launched jet fighters in conjunction with the B-52s arriving from the Anderson Air Force Base in Guam.

Watching and listening to the chief as he masterfully vectored aircraft was impressive to say the least. On the fourth or fifth day of this assignment, as he was directing an air strike, he picked up a SAM launch. Immediately, he began broadcasting, "SAM, SAM, SAM IN THE AIR." Not knowing which aircraft was the intended target, all of the jets began scrambling and executing countermeasures. This particular attack was during daylight hours, so when the chief broadcast his observation, the fighters immediately went vertical and headed directly toward the sun. Fortunately, all of the jet fighters escaped the attack and returned to complete their mission. At the conclusion of their mission, two of the pilots wanted to say thank you by performing a flyby. We were confident the captain, along with every sailor on board, would be excited to have two maverick jet pilots buzz the ship.

Upon learning of the flyby, the 1MC came alive to inform the crew the event would take place in under 10 minutes. The announcement mentioned a pair of Phantom F-4s would be approaching the ship from both the port and starboard sides. All crew members not on duty were encouraged to come out on the main deck to witness the flyby. Several of us took up a position on the 01 Level, a position where both the port and starboard sides of the ship were visible.

Within a few minutes we could see aircraft closing in from both sides. The first amazing feature was their altitude; they were flying under 100 feet above the surface of the water. As they approached, it became apparent they would cross and pass a few hundred feet forward of the bow. Unbeknown to us, they had another surprise up their sleeves. As they were crossing the bow of the ship, the pilots abruptly changed course and went vertical at an incredible rate of speed. A report from the Bridge indicated the aircraft were close enough to see a pilot offer up a salute in the direction of the ship as they executed the maneuver. I would estimate that the

Officially members of the unofficial Tonkin Gulf Yacht Club, a tongue-in-cheek name for the 7th Fleet operating in the waters off Vietnam. (Author's collection)

time from when they first appeared on the horizon to until they were out of sight was in the range of 20 seconds. But I must say, it was an exciting and memorable 20 seconds.

We remained in the area for another week or so, with each day being somewhat hectic. Of course, it paled in comparison to the month we spent in Da Nang. I should also mention that the "Ghosts of Tonkin Gulf," occasionally raised their menacing heads. Each time these little turbulent events occurred, I was drawn back to the sea story about enemy PT boats attacking a destroyer: so, so sad. It was disappointing to witness such conspiracy theories and misinformation being introduced by politicians and believed by the general public. And over the years, the politicians continue with their endless campaign of misinformation and lies. I recall reading the words of one much smarter than I, when he or she so wisely said: "It's easy to realize when a politician is lying; his lips are moving." But the best came from one of the sailors shortly after hearing the specifics involving the Gulf of Tonkin charade. He asked, "What do you call 100 politicians, bound together, at the bottom of the Mariana Trench?" The answer was "a decent start!"

CHAPTER 23

Long Ago Is Never Very Far Away

> Any man who may be asked in this century what he did to make his life worthwhile, I think can respond with a good deal of pride and satisfaction: I served in the United States Navy.
>
> PRESIDENT JOHN F. KENNEDY ADDRESSING A CLASS AT THE U.S. NAVAL ACADEMY IN ANNAPOLIS

Shortly after completing our assignment as watchdog, we returned to the Land of the Blue Dragon and virtually everything had changed. And these changes were dramatic. The Navy put into place an entirely different fighting force, with each signaling a substantial change in posture and approach to the war. As the Navy/Marines learned more about enemy movements and plans, they adjusted and tweaked their assets to meet the changing dynamics. In relatively short order, practically every coastal town and city was under U.S.–South Vietnamese control as the VC began moving further inland.

As we reached the coast, it became apparent that the majority of NGFS missions were preplanned, better coordinated, and more effective. I should also mention, following our return, we supported numerous missions but generally knew little about the targets, whether it be pre- or post mission. Most missions called for fuse quick, which usually meant we were firing against a target involving enemy troops. Importantly, there was an adequate number of naval supply ships in the region, so running short on ammunition, stores, or fuel was never an issue.

Our new assignment had us conducting NGFS missions along the coast north of Da Nang and slowly heading south, ending up at the Mekong Delta. In late October, as we were conducting missions in the area of the Mekong, we received word we would be returning to San Diego in November 1965. At last, the end was in sight.

***

But there's one more piece of unfinished business we have to discuss. The *Stoddard* had departed from San Diego on June 4, 1965, and in just over a month we'd been assigned as Da Nang harbor defense ship. When we departed on our WestPac cruise, I had seven months of active duty remaining in my enlistment. I was scheduled to be separated and enter the Naval Reserve during the latter part of January 1966, roughly two months after returning stateside. In naval terms, a sailor having under six months left in his or her enlistment was classified as a "short-timer." This distinction came with the honor of wearing a short-timer's chain. The chain was a series of small metal balls, the kind you would typically find dangling from a fan. Being a short-timer included having an important daily celebration or ritual. As the number of days decreased, each morning one of the chain links was cut off and tossed into the ocean. Each link removed represented another day counted off before separation and discharge from active duty.

So, in early September 1965, my chain had fewer than 150 links. It was around this time a rumor began circulating that the enlistments of all Navy and Marine personnel may be involuntarily extended by six months. If this were true, my new separation date would change from late January to late July 1966. Several weeks later, we received confirmation that President Johnson approved the extension. Oh my God, let the moaning, groaning, and bitching begin!

Now let's try to put this news into some kind of perspective. Let's say your wife is pregnant and is due in January. In one of her final months, the OB-GYN advises that due to circumstances beyond her control, her pregnancy was being extended for six additional months. Sound crazy or improbable? Well, welcome to the club. And for the record, the sailors involved in the extension reacted more like the women having the baby than the husband; it just doesn't happen! It felt like we were being called up or drafted into the military for six months. Forget about what I said earlier about the Navy never having to "draft" their fighting force.

When we departed in June, our family members were aware of the length of a typical WestPac cruise and planned accordingly. Some short-timer families had planned events, such as weddings and receptions, less than a month following a sailor's return and separation from active duty. Other families were preparing for parties and celebrations to welcome their loved one home. I'm confident you can understand that the news wasn't received very well. It hit us and our families like a 500-pound sack of potatoes.

If you're wondering about its impact on me, I can vividly remember when I realized I was among those affected. I completely lost it! Self-control went out the window; I used words that would grow hair on the palms of your hands and make even a sailor blush. In the end, it failed to help or even lessen the impact of the news. In an absolute fit of rage, I took off my short-timer chain and threw it as far as possible overboard. And even that didn't help. But I should add, the unaffected sailors were considerate by avoiding mentioning it to those impacted. If there was any humor to this unfortunate or disturbing situation, it was when Joseph Heller's novel *Catch-22* came to mind. I had finished it just a week earlier, and it suddenly struck me—son of a bitch, I was Yossarian!

It took more than a few days for this devastating news to fully sink in, well at least to the point where I could rationally begin dealing with it. I assumed my family and friends were aware of my dilemma. God, please no letters expressing how sorry or how bad they felt. If cursing and completely losing it didn't do the job, I can assure you a letter would in no way be helpful. It was one of those occasions where it was best to be simply left alone. I recall sitting on the 01 Level just "talking" to myself. And these talks didn't last for a few hours but continued for days.

Let me mention, it had absolutely no impact on my performance nor the performance of those affected by the extension. If there was any one group to blame, it would be the anti-Americans back home. Rather than supporting the American warrior, these cowards spent their time condemning, belittling, and disparaging these brave Americans. Their goal was to have these courageous combatants disregard and forego the most sacred oath they may ever take: the "Oath of Enlistment for Military Service." Thank God our Founding Fathers, fellow warriors, and veterans didn't follow this ideology; otherwise, we'd still be under England's rule.

Whenever we were conducting NGFS, I was always prepared for whatever came our way. However, in my off-hours I couldn't get the situation out of my mind. As I look back, I'm so glad we were at sea. Had we been in port, I'm confident it could have led to trouble for many of us. As time passed, we had no choice other than to accept the inevitable. For our own sanity, we had to adapt to the hardship it may have caused. And that is exactly what I did. In the end, you finally come to the realization your shipmates aren't responsible for what happened. Life at sea was harsh enough, so why should they have to suffer with a constant barrage of complaining shipmates? It took the better part of a week, but slowly things began returning to normal. Whatever the hell that meant.

Instead, I tried to focus on the positive. I'll be missing another New Jersey winter. But I'll also be missing the planned reunion with Angelo, Chuck, Willard, and Bagofdonuts; all of whom were already home. Just thinking about this reunion made the hurt much worse. For months we'd been making plans to meet at the Robert E. Lee in Morgan, NJ, and order the largest steak on the menu, followed by drinking into the early morning. That would be followed with breakfast at the OB Diner in Point Pleasant, NJ, before retiring "somewhere." The way things were turning out, I would have settled for a hot sausage sandwich at Rocky's Bar and Grill in Rahway, followed by a few hours at Walt's. It was so painful trying to tell them our plans would have to be delayed until July. But the time had come to accept the inevitable and move on.

CHAPTER 24

Can You Believe It? The Bitch Has Yet Another Litter of Puppies!

> The nation which forgets its defenders will be itself forgotten.
>
> PRESIDENT CALVIN COOLIDGE

Several weeks had passed when I was told the XO wanted to see me. This only happened in cases of an emergency (e.g., when my sister was in the car accident). As I was heading up for the meeting, every negative thought was running through my mind. In one way I was in a hurry to meet with him, yet in another I was hesitant. As I approached, I noticed he was cheerful and smiling, even more than usual. I was totally confused or puzzled with what was going on.

After sitting down, the conversation began with "the captain asked me to speak with you." Wait, did I hear that correctly? The captain asked him to speak with me? What in God's name did this mean?

He continued, "The captain asked if you'd consider volunteering to be transferred off the ship." OK, it was worse than I thought. Had my complaining gotten that far out of line? What had I done that was so horrific the captain wanted me off his ship? The XO must have seen my expression and immediately said, "Relax, you did nothing wrong."

Under normal circumstances, the conversation that followed would have been held between me and either the chief radarman or the OI Division officer. I'm confident these two individuals had had an earlier conversation with the XO regarding such a meeting. In the end, they all felt the "XO approach" would yield the best results. For the last several months, both the chief and OI Division officer had been frequently talking to me about "shipping over," aka reenlisting and making the Navy my career choice. No, that's less than accurate; prior to the involuntary extension, they were constantly on my back to reenlist. It was beginning to border on a form of harassment; it got that bad. It had reached the point where I began feeling anger each time the topic was brought up. If either or both men had approached me with what was about to be suggested, I would have immediately and unequivocally replied, "No way, absolutely not" and ended it there!

The XO explained the captain's evaluation of my performance, especially during NGFS missions, exceeded his expectations. He appreciated my effort, commitment, and the long hours spent on duty over the last five months. Resulting from recent events, specifically the extension of my enlistment, he was convinced my "devotion and experience" could serve well and enhance the performance of another destroyer. Bottom line, he was asking me to consider volunteering to be transferred to another destroyer. It would be a ship that would be departing the States in the near future, en route to the Far East and eventually to the coast of Vietnam. After taking a short breath, the XO said he didn't want me to feel any pressure with this request. The decision would be strictly mine and he suggested I take my time before making a decision either way.

Returning once again to my perch on the 01 Level, I began asking the question "why me?" And simply put, I was unable to answer this very basic and simple question. In fact, it remained unanswered for more than 50 years. However, at a ship's reunion in 2018, it was reconfirmed the *Stoddard* was the first ship assigned as Da Nang harbor defense ship. But this reconfirmation came with the knowledge the *Stoddard* was the first destroyer, naval vessel, U.S. warship, to be assigned a combat role and fire a round in the Vietnam War. If you recall, when we assumed the duties of Da Nang harbor defense ship, the entire crew went through and reacted positively to numerous challenges and situations. At the time, many crew members referred to it as "growing pains," while others called it the "school of hard knocks." After more than 50 years, the captain's request finally began to make sense. With the *Stoddard* being the first ship to defend Da Nang harbor and the first to conduct an NGFS mission, every sailor on board became the most experienced naval combat veteran since the Korean War.

Getting back to the XO's "suggestion." Anyone in their right mind would have responded, "No way, absolutely not, out of the question, just ain't gonna happen," or as they say in Brooklyn, "Forget about it!" But over the next few days it was constantly on my mind. No matter what I was doing or thinking about, it always came back to the question, "Should I fill out and submit the transfer request?" Understand, I was fully aware that after it was submitted, there was no turning back. A day or two later I began questioning my sanity. Was I really contemplating a transfer and if so, why? I was only 22 when I learned negotiating with the "inner you" can be very difficult. It's important to mention, following my conversation with the XO, there was never a time when the topic of "volunteering" was brought up by anyone who had knowledge of the captain's request. No one other than the captain, chief, and XO knew, and other than in my conversation with the XO, it wasn't brought up.

Several days later, out of nowhere comes "Pro-John." For the last few days, I'd been dealing with my "Anti-John" inner ego, but soon, out of nowhere, came my "Pro-John" inner ego. I'd fully understood and related closely to "Anti-John," so could there really be a "Pro-John"? Think about it, back in the States there were young people literally fighting over the idea of being drafted. In fact, they were burning their draft cards like it was an Olympic event. On top of that, there were draft dodgers and conscientious objectors willing to leave my country or be imprisoned rather than serve in the military. There were huge and daily protests on most college campuses, as well as in every large American city. Yet here I was contemplating serving a second consecutive tour, in a location most sane individuals were trying to avoid.

But as I continued debating with Pro- and Anti-John, I couldn't help thinking about the honor, privilege, and opportunity afforded to me in serving with such a great and brave group of Marine spotters, support personnel, and my shipmates (including our courageous and fearless UDT sailors). These guys meant so much more to me than just a group of acquaintances. They represented the true spirit of what it was like being an American warrior. That spirit began with the battle fought at Fort McHenry, or when George Washington crossed the Delaware. How fortunate I was to have served with such honorable and brave men. Let me explain what I'm trying to convey. Comparing those with whom you "served" versus those with whom you "fought" was like being asked, "Do you drive to work or take your lunch?" They're just that different! A major element in the equation was, by agreeing to the transfer, could or would my experience save the life of or prevent the injury to even one Marine or serviceperson?

I also wondered what my family and hometown friends would think or say. We never discussed how they felt about the war. How would they react when learning or realizing that rather than coming home, I'd volunteered to go back to a very politically charged and unpopular war? I continued thinking about what was happening back home with all the protesting: how bad was it? When I was finally separated from active duty, knowing all I had experienced and the great people I had the honor of serving with, could I ever rejoin and blend in with the current-day society? How would I react to those referred to as draft dodgers, conscientious objectors, or supporters of what was being called "Un-American activities"? How would I react, after serving my country, to finding out one of my closest friends was one of these cowards? Was I man enough, or even willing, to pick him up off the ground and say, "I'm sorry"?

***

It finally came down to a simple choice. Once the *Stoddard* began heading back to the States, did I want to serve my remaining time enjoying all San Diego had to offer? Or did I want to transfer to another destroyer? This destroyer would consist of a crew of "green" sailors and would likely spend the majority of the next six months at sea. From her departing date of June 4, 1965, until she returned to San Diego in November 1965, the *Stoddard* was away 164 days, of which 135 were spent at sea.

Was this really a choice? After spending many, many hours on Pro- versus Anti-John arguing, I finally decided it this way: "Fuck the cowards hiding behind their shields of being draft dodgers or conscientious objectors; screw the selfish, greedy, self-absorbed, whining college students; as well as the spineless and gutless protestors. In Vietnamese they would be called 'Bui Doi' or the 'dust of life.' Has any one of them earned the right to be called an American? Not in my book, no friggin' way, they sicken me! They're about as American and patriotic as Benedict Arnold; in fact, they're not patriots at all; they're cowardly turncoats.' Yes, war is anything but fair, but did those who were asked to serve in World War I, World War II, or Korea turn their back on their country? No! And probably more importantly, did their country turn its back on these courageous warriors?"

This was especially true of the more than the 58,000 who gave their life for our country. I began wondering where all this disloyalty would eventually take us. As I thought about these anti-war anti-Americans, I found myself hating them. I also realized not only did I hate them at the time, but I'd hate them when I got home, and it was likely I'd continue to hate them until the day I died. And God damn it, that was and is my right! I concluded that turning my back on the brave men I had served and fought with would be less than honorable. The captain asked me to put my personal life on hold to help our war effort, so I filled out and signed the transfer request.

To be perfectly transparent, in less than a day I had buyer's remorse. But it was too late, it was likely the transfer request message had already been radioed to Command and likely received by the Department of the Navy in Washington.

A number of weeks passed and I heard absolutely nothing. It was quite possible, or even probable, that the Navy had trained an adequate amount of NGFS coordinators and didn't require my service or experience. Then, as the *Stoddard* began her return to the States, I received my orders. I would be transferred to the *Samuel N. Moore*, which would be departing Long Beach in a few days for the Far East.

In November 1965, while the *Stoddard* was refueling for her final leg home, I was highlined from the *Stoddard* to an oiler. Two days later, the process was repeated, as I was highlined to the *Samuel N. Moore* during their UNREP operation with the same oiler.

Highlining is a rather unique and challenging means of transferring personnel between ships. It involved connecting a line between ships and securing the transferring sailor to a Bosun's Chair. If an issue develops, the transferee being restrained decreases the likelihood he would be thrown or tossed into the waters between the ships. While it may not sound dangerous, I can assure you that it is an absolutely eye-opening experience.

To increase the sense of uneasiness, add a senior boatswain mate who is also a friend into the mix. As I was leaving the ship, his final words were, "Remember to lift your boondockers to avoid getting them wet during the dip." Oh yeah, that was about as funny as a rubber crutch. Following the pattern of a professional ballbuster, after being about 75 feet into the transfer, I look back to see my boatswain mate friend pointing toward the sea and yelling, "Hey Calder, check out the size of that hammerhead shark." I flipped him the bird, all the while being so, so thankful he was the one in charge of the transfer.

During the process it was impossible to ignore the distance between the *Stoddard* and the oiler, especially as the ships yawed in a constant rhythm of rolling port and starboard. The experience of the transfer from the *Stoddard* to the oiler made the second transfer an order of magnitude more nerve-wracking. Fortunately, the seas and winds were relatively calm during both transfers, so the highlining adventure went off without a hitch. Please be assured, I was beyond relieved when the bosun's chair was unfastened and I stepped onto the deck of the *Samuel N. Moore*.

Following naval protocol, after the restraints were removed from the chair, I stood up, saluted the OOD who just so happened to be the OI Division officer, and requested permission to board. He welcomed me aboard, confirmed I would assume the duties of the ship's NGFS communicator, and told me to report to the mess decks in one hour. The agenda for the meeting included being introduced to the members of OI Division, describing my recent experiences, and a forecast of what life may be like after arriving in the waters off South Vietnam. After completing the refueling operation, we broke away from the oiler and settled in on a westerly course.

As scheduled, the OI Division met on the mess deck. It turned out to be an informative meeting. However, as I was sharing my experiences in Da Nang, I couldn't help but notice a few blank and jaw-dropped expressions. The "meet and greet" concluded with a number of excellent questions. As things wrapped up, I realized it was the first time I had been asked to recap my combat experiences, and yes, it was an eye-opening experience for me as well.

After a brief stop in Subic Bay, the Philippines, we were underway and headed for the coast of South Vietnam. Several evenings later, as we were approaching the coast, the 1MC came to life with the blare of the bosun's whistle, followed by: "Now hear this, now hear this, general quarters, general quarters, all hands man your battle stations. This is not a drill. I repeat, this is not a drill. General quarters."

My second tour began, as we hustled to our assigned GQ stations. I couldn't help but watch as this green crop of fun-loving, foul-mouthed, beer- or whiskey-drinking, women-chasing sailors were about to become professional warriors. For me personally, this call to GQ had somewhat of a calming effect. It was in this moment that I had the overwhelming awareness I had made the right decision; I was where I belonged.

Over the years, I often think about the Marine spotters and shipmates I had the privilege of communicating and serving with. I pray they all made it back safely and are enjoying the wonderful places and opportunities our country has to offer. They certainly earned it! I'll save my tour and experiences on board the *Samuel N. Moore* for another day.

Semper Fortis, Non Sibi Sed Patriae!

U.S.S. SAMUEL N. MOORE DD-747
FLEET POST OFFICE
SAN FRANCISCO, CALIFORNIA
96601

DD747/WKM/qn
1610
Ser: 224
16 APR 1966

From: Commanding Officer, U.S.S. SAMUEL N. MOORE (DD-747)
To: CALDER, John F., 598 58 65, RD3(0000/0000), USN

Subj: Letter of Commendation

1. Prior to the completion of this Southeast Asia cruise, it is proper to reflect on the testimony of your brief tour aboard the MOORE.

2. Since reporting aboard in November 1965, you have performed your professional duties with a flair and competence not often observed. You evidenced talents far beyond those of a normal third class Radarman, skills which were readily recognized by your prompt elevation to watch supervisor. Your widespread familiarity with SEVENTH FLEET Operations has been a valuable liason in MOORE's performing her various missions. Obviously well trained yourself, you have instilled your habits of alertness, prompt and effective reaction, accuracy, and professional excellence in the strikers training under you.

3. Your performance during Naval Gunfire Support has been especially meritorious and gratifying. You have shown an excellent and authoritative familiarity with the entire fire control problem, not merely with your specialized area of communications, and you have helped resolve numerous procedural problems. Since a destroyer's most direct contribution to the Viet Nam war effort is achieved through gunfire support, your personal excellence has reflected well on the ship as evidenced by the high praise we have received for our effective gunfire against the Viet Cong. These commendations in turn have given a real sense of purpose and proud accomplishment to the MOORE during this cruise.

4. My personal congratulations on your short but eminently successful tour aboard the SAMUEL N. MOORE. WELL DONE!!

W. K. Martin
W. K. MARTIN

Letter of Commendation presented to the author by the captain of the USS *Samuel N. Moore* in April 1966. Such letters were awarded for exceptional performance during a specific period, such as a high-stakes mission or deployment. They recognized significant contributions to a ship's readiness or efficiency, as well as actions demonstrating exceptional leadership or initiative beyond the normal requirements of a sailor's rank and responsibilities. The letter was written on official Navy letterhead, and signed by the destroyer's commanding officer, typically a commander in the U.S. Navy. (Author's collection)

Glossary

Military Abbreviations and Acronyms

1MC	1 Main Circuit. The primary public address system used for ship-wide announcements
ARO	Area of Responsibility
ASROC	Antisubmarine Rocket
AWOL	Absent Without Leave. Some define it as: Absent Without Official Leave
ASW	Antisubmarine Warfare
CIC	Combat Information Center
CPA	Closest Point of Approach
CSG	Carrier Strike Group
DI	Drill Instructor
DRP	Dead-Reckoning Position
DRT	Dead-Reckoning Tracer
EMC	Electronic Counter Measures
ET	Electronic Technician
FC/FCS	Fire Control or Fire Control System
GI	Government Issue
GPS	Government Positioning System
GQ	General Quarters
IFF	Identification Friend or Foe
MATS Flights	Military Air Transport Service flights
MAW	Marine Aircraft Wing
NAS	Naval Air Station
NLF	National Liberation Front, aka Viet Cong (South Vietnamese communists)
OC	Operations Communications
OI	Operations Intelligence
OOD	Officer of the Deck
OTC	Officer of Tactical Command
PAVN	People's Army of Vietnam (North Vietnam)
PM	Preventative Maintenance
POOW	Petty Officer of the Watch

RADAR	Radio Detection and Ranging
RD	Radarman designation, aka OS (Operations Specialist)
RDI	Recruit Division Instructors, aka DIs
SEALs	Sea, Air, and Land. The U.S. Navy's primary special operations force
SONAR	Sound Navigation and Ranging
TFC	Task Force Commander, aka CTF
UCMJ	Uniform Code of Military Justice
UDT	Underwater Demolition Team. Originally called "Frogmen"; presently called "SEALs"
UNREP	Underway Replenishment
USS	United States Ship
VC	Viet Cong, aka NLF (South Vietnamese communists)
WestPac	Western Pacific
XO	Executive Officer

Military Terms

01 Level	Refers to the deck immediately above the main deck.
Bandit	An aircraft that has been positively identified as an enemy.
Bogey	An unidentified air radar contact.
Charlie	Viet Cong, aka NLF (South Vietnamese communists).
Junks	A type of sailing boat with distinctive characteristics. Among the most notable of these characteristics are: fully battened sails and flat-bottomed hulls. Junks are traditional boats found throughout Southeast Asia, particularly in China and Vietnam. Their unique way of floating on water, seemingly sliding across the surface, has fascinated people for centuries.
Midrats	Midnight Rations, a meal served late at night to soldiers on duty, particularly those working the graveyard shift.
Port Side	The left side of a ship when facing forward (towards the bow).
Quarterdeck	Considered the main ceremonial and reception area on a ship; it is traditionally a respected place.
Skunk	An unidentified surface contact.
Smoking Lamp	The phrases "the smoking lamp is lit" and "the smoking lamp is out" are used to announce when smoking is permitted or prohibited, respectively. When "the smoking lamp is out," it's largely because munitions, fuel, or combustible materials are being handled.

Starboard	The right side of a ship when facing forward.
Striker	A sailor who is actively working towards earning a specific Navy rating through on-the-job training and potentially, additional schooling.
Weighing Anchor	Signifies the process of raising the ship's anchor from the seabed, signaling the start of a journey or departure. It's the opposite of "dropping anchor," which secures the vessel.

APPENDIX I

USS *Stoddard* 1965—Cruise Consumption[1]

Sine Qua Non

Category	*By the numbers*
Beans	2,000 cans
Beef	19,000 lb
Coffee	3,800 lb
Cola	58,772 cans
Eggs	79,000 dozen
Ice cream	2,000 lb
Mail received	7,445 lb
Mail sent	2,840 lb
Potatoes	42,000 lb
Stamps sold	$1,500

Unreps, Showers, and Seagulls

Category	*By the numbers*
Diesel fuel	1,917,217 gal
Miles steamed	53,465
Potable water	1,034,997 gal

In Memoriam from Vietnam

Category	*By the numbers*
Rounds of high-explosive 5" shells fired	2,600

1 Data summarized from the *STODDARD '65* cruise book, published in 1966.

APPENDIX 2

Vietnam: The Figures[1]

American Casualties

- Hostile deaths: 47,378
- Nonhostile deaths: 10,800
- *Total:* 58,178

Enemy Casualties

During the Vietnam War, the North Vietnamese and Viet Cong deaths were estimated to be between 1,200,000 and 2,000,000.

Analysis of American Casualties

- Eight nurses died.
- 61 percent of the men killed were 21 or younger.
- 11,465 of those killed were younger than 20 years old.
- Of those killed, 17,539 were married.
- Average age of men killed: 23.1 years.
- Five men killed in Vietnam were only 16 years old.
- Missing in action: 2,646.

Miscellaneous Information

- Vietnam veterans had a lower unemployment rate than the same nonveteran age groups.
- Vietnam veterans' personal income exceeds that of nonveteran age group by more than 18 percent.
- 76 percent of the men sent to Vietnam were from lower-middle/working-class backgrounds.

---

1 Statistics on this page from Vietnam Veterans of America Charles S. Kettles Chapter 310, website, https://www.vva310.org/vietnam-war-statistics, accessed August 2025; Vietnam Veteran Project website, https://vietnamveteranproject.org/statistics-2/, accessed August 2025.

- 79 percent of the men who served in Vietnam had a high school education when they entered the military service; 63 percent of Korean War vets and only 45 percent of World War II vets had completed high school upon separation.
- 85 percent of Vietnam veterans made successful transitions to civilian life.
- 97 percent of Vietnam-era veterans were honorably discharged.
- 91 percent of actual Vietnam War veterans and 90 percent of those who saw heavy combat are proud to have served their country. 74 percent say they would serve again, even knowing the outcome.

APPENDIX 3

The Author's Service, in Print

Some people never meet their heroes, but I gave birth to mine.

UNKNOWN NAVY MOM

RAHWAY NEWS-RECORD

With the Armed Forces

Radarman Third Class John F. Calder, son of Mr. and Mrs. Harold F. Calder of 971 Stone St., Rahway, participated on July 22 in a mass firing mission on a suspected Viet Cong assembly area on the Ca De Song River, about eight miles from the De Nang Harbor, while serving aboard a destroyer, U.S.S. Stoddard.

Stoddard, together with another destroyer, U.S.S. John R. Craig, fired more than 40 rounds of five-inch explosives on the target. The action marked the fourth night in succession the Stoddard conducted shore bombardment against Viet Cong guerrillas.

* * *

Midshipman Second Class Richard H. Pelszynski, son of Mr. and Mrs. Stanley A. Pelszynski of 22 Denman Ave., Clark, has been attending a three-week field trip to the Naval Air Station, Corpus Christi, Tex.

Midshipman Pelszynski, a graduate of St. Peter's High School, Staten Island, N. Y., is among the Navy midshipmen from Ohio State University, Columbus, on the trip. He is a junior at Ohio State and is majoring in physics.

* * *

Cpl. George T. Levins, son of Mr. and Mrs. Joseph F. Levins of 279 East Albert St., Rahway, is serving with Marine Attack Squadron 331 at the Naval Air Station, Roosevelt Roads, Puerto Rico.

The squadron, an all-jet attack unit, is undergoing extensive training in the use of rockets and bombs during day and night close air support of Marine Corps ground troops.

* * *

Electronics Technician Phillip W. McDonald Jr., son of Mr. and Mrs. McDonald of 26 Sunset Dr., Clark, is serving aboard a destroyer, U.S.S. Manley, a recovery ship for Project Gemini GT-5, eight-day flight of astronauts Gordon Cooper and Charles Conrad.

Manley occupied a station off the Canary Islands during the crucial liftoff and then relocated to be in a favorable position for recovery in the event of a shortened mission.

News article printed in the local newspaper of the author's hometown, the *Rahway News-Record.* (Author's collection)

Scanned copy of a clipping from a local Rahway newspaper which published an article on the author's service, saved by the author's mother, Agnes Calder. The image is from the author's collection.

Rahway Radarman Returns From Viet Naval Service

RAHWAY — Radarman 3.C. John Calder of 971 Stone St., is home from Viet Nam with an honorable discharge after four years and four months in the U.S. Navy.

The son of Mr. and Mrs. Harold Calder of the same address, he enlisted in January, 1962, and has seen considerable action aboard two destroyers in the Viet Nam area. He is a 1961 graduate of Rahway High School.

Calder was stationed on the USS Stoddard until November, 1965, and was transferred at his own request to the USS Samuel N. Moore in order to serve for an extended period in Viet Nam.

His ship on one occasion laid down "very effective" fire on a Red staging area 120 miles south of Da Nang, Calder related. He also was in an escort with the carrier Independence, when they blasted a powder plant at Thanh Hoa, 75 miles from Hanoi, and was aboard the Stoddard when it blasted 300 shells at a shore target in support of the Marine Corps in the Da Nang area.

Armed Forces

John F. Calder, son of Mr. and Mrs. Harold Calder of 971 Stone Street, Rahway, has returned home after serving ten months in Viet Nam with the U. S. Navy. He served on a destroyer the U.S.S. Samuel N. Moore where he was a Petty Officer 3/c Radarman. John, a Rahway High School graduate enlisted in the Navy in January, 1962.

* * *

Scanned copy of the last news article published about the author's military service. Also from author's collection.

Selected Bibliography[1]

Archives

Naval History and Heritage Command. "Operation Plan 34A." Naval Historical Center, 2022. https://www.history.navy.mil/research/library/online-reading-room/title-list-alphabetically/b/by-sea-air-land-marolda/chapter-2-the-era-of-growing-conflict-1959-1965.html.

Prados, John (ed.). "Gulf of Tonkin Incident, 40 Years Later, Flawed Intelligence and the Decision for War in Vietnam." National Security Archive Electronic Briefing Book No. 132, August 4, 2004. https://nsarchive2.gwu.edu/NSAEBB/NSAEBB132/index.htm.

Books

STODDARD '65, cruise book published in 1966. Believed to have been assembled by the author's shipmates. Such publications were created during every cruise by most, if not all, Navy vessels.

Miscellaneous

Herrick, H. "Chronology of Events: Gulf of Tonkin 4 August 1964." Herrick's memo was dated August 13, 1964, but was only released by the U.S. Navy on July 7, 2005.

Newspaper and Magazine Articles

Hambling, David. "Weatherwatch: Angels of Death." *The Guardian*, August 8, 2014. https://www.theguardian.com/news/2014/aug/08/weatherwatch-tonkin-incident-radar-vietnam-war.

Hanyok, Robert J. "Skunks, Bogies, Silent Hounds, and the Flying Fish: The Gulf of Tonkin Mystery." *Cryptologic Quarterly*, National Security Agency, August 2–4, 1964. https://www.nsa.gov/portals/75/documents/news-features/declassified-documents/gulf-of-tonkin/articles/release-1/rel1_skunks_bogies.pdf.

Paterson, Lieutenant Commander Pat. "The Truth About Tonkin." The U.S. Naval Institute, *Naval History* magazine, Volume 22, No. 1, February 2008. https://www.usni.org/magazines/naval-history-magazine/2008/february/truth-about-tonkin.

Scheer, Robert. "VIETNAM: A Decade Later: Cables, Accounts Declassified: Tonkin—Dubious Premise for a War." *LA Times*, April 29, 1985. https://www.latimes.com/archives/la-xpm-1985-04-29-mn-12824-story.html.

Schuster, Carl Otis. "How North Vietnam's P-4s Missed the Mark." *Military Times*, December 13, 2017. https://www.militarytimes.com/veterans/2017/12/13/how-north-vietnams-p-4s-missed-the-mark/.

1 Note: all hyperlinks referenced in the bibliography were accessed between 2020 and 2025.

Scholarly Works

Landry, Steven M. "'Reds Driven Off': The U.S. Media's Propaganda During the Gulf of Tonkin Incident." *The Cupola*, spring 2020. https://cupola.gettysburg.edu/cgi/viewcontent.cgi?article=1869&context=student_scholarship.

Websites

Bauer, Pat. "The Gulf of Tonkin incident." Britannica, July 26, 2023. https://www.britannica.com/event/Gulf-of-Tonkin-incident.

History.com editors. 2009. "U.S. Marines Land in Da Nang." https://www.history.com/this-day-in-history/u-s-marines-land-at-da-nang.

Schuster, Carl Otis. "Case Closed: The Gulf of Tonkin Incident." HistoryNet, August 7, 2014. https://www.historynet.com/case-closed-the-gulf-of-tonkin-incident/.

Steward, Captain George (ret.). "Life on a Fletcher Class Destroyer in the 1960s." Naval Historical Foundation, July 31, 2013. https://navyhistory.org/2013/07/life-on-a-fletcher-class-destroyer-1950s/.